The Manhattan Project
and the Birth of the Atomic Bomb

A Better You Everyday Publications
email address abetteryoueveryday2022@gmail.com

www.abetteryoueveryday.com

THE MANHATTAN PROJECT AND THE BIRTH OF THE ATOMIC BOMB

From Einstein's Theories to Oppenheimer's Test

By Julian R. Stonebridge

USA
August 2023

CONTENTS

Introduction 1

Einstein's Vision.. 5

Setting the Stage with Einstein's Contributions and the Dawn of the Atomic Age: 9

Chapter 1: The World Before the Atomic Bomb 21

Global geopolitics, scientific advancements, and societal norms before the atomic age .21

Chapter 2: The Global Stage Through a London Lens 29

The Broader Historical Context Influencing the Atomic Age.......................................34

Chapter 3: Theoretical Beginnings - The Science Behind the Bomb 45

Early Scientific Theories and Discoveries 54

Chapter 4: The Manhattan Project - Catalyst of Change.............................. 67

The Geopolitical Landscape and the Rise of Fascism..74

Mobilization of the Scientific Community 83

Key figures: Oppenheimer's, Fermi, Groves, and others...91

Funding and support: The role of the U.S. government 98

Chapter 5: Secret Cities - The Heartbeat of the Manhattan Project......... 109

Establishment of Los Alamos, Oak Ridge, and Hanford 112

Daily life in these secret cities 117

Scientific collaborations and challenges 123

Espionage and security concerns 130

Chapter 6: The Technical Odyssey - Crafting the Bomb 143

The Intricate Physics Behind the Bomb 144

Engineering challenges and innovations 152

The role of raw materials: Uranium and Plutonium 160

The designs: Little Boy and Fat Man 166

Chapter 7: Trials and Triumphs 177

The Trinity test: Preparations, execution, and aftermath 178

The Decision-Making Process: Military and Political Considerations 186

The Flight Crews and Their Training 193

Chapter 8: Hiroshima and Nagasaki - The Bomb's Impact 201

The Immediate Aftermath and Destruction 203

The Human Cost: Stories of Survivors 210

The World's Reaction 218

Chapter 9: Humanity at the Crossroads - Ethical Dilemmas of the Atomic

Age...227

The American Perspective, Hiroshima's Lens, and The Global Ethical Quandary.......228

Chapter 10: Reflections Under Hiroshima's Skies 239

Global responses to the bombings 241

Chapter 11: Geopolitical Implications of the Atomic Age..........................255

The Cold War's inception and the influence of the atomic bomb 256

Chapter 12: The Atomic Renaissance - Science and Society in the Nuclear

Age...269

Positive Advancements from Nuclear Research..271

Chapter 13: The Future of Nuclear Technology 287

Conclusion: Reflections and Resource...297

List of Sources 305

INTRODUCTION

Few events in the history of humanity have left such a lasting impact as the detonation of the bombs over the Japanese cities of Hiroshima and Nagasaki. These pivotal moments not only marked the end of World War II but also ushered in a new era known as the atomic age, forever changing the course of human civilization. At the core of this period lies the Manhattan Project, a secretive mission that brought together some of the brightest minds of that time to achieve what was once considered impossible.

The advent of the age was more than just a scientific and military milestone; it represented a turning point that reshaped geopolitics, ethics, and societal norms. It completely transformed relations as countries grappled with the immense power and responsibility of possessing nuclear capabilities. The ethical questions raised by creating and deploying bombs still echo in present-day discussions, challenging our understanding of what is morally right and humane.

This book titled "The Manhattan Project and the Birth of the Atomic bomb. From Einstein's Theories to Oppenheimer's Test" aims to explore all aspects – scientific, political, and ethical – surrounding this monumental project. With a wealth of research, expert opinions, and firsthand accounts as our guide, we will delve into the history of atomic science. Our journey will take us from the beginnings of this field, led by brilliant minds like Albert Einstein, to the secretive corridors of Los Alamos, where the atomic bomb came into existence.

Albert Einstein, widely recognized as the pioneer of physics, played a crucial role in laying the groundwork for the advent of the atomic age. His revolutionary theories formed the basis for scientific breakthroughs, creating such a powerful weapon. However, this transformation from theory to reality had its share of challenges. Both ethical. The Manhattan Project serves as a testament to innovation and our unwavering pursuit of knowledge fueled by brilliance, ambition, and an atmosphere shrouded in secrecy.

As we embark on this expedition together, expect to gain profound insights into historical events, ideologies, and remarkable personalities that paved the way for one of humanity's most significant projects. The Manhattan Project. From exploring the landscape during the early 20th century to grappling with moral dilemmas arising from advancements in atomic energy. Our narrative aims to be both comprehensive and thought-provoking.

A Glimpse into the Chapters Ahead:

Before we embark on this journey, it's important to give you an overview of what lies ahead. Each chapter has been carefully crafted to provide an understanding of the Manhattan Project and its significant impact. The following chapters offer an immersive experience that sheds light on various aspects of the atomic age through research, expert insights, and firsthand accounts.

Chapter 1 will set the stage by giving you a glimpse into the politics, scientific advancements, and societal norms that existed before the atomic age. This chapter will explore the web of events and ideologies that paved the way for the Manhattan Project.

Chapter 2 will explore the historical context by connecting global politics and the emerging atomic age. This chapter will show how our world stood on the verge of nuclear discovery.

Chapter 3 will dive into early scientific theories and discoveries laying the groundwork for the Manhattan Project. From Einstein's groundbreaking equations to pioneering work by physicists, this chapter will clarify how science shaped our understanding of atomic energy.

As we move into Chapter 4, the focus of the story will shift toward the landscape during that time, the rise of fascism, and how the scientific community got involved. In this chapter, we will meet individuals who played key roles in the project and explore their contributions.

Chapter 5 will take you to the core of the project. We will explore how places like Los Alamos, Oak Ridge, and Hanford were established and operated. This chapter aims to shed light on life in these covert hubs, scientific collaborations, and the challenges those involved face.

Moving on to Chapter 6, we will dive into the intricacies of physics, engineering, and overcoming obstacles to create a functioning bomb. From understanding the importance of materials like Uranium and Plutonium to examining designs such as Little Boy and Fat Man, this chapter provides a comprehensive overview of how these elements came together for bomb development.

Chapter 7 recounts moments including the Trinity test—the preparations leading up to its execution and aftermath. Additionally, we explore the decision-making process behind dropping bombs on Hiroshima and Nagasaki.

The narrative will take on a tone in Chapter 8. In this chapter, we will explore the moral implications of the atomic bomb, considering various perspectives from both the United States and Hiroshima.

Chapter 9 will delve into the immediate and long-term global responses to the bombings. Moving forward to Chapter 10, we will analyze the broader political aftermath that unfolded.

Chapter 11 will shed light on advancements derived from nuclear research and discuss the rise of nuclear activism. Finally, Chapter 12 will highlight the benefits and challenges that lie ahead in nuclear technology.

The atomic age has undoubtedly significantly influenced human history with its nature and profound consequences. As we navigate science, politics, and ethics intricately woven together, this book aims to provide an understanding of the Manhattan Project and its enduring legacy. From its theoretical foundations to global ramifications caused by atomic bombs, our journey promises both enlightenment and thought provocation.

As you embark on this exploration, we invite you to dive and embrace the opportunity to question, contemplate, and fully immerse yourself in the captivating narrative that awaits. Join us on this journey as we uncover the stories, remarkable individuals, and pivotal events that have shaped the atomic age. Prepare to be enlightened and challenged as we peel back the layers of "The Manhattan Project and the Making of the Atomic Bomb; From Einstein's Desk to Hiroshimas Skies." Your curiosity and active participation will guide us in navigating this history together.

Einstein's Vision

The Genius of Einstein:

Albert Einstein, a name with extraordinary intellect, is widely regarded as one of the most influential figures in the history of science. He was born in 1879 in the Kingdom of Württemberg within the German Empire. From an age, Einstein displayed a deep curiosity and an innate ability to think outside conventional boundaries. While he faced challenges during his journey, including disagreements with educators and traditional teaching methods, these experiences only fueled his independent spirit and his relentless pursuit of unraveling the mysteries of the universe.

In 1905, Einstein introduced his Special Theory of Relativity, which showcased his intellectual prowess. By challenging the principles of classical physics, he presented a new framework for comprehending space and time. His iconic equation, $E=mc^2$, goes beyond being a mathematical expression; it represents a revolutionary concept that intertwines energy and mass while suggesting their interchangeability. This theory broke new ground and highlighted Einstein's ability to think beyond established norms and embrace questioning and innovation.

Einstein's brilliance extended beyond concepts and also reflected in his scientific methodology. He firmly believed in harnessing the power of imagination and intuition. For him, science wasn't limited to equations and experiments; it involved understanding nature's language on a deeper level.

He often discussed "thought experiments," where he imagined physical scenarios and then applied his theories to them. One experiment involved envisioning a scenario where he was chasing after a beam of light, which led him to some conclusions about relativity.

Einstein's impact on science extends beyond just his work on relativity. He contributed to fields such as quantum mechanics, statistical mechanics, and cosmology. What set him apart was his ability to navigate various domains of physics, his willingness to challenge established ideas, and his unwavering pursuit of truth. This made him an exceptional scientist and a visionary who revolutionized our understanding of the universe.

Throughout his life, Einstein faced both praise and criticism. However, regardless of the world's opinions, he remained dedicated to his quest for knowledge, always striving to uncover the truths within the universe. In many ways, his genius extended beyond scientific accomplishments; it encompassed his philosophy, ethics, and steadfast belief in the elegance and simplicity of nature's laws.

Turbulent Times and Atomic Energy:

The 1930s and 1940s were not only a time of scientific advancements; they were marked by global unrest, political upheavals, and the looming threat of World War II. The world was on the edge, with nations competing for territorial control and technological superiority.

In this context, Einstein's theories gained greater importance. The significance of his equation $E=mc^2$ was being realized. The concept that a small amount of mass could be converted into an amount of energy was both thrilling and frightening.

This idea became the focus of research, experimentation, and, eventually, weapon development.

To harness this newfound power, the Manhattan Project was initiated as a classified research endeavor by the U.S. Government. Leading scientists and physicists came together to achieve what seemed impossible: creating a bomb powered by nuclear energy. The stakes were incredibly high as the Allies feared that Nazi Germany was also working toward developing a weapon. It became a race to ensure that the Axis powers did not succeed first. Despite his contributions to these theories, Einstein had deep reservations about their practical applications.

Einstein's moral compass was deeply troubled by the devastation that could arise from the misuse of atomic energy. This concern was expressed in his letter to President Franklin D. Roosevelt in 1939, which he co-authored with physicist Leo Szilard. In this letter, they raised awareness about the dangers associated with fission and the development of "extraordinarily powerful bombs of a novel kind." While this influential letter played a role in initiating the Manhattan Project, it also shed light on Einstein's internal conflict and highlighted the ethical dilemmas scientists faced.

As the project advanced, the world remained unaware of the changes that were on the horizon. After years of research and experimentation, a significant milestone was achieved with the testing of an atomic bomb in 1945, specifically at Trinity Site in New Mexico. With its codename "Trinity," this test marked the beginning of an era that forever altered human history.

The subsequent bombings of Hiroshima and Nagasaki were not demonstrations of immense power but were stark reminders regarding ethical considerations and moral implications associated with such advancements. The world witnessed firsthand how Einstein's theories held destructive potential, leading to awe, fear, and deep introspection as humanity entered the atomic age.

Reflections on Hiroshima and Nagasaki:

The bombings that occurred in Hiroshima and Nagasaki in August 1945 impacted the course of human history. These events brought to life the consequences of Albert Einstein's groundbreaking equation, $E=mc^2$. While they marked the end of World War II, they also introduced an era filled with moral and ethical dilemmas surrounding utilizing atomic energy.

Despite his contributions to theoretical physics, Albert Einstein could never have foreseen the immense scale of devastation indirectly caused by his theories. The bombings resulted in the loss of more than 200,000 lives, predominantly innocent civilians. This catastrophe vividly illustrated the connection between energy and mass he formulated four decades earlier. The affected cities were left in ruins, and survivors known as Hibakusha endured enduring psychological trauma forever changed by the catastrophic atomic events.

Einstein's visionary pursuit of comprehension and knowledge became entwined with one of humanity's chapters in the 20th century. The physicist who once marveled at the beauty and complexity of the universe now grappled with ethical considerations arising from his work.

It is said that when Einstein heard about the bombings, he expressed sadness and remarked, "If only I had known, I would have pursued a career in watchmaking."

The bombings of Hiroshima and Nagasaki created a backdrop to Einstein's contributions and the beginning of the atomic age. They emphasize the nature of scientific exploration and its potential for remarkable progress and unimaginable devastation. As the world stood on the cusp of the era, Einstein's reflections on these events served as a poignant reminder of the responsibilities that come with knowledge.

In the aftermath of the bombings, Einstein advocated for global peace and nuclear disarmament. He recognized a need for international cooperation to prevent future nuclear conflicts. His vision initially focused on unraveling mysteries of the universe, expanded to include a desire for a world rid of atomic destruction.

As we set the stage with Einstein's contributions and the dawn of the age, it is vital to acknowledge how profoundly Hiroshima and Nagasaki shaped his perspective. These events showcase science's immense power and underscore ethical dilemmas and moral obligations inherent in our pursuit of knowledge. Einstein's perspective, profoundly influenced by the events of 1945, acts as a beacon underscoring the interplay between exploration and its consequences for humanity.

SETTING THE STAGE WITH EINSTEIN'S CONTRIBUTIONS AND THE DAWN OF THE ATOMIC AGE:

Albert Einstein left a mark in history as an exceptional physicist and a symbol of intellectual brilliance that shone throughout the 20th century. His theories, the Special Theory of Relativity, revolutionized our understanding of the universe. However, his groundbreaking work had far-reaching consequences beyond just theoretical physics. It cast a shadow that defined one of the transformative and tumultuous periods in human history: the dawn of the atomic age.

Einstein's famous equation, E=mc^2, held more significance than being a mere mathematical expression. It was a revelation unlocking the energy concealed within an atom's nucleus. This discovery set in motion a series of pursuits that ultimately led to the Manhattan Project and the subsequent development of atomic bombs. Yet, as humanity raced to harness this newfound power, it grappled with ethical dilemmas. The potential for progress and unparalleled destruction hung precariously in the balance.

The birth of the age brought about mixed emotions. Excitement mingled with apprehension and introspection. The world found itself at a juncture holding both the power to shape its destiny and potentially invite its downfall. The complexities and challenges of our era are closely connected to the contributions of Albert Einstein. Therefore, it is crucial to explore his vision and its impact.

Albert Einstein's influence on the century cannot be overstated. His groundbreaking theories not only transformed the field of physics but also laid the groundwork for the atomic age, drastically changing the course of human civilization. Einstein's intellectual journey was marked by curiosity and a profound desire to comprehend the fundamental truths of our universe. These revelations extended beyond academia, spilling into geopolitics, ethics, and collective consciousness.

Einstein approached physics with intuition and analytical rigor, setting him apart from his contemporaries. While others adhered to norms, he fearlessly questioned existing beliefs and envisioned a universe governed by previously inconceivable principles. His Special Theory of Relativity, proposing that space and time are intricately connected in a framework, was truly revolutionary. However, it was undoubtedly his equation E=mc^2 that had far-reaching implications. This equation hinted at the connection between energy and mass, revealing the immense power hidden within the atom. Once this power was harnessed, it held both the promise of progress and the potential for unprecedented destruction.

The early 20th century was a time of upheaval in science and politics. As nations grappled with the challenges presented by a changing geopolitical landscape, scientists delved deeper into understanding the mysteries of the atom. They discovered that what was once believed to be a nucleus was a complex composition of particles held together by unimaginably strong forces. This realization opened possibilities for harnessing these forces to release energy, sparking a wave of scientific exploration and technological advancements worldwide. Laboratories around the globe became hubs of innovation where physicists, chemists, and engineers collaborated in their quest to unlock the secrets of energy.

However, with this newfound power came an immense responsibility. The ability to tap into energy wasn't just a scientific puzzle; it also posed profound ethical dilemmas. The same energy that could potentially fuel cities and transform industries also carried with it the capability to create weapons of mass destruction. The atomic age was not solely defined by scientific achievements but also encompassed moral and ethical quandaries that accompanied them.

The Manhattan Project, considered one of the most ambitious scientific endeavors of its time, perfectly exemplified this dual nature. However, its main goal was to develop a bomb; the project also brought together some of the brightest minds of that era, fostering a collaborative and innovative environment. The culmination of the project—the bombings of Hiroshima and Nagasaki—served as a reminder of the double-edged sword that atomic energy represented. The world witnessed the immense power unleashed by splitting atoms, leading to awe, apprehension, and deep contemplation.

Einstein, who played a role in developing theories that inadvertently paved the way for the atomic age, found himself deeply entangled in this complex situation. His philosophical tendencies and strong ethical beliefs made him a vocal advocate for peace and disarmament in the years following World War II. For Einstein, it wasn't about harnessing atomic power; it was equally important to comprehend the immense responsibilities of wielding such power.

As we delve further into Einstein's contributions and explore the dawn of the age, we encounter a narrative that encompasses not just human ambition, curiosity, and innovation but also introspection, ethics, and accountability. The era of power, with Einstein as its central figure, is a powerful reminder of the delicate balance between the pursuit of knowledge and our moral obligations.

Einstein: The Visionary Behind the Equation:

Albert Einstein, widely recognized as a symbol of intellect, went far beyond being just the physicist who developed the theory of relativity. His life and work encompassed a range of interests, each marked by deep contemplation and an unwavering dedication to unraveling the universe's complexities.

Born into a family in Ulm within the Kingdom of Württemberg in the German Empire, Einstein's early years didn't necessarily hint at the brilliance ahead. He was slow to start speaking, leading some to perceive him as lacking intelligence. However, once he found his voice, it became evident that his mind operated on a level. His inquiries about the world were not those typically posed by children. By age 12, he had self-taught himself geometry and ignited his passion for unraveling the mysteries of the universe.

Einstein faced obstacles during his academic journey. His disdain for memorization-based learning and clashes with authority figures within the education system often made him an outlier. Yet enough, these very challenges seemed to fuel his independent spirit. He refused to settle for accepting established truths; instead, he relentlessly sought to comprehend the underlying principles.

While at Zurich Polytechnic Institute, he pursued physics and mathematics studies with aspirations of becoming a teacher. He proved transformative.

That's when he started exploring the world of theoretical physics, which eventually became the foundation of his scientific endeavors. His early research papers, those from his remarkable year in 1905, demonstrated a fearless willingness to question established norms. Whether it was his investigations into the effect (for which he later received the Nobel Prize) or his contemplations on the nature of light, Einstein's early writings revealed a scientist who constantly pushed the boundaries of knowledge.

However, it was his work on relativity that truly set him apart. In a world governed by physics, Einstein introduced a groundbreaking change in perspective. His theory of relativity, summarized by the equation $E=mc^2$, proposed a universe where space and time were interconnected and relative. This wasn't simply a way of comprehending the cosmos but an entire revamp of the existing framework. The implications of this theory—both philosophical and practical—were immense. It challenged our understanding of reality, time, and space.

For Einstein, science extended beyond mere equations and experiments—it also encompassed profound philosophical exploration. He believed that beneath all its vastness, the universe adhered to a collection of uncomplicated principles.

Driven by a desire to uncover the underlying principles and decipher the cosmic language, his work reflected a philosophical inclination. This inclination became more apparent in his years when he explored the realms of cosmology, quantum mechanics, and unified field theory. Although he faced criticism for hesitating to accept the probabilistic nature of quantum mechanics, his contributions to these fields were undeniably substantial.

Einstein's personal life was marked by a series of ups and downs. His relationships with his first wife, Mileva Marić, were intricate and often tumultuous. In the 1930s, he moved to the United States due to the rise of Nazism in Germany—a turning point in his life. At Princeton's Institute for Advanced Study in New Jersey, Einstein found solace where he could continue pursuing science without being entangled in Europe's upheavals.

Throughout his lifetime, Einstein remained deeply involved in political matters of his era. Whether it was advocating for rights supporting the Zionist movement or even how his stance on pacifism shifted during World War II—Einstein utilized his influence to champion causes that resonated with him. In aspects, Einstein's brilliance extended beyond scientific accomplishments; it encompassed his approach toward life and continuous learning.

He possessed a range of knowledge, contemplating various subjects and envisioning new possibilities. His impact, defined by a quest for truth and a profound trust in the elegance and comprehensibility of natural laws, still captivates and motivates us. As we explore the depths of the era and its consequences, Einstein's insights, values, and philosophical ponderings remain significant, leading us through the intricate interplay of science, morality, and human existence.

The Atomic Age: A New Era Dawns:

The rise of the Atomic Age wasn't a scientific or technological milestone; it marked a significant shift in society and philosophy that would forever alter the course of human civilization. As the 20th century unfolded, we found ourselves standing at the threshold of an era where we could manipulate the very essence of matter to unleash an extraordinary amount of energy. The implications were both exciting and frightening.

Once believed to be the building block of matter, the nucleus of an atom was now understood as a hub for powerful forces. The revelation that atoms could be split to release amounts of energy had the potential to redefine how we perceive power, progress, and possibilities. If we could harness this energy, it would hold the key to addressing some of our most pressing challenges, from energy scarcity to breakthroughs in medicine. It offered hope for lighting up cities, driving industries forward, and propelling humanity toward a future filled with abundance and innovation.

However, amid these visions for tomorrow, there existed concerns and fears. The same energy that could illuminate our homes and drive economies also carried the capacity for unimaginable destruction within it. The true nature of energy became increasingly apparent as countries worldwide acknowledged its strategic and military importance. The competition to harness and control this newfound power became intertwined with ambitions, national pride, and the looming threat of global conflict.

The Manhattan Project, while a remarkable display of collaboration and innovation, also reflected the urgency and unease of that era. As the world stood at the precipice of another conflict, the stakes in this race for atomic power were extremely high. Shrouded in secrecy, the project served as a crucible where the brightest minds converged, driven by curiosity, duty, and the urgent need to maintain a balance of power.

However, amidst the work conducted by scientists and engineers on the Manhattan Project to unravel the mysteries of atoms, philosophical debates on ethics played out in parallel. Questions regarding what it meant to possess such immense power, its associated responsibilities, and moral considerations surrounding its use emerged as central topics for discussion. The atomic age was not about harnessing energy; it involved grappling with notions of power essence while considering ethical dilemmas and shaping future outcomes. When the first atomic bomb exploded in the New Mexico desert, it marked the beginning of an era for the world. The blinding light from the Trinity test not only showcased human creativity but also shed light on the challenges, dilemmas, and possibilities that came with the atomic age. The world had ventured into territory, and what lay ahead was a journey filled with complexity and transformation.

The Ethical Dilemmas of the Atomic Age:

With its display of human innovation and relentless pursuit of knowledge, the atomic age also brought about a time of deep ethical contemplation. It was an era where the atom held the potential for limitless energy to meet the world's growing power demands yet carried the immense burden of unparalleled destructive capabilities witnessed through the haunting mushroom clouds over Hiroshima and Nagasaki.

The bombings of these cities went beyond military actions; they became events that forced humanity to confront the moral consequences of its progress. The immediate aftermath was devastating; cities were reduced to ruins, countless lives were lost, and survivors known as Hibakusha grappled with long-lasting effects from radiation exposure. However, beyond the devastation lay an even more profound and pervasive trauma. The world had witnessed firsthand the unrestrained power inherent in nuclear energy, leading to a realization that once unleashed, it could never be taken back.

Einstein himself found himself at the center of these debates. While his groundbreaking work aimed to unravel the mysteries of the universe, he could have never foreseen the applications derived from his theories resulting in such catastrophic consequences.

The physicist, known for his pacifist beliefs, faced a dilemma. His letter to President Roosevelt had played a role in initiating the Manhattan Project. However, he was burdened by the consequences of the project, the bombings, which weighed heavily on his conscience.

The global community also grappled with these issues. Was it morally justifiable to use bombs on civilians to end a prolonged and devastating war? Could we defend the bombings considering the loss of lives that would have occurred in an extended conflict? These questions didn't have answers and caused deeply divided opinions.

Furthermore, the bombings had far-reaching consequences as they triggered an arms race during the Cold War era. Countries worldwide recognized the importance of nuclear weapons, resulting in stockpiling and an ongoing threat of mutual destruction. The ethical debates expanded beyond justifying bombings to include discussions on disarmament and nuclear proliferation. Even questioning the philosophy of deterrence that argued possessing nuclear weapons alone would deter adversaries from attacking.

International diplomacy worked hard to navigate these treacherous waters as our world teetered on the edge of nuclear conflicts. Treaties were proposed to control the spread of weapons and promote disarmament. However, ethical dilemmas continued to persist.

The presence of these weapons, even if they are never used, raises ethical questions about our obligations to ourselves and the future of our planet.

The atomic age was not a time of scientific progress but an era that forced humanity to confront its moral limits. The ability to control power came with the duty to use it wisely. As time passed, the lessons from Hiroshima and Nagasaki stood as reminders of the moral consequences of technological advancements and our shared responsibility to prevent such tragedies from happening again.

The era of power has left a lasting impact on human history, bringing many complexities and profound consequences. This book aims to give you an understanding of the Manhattan Project and its enduring significance. From its theoretical foundations to the global impact of the atomic bomb, we invite you to join us on a journey that promises both enlightenment and deep contemplation.

As we embark on this exploration together, we encourage you to delve into the subject matter, ask questions, reflect on what you discover, and immerse yourself in the captivating narrative that unfolds. Join us as we uncover the stories, individuals, and events that shaped this moment in history. Be prepared for enlightenment and challenges as we peel back the layers of "The Manhattan Project and the Birth of the Atomic bomb.

From Einstein's Theories to Oppenheimer's Test." Let your curiosity guide us as we navigate through this chapter in history side by side.

CHAPTER 1: THE WORLD BEFORE THE ATOMIC BOMB

GLOBAL GEOPOLITICS, SCIENTIFIC ADVANCEMENTS, AND SOCIETAL NORMS BEFORE THE ATOMIC AGE

The turn of the century marked a time of significant transformation. As countries dealt with the consequences of World War I, they unknowingly laid the foundation for a more destructive conflict. However, amidst all the military maneuvering, a silent revolution occurred. This revolution aimed to redefine our comprehension of the cosmos and our position within it.

Global Geopolitics:

The geopolitical landscape of the 20th century was full of upheaval with shifting alliances, growing nationalistic sentiments, and the remnants of colonialism. After the First World War, the world had to face the consequences of a conflict that not only changed borders but also global power dynamics.

Europe, which was central to the Great War, experienced transformations. The Austro-Hungarian, Ottoman, and Russian empires collapsed, leading to the birth of new nation-states. While these young countries celebrated their independence, they also faced challenges related to ethnic tensions and economic instability. The Balkans, often called Europe's "powder keg," became a hotbed for competing movements seeking dominance and recognition.

Germany endured hyperinflation and political unrest due to the heavy reparations imposed by the Treaty of Versailles. The

Weimar Republic emerged from the ruins of the German Empire. He struggled to establish a stable democratic foundation. In this climate of despair and disillusionment within society, extremist ideologies gained traction. The rise of Adolf Hitlers Nazi party not transformed Germany but also cast a foreboding shadow over the entire continent.

To the west, both the United Kingdom and France, despite being victorious in the Great War, faced their unique challenges. Their vast empires spanned continents. They were starting to display signs of strain. Movements advocating for independence emerged in colonies ranging from India to Algeria, aiming to challenge European imperialism. The economic consequences of the war, along with the difficulties of maintaining overseas territories, raised doubts about the sustainability and ethical implications of colonial rule.

Across the Atlantic Ocean, the United States emerged from the war relatively unscathed. Was positioned to assume a more prominent role on a global scale. The prosperous and culturally vibrant era known as "The Roaring Twenties" ensued, however, with the crash of Wall Street in 1929, followed by the Great Depression that affected not only America but also had global repercussions. Initially, America adopted a policy of retrenchment and isolationism, which would be tested as tensions escalated toward another major conflict.

In East Asia, Japan's ambitions for expansion were rapidly growing. As they annexed Korea and parts of China, Japan saw itself as Asia's power. Their desires for territories in Southeast Asia and across the Pacific inevitably led to confrontations with powers—most notably with the United States. After the Bolshevik Revolution, Russia was changing to establish a new social order based on communism. The Soviet Union, led by figures like Lenin and later Stalin, aimed to spread their revolutionary ideas, making capitalist Western nations uneasy.

In this network of global geopolitics, the seeds of future conflicts were planted. The ambitions and fears of countries influenced by their past experiences and hopes for the future would eventually come together in a chaotic situation that paved the way for the atomic age.

Scientific Advancements:

The beginning of the century marked a time of remarkable scientific exploration and breakthroughs. Our understanding of the universe was undergoing a transformation as groundbreaking theories and experiments challenged long-held beliefs, opening up new realms of knowledge.

In the 1900s, Albert Einstein introduced his theory of relativity, which revolutionized physics. This theory departed from centuries of Newtonian physics by suggesting that space and time were not absolute but interconnected in a unified framework called spacetime. This concept had implications indicating that time could stretch or contract depending on one's motion. While it was challenging to comprehend, it laid the groundwork for many aspects of modern physics.

Simultaneously, there was another revolution taking place in the study of extremely small particles. Quantum mechanics emerged as a tool to explain phenomena at the atomic and subatomic levels. Visionaries like Max Planck, Niels Bohr, and Werner Heisenberg introduced concepts such as energy levels that occur in quantities and wave-particle duality. Unlike physics, quantum mechanics revealed an inherent probabilistic nature where outcomes could only be described in terms of probabilities rather than certainties. It introduced a world where particles could exist in states at the same time, only settling into one state when they are observed.

While abstract and often counterintuitive, these quantum theories had applications in the real world. The field of electronics, for example, greatly benefited from understanding how electrons behave in materials. Semiconductors, crucial for electronic devices, were developed based on these principles.

Not only physics but also the biological sciences were undergoing significant changes. The discovery of the DNA helix in the 1950s by James Watson and Francis Crick marked a monumental moment in genetics. This complex molecular structure, with its paired bases and spiral staircase design, held the instructions for life itself. It promised to reveal insights into heredity, evolution, and even the origins of life.

Medicine was also on the brink of an era. The development of antibiotics, such as penicillin, by Alexander Fleming, revolutionized healthcare. Once fatal diseases could be cured, combined with advancements in techniques and our understanding of diseases at a molecular level, laid the foundation for a golden age of medical research and treatment.

The early 20th century witnessed scientific breakthroughs and progress. The limits of what we knew were being stretched in ways we had never seen before, paving the way for the progress made in technology and medicine during the latter half of the century. When we look back on this exploration period, it becomes clear that the foundation for the age was laid during the fruitful years of scientific discovery in the early 20th century.

Societal Norms Before the Atomic Age:

The society of the 1900s was a complex interplay of evolving values, changing norms, and emerging movements. After the aftermath of World War I, societies faced the challenges brought by technological and cultural advancements. Cities experienced a rise in urbanization, becoming vibrant centers of innovation and culture. This urban growth brought together ideas, resulting in a flourishing period for art, literature, and music.

The impact of cinema and radio cannot be overstated during this period. It was the time that people from different backgrounds could collectively share cultural experiences. Hollywood's Golden Age was at its peak, with films serving not only as entertainment but also reflecting societal hopes and fears. Radio. Broadcasts connected communities, shaping public opinion while providing a platform for marginalized voices.

The world was also grappling with difficulties following the Great Depression. This downturn prompted a reassessment of principles as people questioned whether unchecked capitalism was sustainable. The rise of communist ideologies, especially in Europe, directly responded to these economic challenges.

Amidst all these changes and uncertainties, there was a sense of optimism—a belief that society stood on the brink of a brighter future. However, this optimism would face challenges in the following decades as the world rapidly approached another worldwide conflict and the beginning of the atomic era.

The world before the bomb was a study in contrasts. It represented the potential for cultural progress, offering hope as we emerged from the aftermath of war. However, it also carried the weight of tensions and societal changes, foreshadowing the challenges ahead. To fully grasp the significance of the Manhattan Project and the creation of the bomb, we must consider this complex backdrop. In this context, pivotal events unfolded during the mid-20th century, forever altering the trajectory of history.

Reflecting upon the world before the atomic bomb, it becomes evident that the stage was set for monumental shifts long before the first mushroom cloud ascended into the skies. The early 20th century was a period of profound transformation, marked by a complex interplay of geopolitical maneuverings, groundbreaking scientific discoveries, and evolving societal norms.

The intricate dance of global geopolitics saw nations grappling with the legacies of past conflicts and the looming shadows of future confrontations. Europe, with its shifting borders and emergent ideologies, was a continent in flux, trying to find its footing in a post-war landscape. The punitive measures imposed on Germany post-World War I, the rise of extremist ideologies, and the challenges faced by colonial powers like the UK and France all contributed to an atmosphere of tension and uncertainty. Across the ocean, the United States, buoyed by economic prosperity but scarred by the Great Depression, was on the cusp of assuming a more assertive role in global affairs. Meanwhile, the Far East, particularly Japan with its imperial ambitions, was charting a course that would significantly impact global peace.

Parallel to these geopolitical shifts, science was abuzz with innovations and discoveries. The groundbreaking relativity and quantum mechanics theories were redefining our understanding of the universe. These scientific advancements, while laying the foundation for the atomic age, also posed ethical and philosophical questions about humanity's place in the cosmos and the responsibilities that come with knowledge.

Society, too, was undergoing a metamorphosis. The cultural vibrancy of the Roaring Twenties, juxtaposed with the economic despair of the 1930s, showcased the resilience and adaptability of the human spirit. Movements for civil rights, gender equality, and decolonization were gaining momentum, challenging established norms and pushing for a more inclusive and equitable world order.

The world before the atomic bomb had contrasts — hope and despair, progress and regression, peace and conflict. Understanding this backdrop becomes important as we delve deeper into the subsequent chapters. It is against this rich and multifaceted occurrence that the events leading up to the Manhattan Project and the detonation of the atomic bombs would unfold, forever altering the course of human history. The world was on the brink of an era that would challenge its moral compass, test its technological prowess, and redefine its geopolitical alliances. The atomic age was not just a chapter in history; it was a testament to humanity's endless quest for knowledge, power, and, ultimately, survival.

CHAPTER 2: THE GLOBAL STAGE THROUGH A LONDON LENS

The 20th century was a period of transformation characterized by rapid technological advancements, changing global power dynamics, and the rise of new belief systems. As the world dealt with the consequences of World War I and the looming possibility of another war, a series of events unfolded, ultimately leading to the advent of the age. London, with its rooted history, vibrant culture, and scientific achievements, provides a special perspective to comprehend the wider historical backdrop that shaped this era of change.

London: The Epicenter of Change:

London was more than just a city at the turn of the century. It was a dynamic entity buzzing with innovation and excitement for discoveries. The streets, paved with cobblestones, were home to both institutions and modern establishments, resonating with the footsteps of pioneers from various fields. The River Thames, which had witnessed centuries of transformation in the city's history, reflected the changing skyline—symbolizing London's evolution from a colonial capital to a global center for science and culture.

Throughout history, London has always attracted individuals. The 20th century was no exception. Scientists fleeing war-torn Europe, visionaries from colonies worldwide, and thinkers escaping regimes sought refuge in this city. They not only brought their expertise but also shared stories of their homelands, adding richness to London's intellectual fabric. Within institutions like Kings College and the Royal Institution, discussions on atomic structures, particle physics, and the enigmatic realm of quantum mechanics reverberated through corridors.

However, it wasn't within academic circles that excitement thrived. London public spaces became arenas where laypeople and experts debated the latest scientific theories. Hyde Parks Speakers Corner and bustling coffeehouses in Soho were among these hubs of intellectual exchange.

In these settings, the concepts of science were transformed into conversations, making London a city where knowledge was not just limited to experts. Still, they were something shared by the entire community.

London's scientific community had an impact beyond its boundaries. They collaborated with institutions, resulting in the exchange of ideas and resources. The city became a hub for scientific pursuits, with its laboratories and research centers often being the first to learn about breakthroughs happening in distant lands.

However, it wasn't the natural sciences that thrived. London's position as a meeting point exposed it to diverse philosophies and worldviews. Eastern philosophies intersected with thought, leading to interdisciplinary explorations aiming to comprehend the workings of the universe not only through equations but also through deep introspection.

Inspired by the Renaissance, London's artistic community began experimenting with new artistic forms and mediums. The abstract art movement found its place in London's galleries as it drew inspiration from the nature of quantum particles. Literature also reflected this evolving understanding of reality as authors crafted narratives that challenged traditional linear storytelling, akin to the nonlinear nature of quantum events.

During the 20th century, London was not just a city but also a hub of diverse ideas. It served as a meeting place for science, art, and philosophy, creating a cultural and intellectual atmosphere. London embraced the complexities of the age, acting as both an inspiration and a critical observer. The city eagerly looked toward the future while recognizing its accompanying responsibilities.

The Geopolitical Landscape:

In London, amidst its famous landmarks and busy streets, one could sense the geopolitical currents of the early 20th century. London, being the center of the British Empire, held more significance than just being a city; it embodied the global tensions and transformations that were reshaping the world order.

After the end of World War I, Europe found itself in a state of uncertainty. The powerful empires of Europe grappled with the realities of a post-war world. The Treaty of Versailles imposed reparations on Germany, leading to economic distress and nationalist sentiments. These circumstances provided ground for extremist ideologies to emerge—fascism in Italy and Nazism in Germany. The rise of these regimes directly challenged Britain and its allies' democratic ideals.

The political elites in London were acutely aware of these shifting dynamics. The British Foreign Office, located at Westminster's heart, became a hub for maneuvering. Prime Minister Neville Chamberlain's policy of appeasement toward Hitler sparked debates within Parliament and featured prominently in newspapers such as The Times and The Guardian. Some people considered it a practical approach to prevent another war, while others, like Winston Churchill, saw it as a risky concession to an aggressive regime.

At the time, the emergence of the United States and the Soviet Union as global superpowers brought another layer of complexity to the geopolitical landscape. The clash between capitalism and communism took the stage and set the foundation for the Cold War. With its connections to Washington, London found itself navigating a delicate balance between nurturing its "special relationship" with the U.S. And being cautious about the growing influence of the USSR.

The mighty British Empire began exhibiting signs of strain as demands for independence from Asian and African colonies grew louder. London became a hub for delegations from territories advocating for self-governance. Representatives from organizations such as the Indian National Congress, African National Congress, and other nationalist movements came to negotiate terms of independence in London, challenging Britain's project at its core.

Economically, Britain was still recovering from the impact of the Great Depression in the 1930s. The City of London's financial district witnessed fluctuations in capital flow with significant efforts by the Bank of England to stabilize Britain's economy.

The challenges made political tensions worse as discussions about protectionism, economic reforms, and social welfare policies took center stage in political debates.

London was in a network of political, economic, and ideological hurdles. The choices made within its centers of power, the discussions held in its universities and think tanks, and the public conversations on its streets all played a part in shaping the geopolitical landscape during the Atomic Age.

Cultural and Ethical Implications:

The advent of the era marked by significant scientific advancements triggered a wave of introspection in cultural and ethical realms. London, a city renowned for its intersection of art, philosophy, and science, grappled with the implications of this new epoch.

Already abuzz with the modernist movement, the literary circles in London began to reflect the hopes and fears that accompanied the age. The realization that humanity now possessed the capability to self-obliterate was astonishing and terrifying. This duality found expression in literature as writers crafted dystopian visions of what lay ahead. The works of Virginia Woolf and T.S. Eliot, among others, echoed inquiries prompted by the atomic bomb: What does it truly mean to be human in an era where humanity holds its destruction within reach? How does one discover significance in a world overshadowed by the looming specter of annihilation?

London's West End theaters also embraced these themes through thought-provoking productions. Plays delved into dilemmas faced by scientists, explored responsibilities carried by political leaders, and examined everyday anxieties experienced by citizens living under the shadow of this devastating weapon.

The performing arts played a role in society during the Atomic Age, serving as a platform for people to process, contemplate, and debate the ethical dilemmas of that time.

Art also underwent a transformation. The abstract expressionist movement, which originated during the period between the two World Wars, found new resonance in the aftermath of war. Artists such as Henry Moore and Francis Bacon started creating artworks that captured the prevalent emotions, uncertainty, and existential unease at that time. Their art reflected a changing world where established certainties were being disrupted by emerging scientific realities.

In parallel to these developments, philosophical discussions gained new urgency. Questions about ethics and morality were now being raised within the context of nuclear technology. Seminars, lectures, and debates held at institutions like the London School of Economics and the University of London became hotspots for deliberations on the moral implications of atomic bombs. Prominent philosophers like Bertrand Russell actively engaged with the public by advocating for disarmament and emphasizing the ethical responsibilities held by scientists and policymakers.

The influx of refugees and intellectuals from war-torn Europe greatly influenced London's cultural landscape. These individuals brought perspectives, experiences, and insights into the ethical ramifications of war, science, and technology. Their presence greatly enhanced the intellectual fabric of London, infusing it with a newfound richness and complexity that added depth to the ongoing conversations.

Essentially, the Atomic Age, characterized by a mixture of optimism, anxiety, and uncertainty, had a lasting impact on London's scene. The city, which has a standing tradition of intellectual and artistic exploration, responded to the challenges of that era by engaging in profound introspection, lively debates, and innovative expressions of creativity. It aimed to comprehend and navigate the ethical terrain of the 20th century.

THE BROADER HISTORICAL CONTEXT INFLUENCING THE ATOMIC AGE

The era of power, though significant, on its own did not arise independently. It represented the culmination of a sequence of interconnected occurrences, beliefs, and scientific advancements that spanned decades. To fully comprehend the scale and consequences of the Manhattan Project and the subsequent use of bombs, it is essential to grasp the larger historical context in which these events occurred.

The Scientific Renaissance:

The beginning of the century marked a significant period of scientific exploration, often referred to as the Scientific Renaissance. During this time, there was a desire for knowledge and a willingness to challenge long-standing beliefs about the universe and our role within it.

Physics played a role in this renaissance. While classical physics, with its laws of motion and gravity, had been established in the 19th century, scientists delving into the atom and venturing into space encountered phenomena that couldn't be explained by classical physics alone. This led to the emergence of quantum mechanics and relativity theory, fundamentally reshaping our understanding of reality.

Quantum mechanics explored the world at the level revealing a realm where particles could exist in multiple states simultaneously and where probability rather than certainty governed their behavior—visionaries like Max Planck, Werner Heisenberg, and Erwin Schrödinger introduced ground-breaking and counterintuitive concepts. For instance, they showed that light could exhibit properties of both particles and waves or that determining an electron's position and momentum was impossible.

These new findings not only expanded our knowledge of the atomic and subatomic world but also provided the basis for technologies that we now consider commonplace, such as semiconductors and lasers.

At the time, Albert Einstein's theory of relativity revolutionized our understanding of space, time, and the very fabric of the universe. His famous equation, $E=mc^2$, introduced the idea that matter and energy are interchangeable. This realization was crucial because it hinted at the amount of energy stored within atoms, energy that could be harnessed or released with significant consequences.

In addition to advancements in physics, this era also saw progress in other scientific fields. Chemistry made strides with the development of the table, enabling a deeper understanding of element relationships and leading to the creation of new materials and modern industries. Biology leaped forward with the discovery of DNA structure, setting us on a path toward unraveling life's fundamental code.

This period was not solely characterized by scientific discoveries and theories; it was also marked by introspection and philosophical debates. The deterministic worldview upheld by physics gave way to the probabilistic nature of quantum mechanics, sparking profound questions about causality, determinism, and even reality itself. Both philosophers and scientists engaged in contemplation of these profound questions, resulting in fruitful interdisciplinary conversations that connected the realms of science, philosophy, and even theology.

Essentially, the Scientific Renaissance was an era characterized by immense intellectual enthusiasm. It was a time when boundaries were pushed, established paradigms underwent transformative shifts, and the foundations for the age were laid. Humanity found itself on the cusp of an era armed with newfound knowledge and poised to unlock the mysteries of the universe. These discoveries held the potential for both creation and, unfortunately, destruction.

The World at War:

The early 20th century was marked by global changes that profoundly impacted the world. Two World Wars reshaped the social and economic landscapes, leaving lasting effects. The First World War, often referred to as the "Great War," was an event that witnessed major powers engaged in a brutal conflict. Its aftermath led to instability, economic turmoil, and deep-rooted resentments that served as precursors to future conflicts.

The Treaty of Versailles concluded the First World War. They imposed heavy reparations on Germany while also redrawing Europe's map. Although designed to establish peace, the punitive measures worsened Germany's economic hardships and created fertile ground for extremist ideologies. This allowed Adolf Hitlers Nazi Party to rise in power with their expansionist policies, ultimately leading Europe into another devastating conflict.

During this period in Asia, significant geopolitical shifts were taking place. Japan emerged as an imperial power following its victories in the Russo-Japanese War and World War I. Seeking to expand its territories in Asia, Japan invaded Manchuria in 1931 and subsequently displayed aggression toward China. These actions marked the beginning of Japan's ambitions, which culminated in the Pacific theater of World War II.

The Spanish Civil War, which took place from 1936 to 1939, served as an indication of the ideological divides that existed during that time. On one side were the Republicans, who received support from brigades, and on the other side were the Nationalists, led by General Francisco Franco. This conflict foreshadowed the ideological battle of World War II, with opposing powers, such as fascists and communists, lending their support to different factions.

As countries rearmed themselves and formed alliances, the world moved closer to yet another global conflict. The Munich Agreement of 1938 exemplified the policy of appeasement adopted by Britain and France, allowing Germany to annex parts of Czechoslovakia. However, this approach only strengthened the Axis powers' resolve, leading to Germany's invasion of Poland in 1939 and subsequently triggering World War II.

The Second World War proved more devastating than its predecessor, spreading across Europe, Asia, and Africa. It witnessed the rise of two superpowers—the United States and the Soviet Union—which set the stage for what would become known as the Cold War era. Significant technological advancements emerged from this conflict, including jet engines, radar systems, and, notably, nuclear technology.

With its conclusion came a new global order where international cooperation was fostered by establishing organizations, like the United Nations, to prevent conflicts. However, the deep division between the nations of the Western world and the communist countries of the Eastern bloc, symbolized by the Iron Curtain and the Berlin Blockade, marked the start of a different kind of conflict. A Cold War that would shape global politics for the next forty years.

Against this backdrop of uncertainty, securing power became a crucial objective. The potential of technology as a deterrent and its far-reaching implications for global power dynamics made it a central focus in geopolitical strategies, culminating in the Manhattan Project and ushering in an era defined by atomic energy.

The Ethical Quandary.

The rise of the era not only brought remarkable scientific achievements but also raised profound ethical dilemmas that continue to resonate throughout history. The essence of research, with its potential to harness unparalleled energy, gave rise to questions that extended beyond the boundaries of science and ventured into the realms of ethics, philosophy, and human accountability.

The atomic bomb, as a result of this research, was more than just a weapon; it represented humanity's ability to wield the very forces that shape our universe. However, this newfound capability brought forth inquiries about intentionality, purposefulness, and consequences. Should we use this power exclusively for purposes like energy generation? Was its destructive potential an inevitable outcome tied to its discovery?

Prominent scientists and thinkers of that time grappled with these inquiries. Icons such as J. Robert Oppenheimer, often known as the "father of the bomb, " experienced deep internal conflicts. Oppenheimer's contemplation after witnessing the first successful atomic bomb test—quoting from the Bhagavad Gita, "Now I am become Death, the destroyer of worlds"— summed up the moral turmoil experienced by many. It marked a realization of the weightiness associated with their creation and a confrontation with the implications arising from their work.

The ethical debates surrounding the bombings of Hiroshima and Nagasaki were further intensified. The immediate devastation and the long-term ramifications of radiation raised moral questions about using such weapons against civilian populations. Can we justify inflicting enduring suffering upon innocent inhabitants to swiftly end the war and potentially save countless lives from prolonged combat?

This dilemma extended beyond the immediate aftermath of the bombings. With the advent of the Cold War and an escalating arms race, humanity teetered on the edge of nuclear annihilation. The concept of Assured Destruction (MAD) emerged, hinging on the belief that nuclear weapon's sheer destructive power would deter nations from using them out of fear of their destruction in return. However, this strategy itself was laden with concerns. Were we to build security on a delicate balance wrought by terror?

The atomic age also sparked philosophical discussions regarding scientific responsibility. Should scientists pursue knowledge without considering its applications? Do they bear a moral duty for any consequences that arise from their discoveries? Philosophers, ethicists, and the scientific community actively participated in discussions, delving into the limits of scientific investigation and the ethical responsibilities of those leading the way in research.

Fundamentally, the ethical dilemma presented by the age reflected humanity's struggle with its potential. It confronted us with the conflicting aspects of exploration – its capacity to bring both progress and devastation. The atomic age compelled society to confront the consequences of our actions, prompting us to navigate carefully between advancement and accountability.

The Global Response.

The atomic bombings of Hiroshima and Nagasaki not only marked the end of World War II but also signaled the start of a new era in global politics. The world witnessed the destructive power of nuclear weapons, and its implications were profound and far-reaching.

After the bombings, there was a palpable sense of shock and awe worldwide. Nations, both allies and adversaries, recognized the game-changing nature of weapons. The balance of power shifted, creating uncertainty in the order. While the United States was the first to utilize bombs in warfare, it became clear that other countries would soon strive to develop their nuclear capabilities.

Observing how the U.S. Gained an advantage through its nuclear arsenal, the Soviet Union expedited its atomic research program, culminating in its successful nuclear test in 1949. This event marked the beginning of an era known as the Cold War— a rivalry between these two superpowers. The world effectively split into two factions competing for dominance and influence.

The subsequent arms race unfolded rapidly. It caused great alarm. Both superpowers amassed stockpiles of nuclear weapons, resulting in a state known as Mutually Assured Destruction (MAD).

The reasoning behind it was quite straightforward; if one side were to initiate an attack, the other would retaliate, destroying both. This delicate balance of power paradoxically served as a deterrent preventing conflicts between the United States and the Soviet Union.

However, the Cold War was not a two-sided competition. Other countries acknowledged the significance of nuclear weapons and aimed to enhance their capabilities. The United Kingdom, France, and China conducted their nuclear tests, joining the group of nations armed with nuclear weapons. This spread caused concerns about disputes escalating into full-blown nuclear confrontations.

To address the worries about the proliferation of nuclear weapons, international efforts were launched to promote disarmament and prevent further spread. The Nuclear Non-Proliferation Treaty (NPT), signed in 1968, was a milestone in this endeavor. With participation from 191 countries, this treaty aimed to curb weapons proliferation while fostering cooperation in peaceful applications of nuclear energy and working toward complete disarmament.

Although the NPT played a role in restraining nuclear proliferation, it faced certain challenges. Countries such as India, Pakistan, and Israel opted not to sign this treaty and proceeded to develop their stockpiles of nuclear weaponry. North Korea initially agreed to the treaty. Later, he withdrew and carried out nuclear tests.

In addition to treaties and efforts to disarm, the atomic era also witnessed the emergence of movements advocating for peace and the elimination of nuclear weapons. Civil society organizations, activists, and concerned individuals united against testing, calling for a world without nuclear arms. The devastating images of Hiroshima and Nagasaki became symbols for these movements, highlighting the human toll of nuclear warfare.

The global response to the age was multifaceted. While nations grappled with the implications of nuclear weapons, there was an increasing recognition of the importance of cooperation, disarmament, and diplomatic efforts. The challenges posed by the age emphasized how interconnected our global community is and reinforced our shared responsibility to prevent a recurrence of the horrors unleashed by nuclear warfare.

As we come to the end of this chapter, it is crucial to reflect on the web of events, beliefs, and reactions that shaped the early

20th century and set the stage for the atomic age. With its historical significance and global impact, London offered a unique perspective that allowed us to explore the broader historical context that influenced this transformative era.

The city's vibrant community of intellectuals, characterized by debates and groundbreaking research, provided valuable insights into the scientific revolution that paved the way for the atomic age. From the bustling streets of London to the corridors of Los Alamos, the journey of atomic science was marked by brilliance and ethical dilemmas. The world before the advent of bombs was filled with hope, ambition, and occasional profound uncertainty.

The section on historical context further sheds light on global dynamics in play during this period. The world was in flux, with nations grappling with war repercussions, the emergence of new ideologies, and the onset of the Cold War era. While being a testimony to innovation and genius, atomic bombs also posed significant ethical and geopolitical challenges. The global response demonstrated the awareness of the world with efforts focused on promoting peace, controlling nuclear proliferation, and addressing the moral complexities of the atomic era.

The stories of Hiroshima and Nagasaki, the race for arms, the rivalries during the Cold War, and the global movements for peace are interconnected elements within this narrative. They highlight how the atomic age had a nature – promising limitless energy while casting a shadow of immense destruction.

As we move forward, it is crucial to carry forward the knowledge and lessons acquired from this exploration. The Manhattan Project and the creation of bombs were not isolated incidents; they were significantly influenced by historical events, scientific advancements, and ethical considerations of that time. Understanding this context becomes vital as we delve deeper into understanding aspects and significant implications of the atomic age.

In chapters, our journey will take us through seats of power, revered scientific institutions, and society itself. We will explore the events and challenges of that era while pondering their lasting impacts.

Now that we have established the groundwork in this chapter, we can comprehend and value the intricacies, accomplishments, and ethical dilemmas surrounding the Manhattan Project and its profound global influence.

CHAPTER 3: THEORETICAL BEGINNINGS - THE SCIENCE BEHIND THE BOMB

Throughout history, the atomic age shines as a remarkable period of scientific breakthroughs and ethical dilemmas. The bombings of Hiroshima and Nagasaki were not the culmination of extensive research and experimentation but also raised profound questions about our responsibility in wielding such immense power. The Manhattan Project, at its core, was not solely focused on creating a weapon; it represented the convergence of minds, geopolitical pressures, and an unwavering thirst for knowledge.

The atom, a subject of philosophical contemplation in ancient Greece, had by the 20th century become the center of intense scientific scrutiny. As scientists delved deeper into its mysteries, they unraveled the choreography of particles and forces with the promise of limitless energy. However, this promise came with a side. While there was potential for peaceful applications like energy production, there was also the looming threat of unprecedented destruction.

The early 20th century witnessed a surge in scientific advancements that pushed traditional boundaries of knowledge and gave rise to new fields of study. Quantum mechanics emerged with principles that challenged our very perception of reality.

The electron proton and neutron discovery gave us insights into how atoms work. Additionally, Einstein's groundbreaking research on relativity emphasized the interconnectedness between energy and matter.

However, despite progress, the journey toward developing the atomic bomb was not solely about scientific principles. It was equally influenced by the people involved. Behind every experiment and theory were individuals driven by curiosity, ambition, and, at times, fear. The political climate of that era was marked by conflicts and the looming shadow of World War II, which added a sense of urgency to unravel the potential of atoms.

This book explores this journey—from its earliest theoretical foundations to the ethical considerations arising from the atomic age. We will navigate through science, politics, and ethics to comprehend how it happened and why it happened during one of history's most crucial periods.

As we embark on this exploration, it is important to acknowledge that the story of the age is not limited to history books; rather, it continues to have relevance in today's world.

The inquiries raised by the Manhattan Project regarding the obligations associated with knowledge and the ethical implications of progress remain just as pertinent today as they did in the past. Our aim is not only to offer insights into past events but also to provide a basis for contemplating the difficulties and possibilities that lie ahead in the present and future.

The Atom: A Universe in Itself:

The atom, which has long been considered the building block of matter, has fascinated humans for centuries. Its transformation from a concept to a well-defined scientific entity demonstrates our evolving understanding.

Although ancient Greek philosophers like Democritus and Leucippus were among the first to propose the existence of particles, it wasn't until the late 19th century that we began unraveling the mysteries of the atom—advancements in techniques provided scientists with unprecedented precision in exploring its nature.

J.J. Thomson's experiments with cathode rays in the 1800s were crucial in this process. Through studying how these rays behaved in magnetic fields, Thomson deduced the presence of negatively charged particles initially called "corpuscles" but later identified as electrons. This discovery was groundbreaking as it challenged the prevailing belief that atoms were solid and indivisible, suggesting a complex structure where electrons orbited around a central core instead.

However, we did not gain further insight into this central core until Ernest Rutherford's experiments in the 20th century. Rutherford concluded that an atom's mass and positive charge were concentrated within an incredibly small nucleus by bombarding gold foil with alpha particles and observing their deflection patterns.

According to his proposal, the center of an atom, known as the nucleus, is surrounded by electrons, similar to how planets orbit the sun. Then, being a solid sphere, the atom takes on a structure resembling a miniature solar system.

Further experimentation revealed insights into the internal makeup of atoms. It became clear that the nucleus itself is not elementary but composed of particles: protons with positive charges and neutrons that are electrically neutral. The balance between protons and electrons determines an atom's neutrality, while the number of protons defines its elemental identity.

As we progressed, our understanding of atoms continued to deepen. The introduction of quantum mechanics revolutionized physics. They have provided us with tools to comprehend electron behavior within atoms. Niels Bohrs 1913 Bohr model proposed that electrons orbit around the nucleus in energy levels or shells. However, this model was later refined by quantum mechanics principles; it served as a framework for comprehending atomic structure and behavior.

Research began focusing on unraveling the particles within atoms governed by fundamental forces. Understanding these forces and energy transitions within atoms opened doors for harnessing energy for both peaceful purposes and, unfortunately, warfare. Essentially, the atom, which was once a topic of discussion, has evolved into its miniature world, unlocking the secrets of nature and possessing great power.

The Birth of Quantum Mechanics:

The emergence of quantum mechanics changed the field of physics, challenging long-standing beliefs and introducing concepts that continue to defy our intuitive understanding even today. The scientific community experienced a period of upheaval during the 20th century when experimental results started to defy explanations provided by classical physics. It became evident that a new framework was needed, giving rise to the field of quantum mechanics.

One pivotal moment was Max Planck's investigation into radiation, which revealed that the classical worldview was incomplete. In his attempt to understand the distribution of radiation emitted by a black body, Planck introduced the idea of quantized energy levels. This revolutionary notion suggested that energy existed in packets or "quanta " rather than being continuous. Although this hypothesis was considered radical then, it accurately described blackbody radiation. He laid down the initial foundation for quantum theory.

However, Albert Einstein's research on the effect truly paved the way for the quantum revolution. By observing how electrons were emitted from metals when exposed to light, Einstein proposed that light had quantized properties. He introduced photons as units of energy and suggested that light exhibited characteristics resembling waves and particles simultaneously. The nature of light with its characteristics marked a significant departure from classical theories and hinted at a deeper and more intricate reality beneath the surface.

While Planck and Einstein inspired, it was the contributions of other scientists that truly shaped quantum mechanics into a comprehensive theory. Niels Bohr's atom model, which proposed energy levels quantized for electrons, represented a stride forward. Bohr's model successfully explained the lines of hydrogen, an aspect that classical physics had struggled to comprehend.

However, as groundbreaking as the Bohrs model was, it merely scratched the surface. The true complexity and profoundness of quantum mechanics began to reveal itself through the development of wave mechanics. Led by pioneers such as Louis de Broglie, Erwin Schrödinger, and Werner Heisenberg, wave mechanics established a mathematical framework for understanding particle behavior at the quantum level. De Broglie suggested that matter exhibited both particle and wave properties— to light—which Schrödinger further expanded upon with his wave equation. Heisenberg introduced matrix mechanics and the uncertainty principle that stated physical properties (like position and momentum) could not be precisely measured simultaneously.

These advancements portrayed a world fundamentally governed by probabilities. At this level, certainty was replaced by probability, and determinism gave way to unpredictability. Particles existed in states simultaneously, only collapsing into a definite state when observed. This departure from determinism was famously demonstrated through Schrödinger's cat thought experiment, which revealed the puzzling nature of quantum superposition.

The emergence and development of quantum mechanics were not a series of scientific breakthroughs; they represented a significant shift in our comprehension of reality. The quantum realm was peculiar, defying sense and often conflicting with classical intuition. However, this peculiarity held the key to unraveling the profound nature of the universe, spanning from minute particles to immense galaxies.

Moving forward, it is crucial to acknowledge the role of quantum mechanics in shaping 20th-century science. Though its principles can be challenging to grasp, they form the foundation of technology and have far-reaching implications for our understanding of the cosmos.

The Nucleus and the Forces that Bind:

The tiny atomic nucleus, which exists at the center of every atom, is truly fascinating. Even though it occupies a space smaller than the atom, it holds more than 99.9% of its mass. This compact core consists of protons and neutrons. It is a hub of activity governed by mysterious forces.

During the 20th century, scientists had limited knowledge about the nucleus. They were aware of protons thanks to Rutherford's experiments. James Chadwick's discovery of neutrons in 1932 added a new dimension to nuclear physics. The coexistence of these particles protons with similar charges in such proximity posed an important question: How do they stay together without repelling each other?

The answer lies in a force entirely different from any force known at that time – the strong nuclear force. As its name implies, this force is incredibly powerful. Overcomes the electromagnetic repulsion between protons to bind the nucleus together. However, its influence diminishes rapidly as you move away from the nucleus, limiting its reach to its surroundings.

The discovery of the nuclear force marked a significant milestone in physics. Not only did it help us understand why the nucleus remains stable, but it also allowed us to explore more complex nuclear phenomena. Take fission, for example. Some atomic nuclei can break apart when given energy, overcoming the force that holds them together. On the other hand, under specific circumstances, smaller nuclei can merge in a process called nuclear fusion, releasing even more energy than fission.

To hold protons and neutrons together, particles known as gluons act like glue. These gluons and quarks (the building blocks of protons and neutrons) form the foundation of quantum chromodynamics (QCD). QCD is a theory that explains how strong interactions occur at the level. It is a part of the Standard Model of particle physics and gives us a comprehensive understanding of how quarks and gluons behave and interact within the nucleus.

As scientists explored the intricacies of the nucleus, they discovered particles and resonances, each with its unique properties and behaviors. For instance, mesons consist of a quark and an antiquark. Play a role in mediating the strong force between nucleons (protons and neutrons).

The investigation of these particles and how they interact, which is referred to as hadron physics, has given us insights into the nature of the strong force and the rules that govern the atomic nucleus.

Essentially, the atomic nucleus serves as a small-scale representation of the forces and particles in the universe. Its exploration has not only unveiled the secrets of atoms but has also deepened our understanding of how the universe is structured. The knowledge gained from studying the nucleus and its binding forces has had implications ranging from advancements in nuclear energy to the development of atomic weaponry, which has forever changed humanity's connection with nature.

Einstein, Energy, and the Famous Equation:

When we think of a genius, one image often comes to mind is Albert Einstein with his wild hair and deep-set eyes. Beyond the portrayals and cultural references, Einstein's contributions to science were revolutionary. Among his groundbreaking works, one equation stands out not only for its simplicity but also for its profound implications: $E=mc^2$.

This equation, part of his Special Theory of Relativity, published in 1905, represents a concept that completely reshaped our understanding of energy and matter. At its core, $E=mc^2$ suggests a connection between an object's energy (E) and its mass (m), with 'c' representing the speed of light in a vacuum—an astronomical value approximately equal to 299,792,458 meters per second. When squared, this number becomes incredibly large, implying that even a tiny amount of mass possesses the potential to release an amount of energy.

What did this mean practically? For most of the 20th century, this equation remained a theoretical marvel appreciated by physicists but largely divorced from tangible applications.

However, as research advanced in nuclear physics, the true potential behind $E=mc^2$ started to reveal itself.

Scientists realized that the tremendous energy generated during reactions like those occurring naturally in the sun could be explained by converting a tiny amount of mass into energy, as Einstein's equation describes.

This discovery played a role in the pursuit of harnessing nuclear energy. If even a small portion of an atom's nucleus mass could be transformed into energy, the resulting release would be significantly more powerful than chemical reactions such as combustion. This principle formed the foundation for exploring fission, where heavy atomic nuclei like uranium or plutonium were split into lighter elements, unleashing an immense amount of energy.

However, Einstein's equation also introduced ethical and philosophical dilemmas. The potential to extract amounts of energy from minuscule amounts of matter offered unlimited possibilities for clean energy. At the time, it carried with it unparalleled destructive capabilities. The atomic bomb exemplifies this dual nature – a direct application of $E=mc^2$. The enormous release of energy during explosions can level entire cities and leave long-lasting environmental and health consequences—an undeniable manifestation of Einstein's theoretical contributions.

Einstein himself was acutely aware of these implications. Though his contributions laid the groundwork for physics, he was also a vocal advocate for peace, particularly in the aftermath of the bombings of Hiroshima and Nagasaki. The equation $E=mc^2$ stands as a reminder of the dual nature of scientific discovery, offering immense potential for progress and well-being but presenting significant ethical challenges.

Within the context of our examination of the Manhattan Project and the development of weaponry, Einstein's equation serves as a fundamental cornerstone. It highlights the principles that facilitated the creation of such destructive weapons while encouraging us to contemplate the broader consequences of harnessing atomic power. As we progress through the chapters, this interplay between science, ethics, and history will emerge as a recurring theme, emphasizing how a complex web of events and decisions shaped the era defined by atomic energy.

EARLY SCIENTIFIC THEORIES AND DISCOVERIES

For years, humans have been driven by a deep curiosity to unravel the mysteries of the universe. From the ponderings of thinkers to the rigorous experiments conducted by modern scientists, we have embarked on an arduous yet exhilarating journey to comprehend the true essence of our world. In this chapter, we will travel through time, retracing the footsteps of minds who dedicated themselves to understanding the intricate workings of atoms.

The atom, often hailed as the building block of matter, has captivated and sparked speculation for centuries. While ancient civilizations contemplated its existence, it wasn't until modern science emerged that we began to uncover its nature. Each discovery and breakthrough acted as a puzzle piece in a mosaic that gradually revealed a world far more complex and captivating than anything previously imagined.

The late 18th and 19th centuries marked a pivotal period in atomic exploration. As scientists delved deeper into studying matter, they encountered phenomena that defied understanding. The identification of electrons, recognition of nuclei, and birth of quantum mechanics were not isolated incidents but interconnected milestones forming part of an extraordinary scientific narrative.

This narrative was not about dry facts; it encompassed emotions and wonderment, too. It had stories of ambition, collaboration, competition, and unexpected discoveries. Every theory and experiment had its group of extraordinary individuals. The visionaries who dared to challenge the norms question everything, experiment, fail, and never give up. Their personal stories intertwined with their pursuits bring a human touch to the fascinating tale of atoms.

As we dive into this section, we invite you to travel in time and walk alongside remarkable figures like Dalton, Thomson, Rutherford, and Bohr. Witness their "eureka" moments, engage in debates, and witness paradigm shifts that shaped our understanding of the world. Through this journey, we aim not only to present a chronicle of accomplishments but also to pay homage to the unyielding spirit of human curiosity and the relentless quest for knowledge.

With this groundwork established, we will navigate the paths of discovery—examining how each puzzle piece related to atoms found its place on our knowledge canvas. This sets the stage for events in the 20th century and marks the beginning of an era—the atomic age.

Ancient Philosophical Musings:

The concept of the atom, considered an indivisible building block of matter, is deeply rooted in ancient thinking. Before the development of modern scientific methods, ancient civilizations pondered over the nature of the universe and the essence of reality. While their contemplations were not based on scientific approaches, they laid the philosophical groundwork for future investigations.

In Greece, the idea of the atom emerged as an answer to a philosophical puzzle: how can something arise from nothing? This inquiry, central to understanding creation and transformation, led to speculations. Some philosophers believed that everything originated from a primal substance, while others proposed the existence of multiple elements. Amidst these debates, the concept of the atom began to take form.

Democritus is often recognized as one of the figures in this discourse on atomic theory. Expanding upon ideas from his mentor, Leucippus, Democritus proposed that all things in the universe were composed of particles known as "atoms" that could not be further divided. According to him, these particles moved through space and combined or rearranged themselves differently to give rise to all kinds of objects and substances we perceive today. Democritus believed that these atoms' properties—such as shapes, sizes, and arrangements—determined the characteristics exhibited by the matter they constituted.

While Democritus' ideas were groundbreaking, they did not receive acceptance. Plato, for example, rejected the theory and favored his theory of ideal forms. Similarly, Aristotle had reservations. He believed in the existence of five fundamental elements. Earth, water, air, fire, and aether. Rather than indivisible atoms.

However, there was a renewed interest in the theory through the works of Epicurus and the Roman poet Lucretius. Lucretius's epic poem "On the Nature of Things" explained Epicurean philosophy and the atomistic theory. He portrayed atoms as indestructible entities in perpetual motion that beautifully intertwined to form the natural world.

Although ancient atomists lacked evidence to support their claims, their philosophical insights were profound. They challenged prevailing beliefs about divisibility and continuity by introducing concepts that continued to inspire generations of thinkers. These speculations laid the groundwork for advancements and empirical investigations that ultimately validated and refined our understanding of atoms.

The contemplations of these philosophers stand as a testament to humanity's enduring pursuit of knowledge. They serve as a reminder that exploration often commences with conjecture, with intellectuals venturing to envision the invisible and challenge conventional wisdom. The atom, merely a concept in philosophy, would eventually play a crucial role in our comprehension of the cosmos, connecting the realms of abstract thinking and empirical scientific inquiry.

The Dawn of Modern Atomic Theory:

The beginning of the century marked a significant period in the development of atomic theory. While the ancient Greeks had speculated about the existence of particles, it was during this time that a more precise and scientific understanding of atoms began to take shape.

John Dalton, a scientist specializing in meteorology and chemistry, played a crucial role in this shift. His curiosity about gases led him to contemplate the nature of matter. Dalton noticed patterns in how elements combined to form compounds through observations and experiments. This led him to propose that each element consisted of atoms, which combined in consistent proportions to create compounds. For example, water would always have two hydrogen atoms for every oxygen atom, which resulted in its formula H_2O.

Dalton's atomic theory was groundbreaking for several reasons. Firstly, it suggested that atoms of an element had identical mass and properties. This departure from vague notions provided a concrete identity for each element. Secondly, Dalton's theory proposed that chemical reactions involved rearranging these atoms while keeping them unchanged. This idea revolutionized our understanding of reactions at a microscopic level.

Dalton introduced the notion of weights. By examining the ratios in which various elements combined, he could assign weights to different atoms. For example, he found that an oxygen atom was eight times heavier than a hydrogen atom. However, these values may not align perfectly with standards; they laid the foundation for the periodic table and our present comprehension of atomic masses.

Nevertheless, like any pioneering theory, Dalton's ideas faced opposition from critics. Some scientists were skeptical about atoms during that era due to a lack of direct observational evidence. However, as time progressed through the century, additional experimental evidence emerged that supported and refined Dalton's theories.

One such piece of evidence was the discovery of isotopes. While Dalton initially proposed that all atoms of an element were identical, later experiments revealed that this was not entirely accurate. Certain elements possessed atoms with varying masses called isotopes. This discovery added complexity to theory and deepened our understanding of the atomic realm.

Overall, the 19th century marked a period of rapid exploration and refinement in modern atomic theory. The groundbreaking research conducted by John Dalton established the basis for our comprehension of the atom, paving the way for even more groundbreaking discoveries in the 20th century. By merging his theories with the contributions of numerous other scientists, they could transform the atom from a mere philosophical idea into an empirically verifiable scientific entity, indefinitely altering the trajectory of scientific progress.

Electrons, Cathode Rays, and the Plum Pudding Model:

During the part of the 19th century, scientists were filled with excitement and curiosity regarding the enigmatic "cathode rays." These peculiar rays were observed when an electric current passed through a low-pressure gas, sparking debates. The scientific community pondered whether these rays resembled waves like light or possessed properties of particles with mass and charge.

Among the pioneering scientists was Sir William Crookes, a researcher who extensively experimented with cathode ray tubes. He noted that these rays traveled in lines and cast shadows, indicating a particle-like behavior. However, J.J. Thomson, a physicist from the University of Cambridge, conducted a defining experiment.

Thomson's experiments involved directing cathode rays through magnetic fields. By measuring how much the rays deflected under known field strengths, he made two determinations: cathode rays carried negative charges and had significantly less mass than even hydrogen—the lightest known atom. This groundbreaking revelation led Thomson to name these unknown negatively charged particles "electrons."

The discovery of electrons held significance. It indicated that atoms, which had long been considered the smallest indivisible units of matter, actually had smaller components. However, this discovery presented a puzzle. Atoms were known to have no charge, so how could they contain negatively charged electrons? To solve this dilemma, Thomson proposed the "plum pudding" model of the atom in 1904.

According to this model, the atom was envisioned as a sphere with a charge resembling a pudding or dough. The charged electrons were embedded within this sphere, similar to how plums are embedded in a traditional English plum pudding. The overall neutrality of the atom was maintained by balancing the charge of the electrons with the positive charge of the surrounding "pudding."

Thomson's model explained the presence of electrons within atoms while preserving their overall neutral nature. However, as is common in sciences, evolving domains, new experiments, and discoveries would soon challenge and refine our understanding of atomic structure. Eventually, the plum pudding model would be replaced by an accurate representation that paved the way for further groundbreaking discoveries in atomic physics.

Rutherford's Gold Foil Experiment:

Ernest Rutherford, often called the father of physics, conducted an experiment in 1909 that challenged the prevailing understanding of how atoms are structured. During that time, J.J. Thomson's "plum pudding" model was widely accepted, which suggested that an atom resembled a diffuse cloud of charge with embedded electrons, similar to plums in a pudding.

Rutherford and his assistants Hans Geiger and Ernest Marsden decided to test this model. Their experiment involved shooting charged alpha particles at an extremely thin sheet of gold foil. According to the "plum pudding" model predictions, they expected these alpha particles to pass through the foil with little deflection since they would travel through a mostly uniform charge distribution.

However, the results were astonishing. While most alpha particles did pass through the foil as anticipated, a small fraction experienced significant deflection at large angles, and some even bounced back toward their source. This outcome was completely unexpected. The existing atomic model couldn't explain it.

Rutherford compared this experience to firing an artillery shell at tissue paper only for it to rebound back. The implications were clear; the atom's mass and positive charge were concentrated in a central area, which Rutherford called the "nucleus." On the other hand, the electrons must be orbiting this nucleus at relatively large distances, resulting in an atom that consists mostly of space.

This discovery was truly groundbreaking. It signified that of being a solid mass of positive pudding with embedded electrons, the atom had a central nucleus of protons (later understood to include neutrons) surrounded by a cloud of electrons. The majority of the atom's volume was space.

Rutherford's gold foil experiment marked a moment in the history of atomic physics. Not only did it disprove the "plum pudding" model, but it also laid the foundation for our current understanding of the structure of atoms. The discovery of the nucleus led to investigations into its composition and the forces holding it together, paving the way for subsequent breakthroughs in nuclear physics and quantum mechanics.

What made this experiment truly elegant was its simplicity. Using alpha particles, gold foil, and a detector, Rutherford and his team completely transformed how scientists looked at atoms. It demonstrated how curiosity-driven research can yield valuable discoveries even from simple experiments.

Bohr's Quantum Leaps:

Niels Bohr contributed to the atomic theory field, which marked a departure from classical physics and paved the way for quantum mechanics. His work played a role in understanding how electrons behave within atoms and laid the foundation for subsequent advancements in quantum theory.

Bohr's model centered around the concept of quantized energy levels. Unlike orbits, where planets can freely revolve at any distance from a star, electrons in the Bohrs model were restricted to specific fixed orbits around the nucleus. Each orbit corresponds to an energy level, with closer orbits having lower energy and vice versa.

One of the groundbreaking aspects of Bohr's model was the idea of quantum leaps or transitions. According to Bohr, electrons could transition between energy levels but couldn't exist between them. When an electron moves to an energy level, it absorbs a precise amount of energy, often light photons. On the other hand, when it dropped to a lower energy level, it emitted photons.

This concept beautifully explains the spectral lines observed in light emitted or absorbed by atoms.
Each element had its distinct set of spectral lines, as the Bohrs model revealed that these lines resulted from electrons transitioning between different energy levels. The specific energy values of the photons absorbed or emitted correspond to the variations in energy between these levels.

Additionally, Bohr introduced the concept of quantized momentum. He proposed that the momentum of an electron while orbiting was restricted to specific values. This quantization helped explain why only certain orbits were permissible within his model.

Although the Bohrs model represented an advancement, it did have its limitations. While it worked well for hydrogen, the simplest atom with just one electron, it struggled to describe atoms with multiple electrons accurately. The model couldn't account for the structure observed in spectral lines or phenomena like the splitting of spectral lines known as the Zeeman effect, which occurs in the presence of a magnetic field.

Nevertheless, it is essential to recognize the significance of Bohr's work. It served as a stepping stone and laid the groundwork for more comprehensive quantum mechanics that would soon emerge. The concepts of quantized energy levels and quantum leaps became principles within quantum theory. They guided future physicists in their pursuit to unravel the enigmas of the atomic and subatomic realms.

The Uncertainty Principle and Quantum Mechanics:

The discovery of quantum mechanics in the 20th century significantly changed how we understand the world of atoms and particles. This new field of physics aimed to explain phenomena that classical physics couldn't account for at the smallest scales. One revolutionary and sometimes counterintuitive idea to come out of this field was Heisenberg's uncertainty principle.

In 1927, Werner Heisenberg, a physicist, proposed that there are limits to how precisely we can know certain pairs of physical properties of a particle simultaneously. The well-known example is position and momentum. Essentially, if we know one property accurately, we will have less accuracy in knowing the other. This isn't because our measuring tools are flawed. Rather, it is an inherent characteristic of quantum systems.

This principle challenged held beliefs about predictability in physics. In mechanics, if you knew the initial conditions of a system, you could predict its future behavior with great precision. However, the uncertainty principle introduced an element of unpredictability into quantum mechanics. It suggested that at the quantum level, reality doesn't exist in a state but exists as a combination or superposition of states until observed and measured.

This concept was further investigated in a known thought experiment called Schrödinger's cat. Erwin Schrödinger, a figure in quantum mechanics, presented a scenario where a cat inside a sealed box could exist simultaneously as both alive and dead depending on an unpredictable event that occurred earlier until the box is opened and the cat is observed. This experiment highlighted the often counterintuitive nature of quantum mechanics.

Another important idea in quantum mechanics is the notion of wave-particle duality. Experiments like the slit experiment demonstrated that particles, such as electrons, can exhibit characteristics of both particles and waves. When electrons were directed at a barrier with two slits, they produced an interference pattern typically associated with waves when fired one at a time. However, when attempts were made to determine which slit, each electron went through the interference pattern. They behaved like particles.

These experiments and theories have revolutionized our understanding of the universe on its fundamental level. They propose a world where probabilities hold sway over certainties, and observation plays an essential role in shaping reality.

The implications of quantum mechanics extend beyond theoretical physics alone. They have led to advancements in chemistry, material science, and even biology. Additionally, they have paved the path for advancements, such as lasers, MRIs, and computers.

In the context of our account of the Manhattan Project and the atomic bomb, comprehending the quantum realm is crucial. The behaviors and interactions of particles at this level played a role in developing nuclear fission and eventually creating the bomb. As we delve deeper into this narrative, it will become more apparent how significant these quantum phenomena are, highlighting the relationship between theory and application in atomic physics.

The exploration into the atom's core, from its concepts to the intricate movements of tiny particles, reflects humanity's unquenchable curiosity and unwavering pursuit of knowledge. The ancient Greeks laid the groundwork for a quest that would span centuries, with their ponderings on "atoms" or indivisible particles, planting the seeds of inquiry that would eventually bear fruit.

The rise of atomic theory, led by John Dalton's theories, marked a significant transition from philosophy to science. Dalton's insights, based on observations, provided a framework for comprehending the nature of matter and paved the way for groundbreaking discoveries. The late 1800s and early 1900s witnessed progress as scientists such as J.J. Thomson and Ernest Rutherford reshaped our understanding of atomic structure. Thomson's identification of electrons and Rutherford's unveiling of the nucleus were pivotal moments that challenged and refined our perceptions of atoms.

However, it was quantum mechanics that truly transformed physics. Visionaries like Niels Bohr, Werner Heisenberg, and Erwin Schrödinger introduced concepts that offered a deeper and more comprehensive grasp of atomic behavior.

Bohr's discovery of energy levels that occur in increments, Heisenberg's principle of uncertainty, and Schrödinger's equations describing the behavior of waves all came together to present a captivating yet intricate picture of the atom.

When we reflect upon the scientific theories and breakthroughs, it becomes clear that our exploration into the atomic realm was far from straightforward. It was a journey marked by obstacles, debates, and shifts in thinking. However, each new. Theory built upon the previous ones, forming a mosaic of knowledge that eventually led to the creation of the atomic bomb through projects like the Manhattan Project. These fundamental understandings of how atoms functioned played a role in harnessing their immense power and forever changing human history.

As we venture further into chapters, we will explore how these theoretical foundations were translated into practical applications with significant implications for science, politics, and ethics. The atomic age presented us with complexities and far-reaching consequences; it invites us to gain insights, ponder upon reflections, and develop a deeper understanding of one of history's most transformative eras.

CHAPTER 4: THE MANHATTAN PROJECT - CATALYST OF CHANGE

Few endeavors in 20th-century history stand out as prominently as the Manhattan Project. It wasn't a scientific mission but an enormous undertaking that captured the aspirations, anxieties, and ambitions of an era on the verge of unprecedented change. As nations grappled with the aftermath of a world war and the emergence of global powers, the race to harness atomic power became symbolic of a larger struggle: the pursuit of dominance in a rapidly evolving geopolitical landscape.

The Manhattan Project was far more than its name implies. It went beyond New York City's boundaries. It transcended mere project status. The initiative spanned multiple cities, involved thousands of individuals, and consumed extensive resources. At its core, it represented determination, resourcefulness, and an unwavering quest for knowledge even when confronted with profound ethical dilemmas.

This chapter aims to delve into the essence of the Manhattan Project by exploring its origins, the key figures involved, and the myriad obstacles it encountered. We will embark on a journey through the geopolitical landscape of the early 20th century characterized by fascism's rise and the looming threat of another global conflict.

We will witness a gathering of scientists motivated by fear, ambition, and curiosity. By delving into the stories of figures such as Oppenheimer, Fermi, and Groves, we will gain insights into the human aspects of this immense endeavor. The emotions, conflicts, and collaborations that propelled the project forward.

We will delve into the role played by the U.S. Government in financing and supporting the project. This will illuminate the connection between politics, science, and military strategy. As we navigate through this chapter, we aim to provide an understanding of the Manhattan Project, not just as a historical event but also as a catalyst for transformative change that continues to impact

Join us on this exploration as we retrace the footsteps of minds who dared to unlock the secrets held within atoms. Their groundbreaking efforts forever altered the course of history.

The Genesis of a Revolutionary Endeavor:

The Manhattan Project, although often simplified to its result. The atomic bomb. It was a series of events, choices, and necessities that unfolded over several years. Its origins can be traced back to a world grappling with the pace of technological progress and the looming specter of conflict.

The early 20th century witnessed scientific breakthroughs. Our understanding of atoms and their potential energy was still in its stages, but the implications of harnessing such power became increasingly clear. As nations raced to progress in fields, atomic energy emerged as a focal point not only for its military applications but also for its potential to shape the future of energy and technology.

However, the drive to delve into research was not solely fueled by scientific curiosity. The geopolitical landscape at that time played a role. The emergence of fascist regimes in Europe with their expansionist ambitions threatened global peace. The balance of power shifted, leading to an outlook on what lay ahead. In this context, the United States faced a dilemma after maintaining a stance for so long. The realization of the importance of being prepared for an escalating conflict and gaining an advantage in the war became clear.

It was within this context that the concept of the Manhattan Project was born. The project wasn't a response to immediate threats then but a forward-thinking initiative. Leaders and visionaries recognized that the world stood on the brink of an era, understanding that the nation that could harness atomic power first would not only possess a significant military edge but also wield influence in shaping the post-war global order.

Therefore, the decision to embark on the Manhattan Project held both significance and required a leap of faith. It represented a commitment to venture into the territory, investing resources and intellect into an endeavor with uncertain outcomes. However, it also reflected a belief in creativity and confidence that innovation and collaboration could pave a path forward when confronted with unprecedented challenges.

In retrospect, we can see that the origins of the Manhattan Project were shaped by both the spirit of its time and the urgent needs of a world in turmoil. It represented a stride toward an uncertain future during a period filled with uncertainties and obstacles.

A Confluence of Disciplines:

The Manhattan Project was a massive endeavor and a deliberate strategy to address its complex challenges by bringing together experts from various fields. The project recognized the need for collaboration and integration of scientific disciplines to achieve its ultimate goal.

While physics laid the foundation for understanding fission and atomic reactions, it became clear that creating a working atomic bomb required expertise beyond just physics. Chemists played a role, especially in the intricate process of enriching uranium. Separating uranium 235 from the abundant uranium 238 posed significant difficulties that demanded deep knowledge of chemical processes, material properties, and innovative techniques such as gaseous diffusion and electromagnetic separation.

Engineers and metallurgists were responsible for designing and constructing the bomb to withstand the conditions of a nuclear detonation. Their expertise ensured that all physical components could perform effectively under pressure.

Overall, the success of the Manhattan Project relied on collaboration among scientists from different disciplines who brought their unique perspectives to achieve the project objectives collectively. They faced challenges concerning the integrity of materials, reducing size, and achieving precision. They made sure that every component, the smallest detail, worked perfectly.

The mathematicians, who often go unnoticed in this project, provided the foundation. In a time when modern computers didn't exist yet, they carried out calculations and simulations to predict how nuclear reactions would behave and refined the bomb design based on those predictions.

Apart from these aspects, the project also relied on logistics, project management, and even psychology experts. Understanding behavior was crucial, particularly in maintaining secrecy and keeping the large workforce motivated and aligned with the project goals.

These diverse disciplines intertwined with each other and formed the essence of the Manhattan Project. It was like a symphony where every mind played an indispensable role. This project's success showcased human creativity and demonstrated how collaboration among diverse minds with a shared vision could achieve what seemed impossible.

Challenges Beyond Science.

The Manhattan Project, despite being focused on scientific exploration, faced numerous complexities that went well beyond the confines of laboratories and research facilities. The scale of this undertaking brought forth a range of ethical and geopolitical challenges that were just as intricate, if not more so, than the scientific issues the project aimed to solve.

From a standpoint, the project was an unprecedented endeavor. The demand for raw materials such as uranium and plutonium was immense, and procuring them in the required quantities, often under covert circumstances, proved to be a monumental task. The secretive nature of the project meant that substantial resources had to be mobilized without attracting attention. This level of secrecy also extended to the workforce involved. Numerous individuals from backgrounds. Including construction workers and leading scientists. We were employed across different sites without fully understanding the project's true nature. Maintaining confidentiality among such a diverse group presented its own set of challenges.

Selecting locations for research and testing facilities posed additional obstacles due to security and safety concerns. Building cutting-edge laboratories and accommodations in places like Los Alamos, perched on a plateau in New Mexico, demanded meticulous planning and flawless execution. The isolation also meant that everything people needed, like food and special equipment, had to be brought from away. They had to build roads or railways to transport these necessities.

Besides dealing with challenges, the project faced significant ethical dilemmas. The scientists and leaders involved were well aware of the consequences of their work. Creating a weapon of destruction weighed heavily on many minds, leading to intense debates and personal conflicts. Dr. J. Robert Oppenheimer, who led the side of the project, famously quoted from the Bhagavad Gita after witnessing the first successful test; "Now I am become Death the destroyer of worlds." This quote reflected the struggles experienced by many involved in the project who were torn between their duty and moral considerations.

From a standpoint, the Manhattan Project was like a high-stakes gamble. Developing a bomb wasn't just a scientific competition but also a strategic one with global domination at stake. The United States knew that other countries, Nazi Germany, were also researching nuclear weapons. This added more urgency and pressure to succeed in this project because delays or failures could have disastrous consequences.

The Manhattan Project represented a small-scale version of what was happening then. It captured the dreams, anxieties, obstacles, and moral dilemmas of a period teetering on the edge of a global arrangement. The scientific hurdles, though massive, were one aspect of this intricate undertaking. The true intricacy of the project resided in its connection with the social, political, and ethical context of that era.

A Legacy Beyond the Bomb.

The legacy of the Manhattan Project is extensive and diverse, extending beyond the mere creation of the atomic bomb. While the bomb became a symbol of the project's success and the awe-inspiring energy potential, its broader implications touched various aspects of society, politics, and science.

In terms of relations, the existence of the atomic bomb reshaped power dynamics. Nuclear deterrence became an element in defense strategies, resulting in a delicate balance of power during the Cold War era. The concept known as " Assured Destruction" emerged, where merely possessing nuclear weapons acted as a deterrent against their use by opposing nations. This emphasized the significance of diplomacy and dialogue in preventing catastrophe.

On the front, the Manhattan Project spurred advancements across multiple fields. The research conducted during this project deepened our understanding of reactions, which later paved the way for developing nuclear power plants. These plants offered an energy source that could reduce humanity's reliance on fossil fuels. Additionally, this project made significant progress in particle physics, leading to discoveries regarding subatomic particles and enhancing our understanding of fundamental building blocks.

Apart from the scientific advancements, the Manhattan Project profoundly impacted the ethos of research and collaboration. This endeavor showcased how experts from different fields could come together to solve intricate problems on a large scale. This collaborative spirit became a model for scientific projects ranging from space exploration missions to the development of massive particle accelerators.

However, it's crucial to acknowledge that the project's legacy brings forth implications. The remarkable success of the Manhattan Project triggered introspection regarding the responsibilities of scientists. The devastating power of the atomic bomb raised questions about the boundaries of scientific exploration and the ethical considerations that must accompany it. Consequently, this project served as a point for ongoing debates surrounding science's role in society and striking a balance between progress and ethical responsibility.

In a cultural context, art and literature were significantly influenced by the Manhattan Project and its aftermath. The atomic age, characterized by a blend of hope and fear, became a theme in various artistic expressions. From thought-provoking works grappling with nuclear power's moral implications to films depicting post-apocalyptic scenarios, this project's influence permeated popular culture.

Ultimately, while the immediate outcome of the Manhattan Project was creating a bomb, its legacy represents an intricate interplay between science, society, and ethics. It serves as a reminder of how scientific endeavors have impacted human history and the responsibilities of having transformative power.

In essence, the Manhattan Project went beyond building a bomb. It stood as a testament to resilience, collaboration, and an unwavering pursuit of knowledge. It demonstrated the extent to which humanity could push itself when faced with threats and what it could achieve when people from diverse backgrounds united for a common goal. With its successes and challenges, the project serves as a reminder of both the potential and risks involved in unrestricted scientific exploration.

THE GEOPOLITICAL LANDSCAPE AND THE RISE OF FASCISM

The Post-War World and the Seeds of Unrest:

The end of World War I brought relief, but the peace that followed was fragile at best. The world had witnessed the effects of modern warfare, which left deep physical, psychological, and societal scars. This "war to end all wars" reshaped the global landscape, setting the stage for political and social upheavals throughout the 20th century.

At the heart of this war situation was the Treaty of Versailles. Designed to prevent conflicts, many viewed its provisions as an imposed peace, particularly in Germany, where it was seen as a "dictated peace" or "Diktat." The harsh reparations imposed on Germany and losses and military restrictions inflicted a profound sense of national humiliation. It wasn't a financial burden; it struck the core of Germany's pride as a prominent European power.

The consequences for Germany's economy were far-reaching. Already strained by the war, these reparations further weakened their economy. Hyperinflation skyrocketed to levels; stories circulated about individuals needing wheelbarrows full of money to buy necessities. An image that symbolized the economic despair that gripped the nation. However, it's important to note that this economic instability wasn't limited to Germany.

The 1920s marked a period of economic uncertainty, eventually leading to the Great Depression in the 1930s. As economies crumbled, unemployment rates increased. People's trust in democratic institutions wavered.

Simultaneously, the political landscape changed this economic turmoil. The monarchies of Russia, Germany, and Austria-Hungary gave way to political entities and ideologies. The void left by these fallen empires became a battleground for political ideologies ranging from far-left communism to far-right fascism.

Societal norms were also in a state of flux. The war brought women into the workforce, challenging gender roles. A generation traumatized by war began questioning the values and beliefs upheld by their predecessors. Known as the "Lost

Generation, " they sought solace through art, literature, and music movements such as Dadaism and Surrealism that expressed their disillusionment with the era.

Extremist ideologies found fertile ground in this mix of despair, political upheaval, and societal transformation. Desperate for stability and a return to pride, people were drawn to charismatic leaders who promised an escape from chaos. The aftermath of the war had planted the seeds of discontent. They were beginning to sprout, bringing the world to the edge of another significant transformation.

Emergence of Fascism:

The rise of fascism during the 1900s was not an isolated event but a response to social, economic, and political factors. After World War I, nations faced challenges and found that their traditional political systems were insufficient; at that time, the world was uncertain and in flux. Fascism presented itself as a source of stability and order.

In Italy, where fascism originated, Benito Mussolini became its figure. Despite being on the winning side in World War I, Italy felt dissatisfied with the peace settlements. Economic. Perceived lack of territorial gains led to disillusionment among Italians. Mussolini capitalized on this prevailing sentiment with his leadership and promised to restore national greatness. Many Italians were drawn to his vision of a "New Roman Empire."

What distinguished fascism was its foundation? It rejected both wing ideologies, such as socialism and communism, and liberal democratic principles prevalent in the West. Instead, it promoted a form of authoritarian nationalism. Under a ruling party and leader, the state held supreme authority, with individual rights and freedoms taking a backseat to the collective will of the nation.

To strengthen this sense of unity, fascist regimes employed propaganda tactics. Mass gatherings, parades, and public speeches were utilized to rally support and foster nationalistic fervor. The state-controlled media promoted fascist ideals as the sole solution to the nation's challenges.

However, beneath this facade of unity and power lurked an aspect of fascism: its inclination toward violence and suppression. Dissent was not tolerated, leading to persecution, imprisonment, or even elimination of opponents—especially communists and socialists. Minority groups also faced discrimination; for instance, the Jews in Nazi Germany endured unimaginable suffering during this period.

The allure of fascism extended beyond Italy—it also resonated with parts of Europe. Adolf Hitler's Germany and Francisco Francos Spain embraced principles within their unique national contexts while upholding core tenets such as authoritarianism, nationalism, and disdain for liberal democracy.

Essentially, the rise of fascism can be seen as a response to the times. It offered a sense of stability amidst a world, a way to restore order amid chaos, and a chance for national pride following perceived humiliation. However, this promise came at a price. It required sacrificing individual freedoms, democratic values, and human lives.

Germany and the Rise of Hitler.

After World War I, Germany was tasked with establishing the Weimar Republic, a delicate democracy that grappled with numerous challenges. The nation's pride suffered greatly due to the Treaty of Versailles, which imposed reparations, territorial losses, and military limitations. This sense of humiliation was further compounded by rampant hyperinflation during the early 1920s, causing significant financial hardships for the middle class and plunging many into poverty.

Amid this turmoil, disillusioned Germans turned to political parties that promised stability and a restoration of national pride. One such party was the Nazi Party, led by Adolf Hitler, who was known for his leadership. Hitler's rhetoric combined anti-communist sentiments with a disdain for the Weimar democracy and rooted anti-Semitism. He envisioned a pure Germany free from what he perceived as corrupting influences brought by Jews and communists.

However, it is important to note that the Nazi's ascent to power did not occur immediately. Throughout the 1920s, they remained on the fringes of politics, often disregarded by mainstream politicians. It was with the onset of the Great Depression in the 1930s that their political fortunes dramatically changed. As unemployment soared and public discontent peaked, the Nazis positioned themselves as champions of citizens by promising employment opportunities, access to necessities like bread, and an overall revitalization of the national spirit.

By 1933, Hitler became the Chancellor of Germany through maneuvering, intimidation tactics, and gaining public support. In power, the Nazis wasted no time in strengthening their control. Taking advantage of the Reichstag Fire incident in February 1933, Hitler used it as an opportunity to pass the Reichstag Fire Decree, which effectively suspended liberties and allowed for the arrest of political opponents. This was followed by the Enabling Act, which gave Hitler the authority to create laws without involving the Reichstag, essentially granting him powers.

Over the years, the Weimar Republics democratic institutions were systematically dismantled by the Nazis. The press faced censorship, and political adversaries were persecuted relentlessly. An extensive propaganda machine was put into motion to indoctrinate the German population: the SS and Gestapo. Nazi paramilitary and secret police organizations ensured that dissent was swiftly and brutally crushed.

Alongside these maneuvers, Hitler initiated a bold program for rearmament that directly violated the Treaty of Versailles. The German military was expanded significantly while compulsory military service was reintroduced. These measures not strengthened German military power but also provided employment opportunities for many citizens consolidating public support for the Nazi regime.

However, behind this facade of recovery and patriotic zeal lurked darker elements of Nazi ideology. The Nuremberg Laws enacted in 1935 took away the citizenship of Jews, setting the foundation for the widespread persecution that would intensify over time. Hitler's desire for Lebensraum drove him to pursue policies aggressively, which eventually led to the annexation of Austria and the Sudetenland, ultimately triggering World War II.

In essence, the rise of Hitler and the Nazi Party was an interplay between economic hardships, political opportunism, and deep-seated prejudices. Their impact on Germany and the world was significant, creating conditions for a conflict of immense scale and devastation.

Fascism Beyond Europe:

Although Europe played a role in the development and spread of fascism, its influence extended far beyond its borders, resonating in various parts of the world. The appeal of fascism on a scale reflected the broader challenges nations faced during a turbulent period encompassing socio-political and economic realms.

In Asia, Japan emerged as an example of a country influenced by ideologies resembling fascism. The 1920s and 1930s witnessed Japan grappling with economic hardships, political assassinations, and the growing influence of militarism in governance. Driven by ambitions fueled by the desire for economic self-reliance and regional dominance, Japan's actions bore similarities to fascist doctrines centered around territorial expansion. The concept of Hakko Ichiu, meaning "Eight Corners of the World under One Roof," encapsulated Japan's vision for Asia under Japanese leadership. This ideology justified Japan's expansion into Manchuria, Korea, and Southeast Asia territories.

Similarly, South American countries, like Brazil and Argentina, experienced the rise of regimes that drew inspiration from European fascist movements. In Brazil, Getúlio Vargas Estado Novo or "New State" (1937- 1945) was characterized by a concentration of power state-driven economic policies and the suppression of opposition. While it cannot be purely classified as fascist, the Vargas regime shared characteristics with the ideology, such as corporatism, state propaganda, and a strong emphasis on national pride.

Similarly, Argentina under Juan Domingo Perón displayed traits of European fascism. Known as Perónism, it emphasized justice, labor rights, and nationalism. While Perón's regime had its unique focus on social welfare and its relationship with the working class, its authoritarian nature, press censorship, and suppression of dissent drew parallels to fascist governance.

However, it is important to acknowledge that these regimes and movements outside Europe were also influenced by their cultural backgrounds and historical and socio-political contexts. The global dissemination of fascist-like ideologies during this period highlights the broader challenges faced in the interwar years, including economic downturns, political instability, and widespread disillusionment with what was perceived as failures of liberal democracy.

Essentially, the attraction of fascism outside of Europe emerged as a result of and reaction to the difficulties encountered by nations during this era. Although originating from ideologies, its impact took on various forms that mirrored the intricacies of a changing world.

The Global Response:

As the grip of fascism tightened its hold over regions of Europe and Asia, the world observed with a mixture of concern and determination. The rapid expansion of ideologies and territories posed a regional threat and endangered the essence of international relations and the principles of democracy and self-determination.

In the United States, there was initially an inclination toward isolationism. The painful memories from World War I and the strong desire to avoid another conflict contributed to a reluctance to get involved in European affairs. However, as the 1930s progressed and fascist regimes displayed aggressive actions, public opinion shifted. Under President Franklin D. Roosevelt's leadership, though still officially neutral, the U.S. Government recognized the necessity for a proactive approach. Consequently, indirect support was provided to nations resisting aggression through initiatives like the Lend-Lease Act, which supplied crucial military aid to countries such as Britain and the Soviet Union.

Britain and France, being democratic powers in Europe then, faced their unique challenges. Initially adopting a policy of appeasement, they sought to prevent large-scale conflicts by concessions to Nazi Germany's demands. The Munich Agreement of 1938 epitomizes this approach as it permitted Germany's annexation of parts of Czechoslovakia. However, hopes for peace were shattered when Germany occupied Czechoslovakia and invaded Poland in 1939. This prompted Britain and France to declare war on Germany, marking the start of World War II.

The Soviet Union, led by Joseph Stalin, had a complicated relationship with the rise of fascism. Initially, they signed an aggression treaty called the Molotov Ribbentrop Pact with Nazi Germany, which allowed both countries to divide up Eastern Europe. However, this alliance didn't last long. In 1941, Germany invaded the Soviet Union, resulting in one of the deadliest fronts during the war. Despite setbacks, the Soviets played a vital role in defeating Nazi Germany.

The League of Nations attempted to restrain Japan's expansionism in Asia after it invaded Manchuria in 1931. However, due to a lack of enforcement mechanisms and major powers like Japan, Germany, and Italy withdrawing from the organization, its impact was significantly diminished. In response to Japan's aggression in Asia, the United States imposed economic sanctions, such as an oil embargo that pushed both nations toward confrontation. Culminating in Japan's attack on Pearl Harbor in 1941.

The global response to fascism took forms and evolved over time. Initially, people had reactions ranging from trying to make peace with fascist powers to isolating themselves. However, as the aggressive actions of these powers intensified, it motivated nations to take action; they formed alliances, adjusted their strategies, and prepared for a conflict on a scale. The rise of fascism and how the world responded to it created the conditions for a war that would completely reshape geopolitics and lead to the dawn of the age.

To summarize, during the 20th century, there were significant shifts in power dynamics in the geopolitical landscape. A combination of hardships, nationalism, and political opportunism drove the emergence of fascism. This reshaped the order as countries grappled with these challenges. These circumstances set the stage for a series of events that eventually led to another conflict—a backdrop against which the Manhattan Project emerged.

MOBILIZATION OF THE SCIENTIFIC COMMUNITY

The Imperative for Collaboration:

The Manhattan Project, although rooted in the worlds of science and military strategy, was primarily an undertaking. Its success relied on technical skills and individuals coming together and surpassing personal, cultural, and academic boundaries. Collaboration was not a practical necessity for the project; it was its lifeblood.

In the 20th century, scientific research often involved solitary pursuits with individual scientists or small teams working in relative isolation. However, the magnitude and complexity of the Manhattan Project necessitated a departure from this approach. The stakes were high. The challenges were multifaceted. No single person could hope to tackle them, no matter how brilliant they may be. The project demanded a convergence of expertise from different fields: nuclear physics, engineering, metallurgy, and even espionage.

Collaboration within the context of the Manhattan Project extended beyond numbers or multidisciplinary knowledge. It revolved around creating an environment where ideas could flow freely, and failures were seen as stones toward success. It thrived on perspectives merging to form a comprehensive solution. This collaborative ethos was cultivated at every level, with leaders like Oppenheimer emphasizing dialogue and collective problem-solving.

The global nature of the threat presented by regimes necessitated worldwide cooperation. The initiative emerged as a symbol of collaboration, attracting scientists from war-ravaged Europe who brought their unique perspectives and expertise. This global dimension added depth to the efforts by introducing a fusion of cultural viewpoints and scientific methodologies.

However, collaboration was not without its obstacles. Given the proximity of brilliant minds, clashes of ego and divergent opinions were unavoidable. Skillfully navigating these dynamics was as vital to the project's success as any scientific breakthrough. It demanded an equilibrium of diplomacy, mutual respect, and a shared sense of purpose.

Ultimately, the Manhattan Project is evidence of the power unleashed through human collaboration. It emphasizes that when individuals unite behind an objective with an urgent drive, they can accomplish extraordinary, inconceivable achievements in isolation. The triumph achieved by this project transcended scientific advancements; it embodied the indomitable spirit of humanity and reinforced our belief in our collective potential surpassing individual capabilities.

The European Exodus:

The 1930s and 1940s were challenging times for Europe, marked by turmoil and uncertainty. After the First World War, the continent was on the brink of another conflict. The rise of regimes, particularly under Adolf Hitler in Germany, brought about a period filled with persecution, intolerance, and aggression. This hostile environment posed a threat to both the Jewish community and intellectuals who openly opposed fascist ideologies.

Germany had previously been known for its advancements and renowned research institutions, but it began to experience a notable loss of intellectual talent. The Nazi's implementation of laws and rejection of "Jewish physics" resulted in many leading scientists being expelled from their academic positions. This purge targeted not Jews but also individuals considered non-Aryan or those with opposing political views to Nazi doctrine.

One prominent scientist who fled the regime was Albert Einstein, a renowned physicist whose groundbreaking work on the theory of relativity had already gained him global recognition. Sensing the danger, Einstein left Germany in 1933 and eventually settled in the United States. His departure was more than a personal escape; it symbolized the broader exodus of scientific talent from Europe.

Enrico Fermi, a physicist renowned for his groundbreaking research on nuclear reactions, stands out as a noteworthy figure. Although he was not Jewish, his wife's Jewish background put his family at risk due to the laws imposed by Mussolini's fascist regime in Italy. Recognizing the growing dangers, Fermi decided to accept the Nobel Prize in Physics in 1938 and utilized his trip to Stockholm as an opportunity to escape, eventually finding refuge in the United States.

Similarly, Niels Bohr, a physicist who contributed significantly to our understanding of atomic structure and quantum mechanics, faced a precarious situation. As Denmark fell under Nazi occupation in 1940, Bohrs Jewish heritage placed him at risk despite being a Christian. In an escape plan, he fled to

Sweden before journeying to the United States and later the United Kingdom. He continued his endeavors there and played a vital role in atomic research efforts.

These individual stories represent a small fraction of a larger narrative. The departure from Europe entailed more than people seeking safety; it involved the transfer of knowledge, expertise, and intellectual capital. The scientists who sought sanctuary in countries brought invaluable experience and insights that enriched their host nation's scientific communities. Their contributions would be extremely valuable in the context of the Manhattan Project, where these émigrés collective knowledge played a crucial role in the race to harness atomic energy.

The departure of Europeans, although a tragic outcome of the turmoil at that time, unintentionally paved the way for a new era of scientific collaboration in the Western world. The blending of expertise with American resources and creativity resulted in a powerful alliance that drove the Manhattan Project and permanently changed the trajectory of history.

Convergence at Los Alamos.

Nestled amidst the landscapes of New Mexico, Los Alamos took on a significance that surpassed its mere geographical location. It became the crucible in which the atomic age was born and shaped. The deliberate choice of this town was not coincidental; it offered a cloak of secrecy that shielded the project from prying eyes and potential espionage. Beyond its strategic advantages, Los Alamos provided an environment where some of the world's brightest minds could come together, collaborate, and unleash their innovative potential.

The establishment of the Los Alamos Laboratory brought about a shift in the trajectory of the Manhattan Project. This laboratory buzzed with activity under the supervision of military personnel and led by J. Robert Oppenheimer. Scientists from corners of Europe who had sought refuge from persecution worked side by side with their American counterparts. This unique mix of cultures, experiences, and expertise fostered an intellectually stimulating atmosphere.

Nevertheless, life at Los Alamos came with its share of challenges. The pressure to produce results was immense as every moment counted in the race against time during wartime. Scientists worked tirelessly for hours that often blurred into one another. Being situated in a location meant limited access to external resources—necessitating resourcefulness and ingenuity to overcome technical obstacles.

However, amidst the pressure and difficulties, stories of camaraderie and resilience emerged. Informal conversations during meal times or walks often led to breakthroughs. The laboratory's communal atmosphere fostered a culture of dialogue and exchanging ideas. It was not uncommon for physicists to engage in debates challenging each other's theories only to collaborate on experiments the following day.

Beyond the pursuits, Los Alamos became a reflection of society itself. Families of scientists settled in schools. Social events were organized. This sense of normalcy provided a needed break from the intense work. It also created a sense of community that united the residents in their shared mission.

As the project progressed, Los Alamos witnessed a convergence of scientific minds and a coming together of ideologies and aspirations. It became a symbol of hope—a beacon pointing toward an end to the war. Simultaneously, it provided evidence for the complexities and ethical dilemmas that arise with scientific progress.

Looking back, the convergence at Los Alamos was more than a strategic decision; it was, at its core, both the heart and soul of the Manhattan Project. Here, we saw the birth of an age shaped by collective efforts, dreams, and moral difficulties faced by those who called it home.

Challenges and Triumphs:

The journey toward harnessing energy was far from easy. While the Manhattan Project is widely known for its achievements, the road to success was filled with various obstacles, some expected and others unforeseen.

One of the difficulties stemmed from the groundbreaking nature of the endeavor. Although theoretical frameworks existed, translating them into applications was unexplored territory. Each experiment was an expedition into territories where both failures and successes played integral roles. For example, initial bomb designs underwent iterations due to many ineffective or unstable prototypes.

Additionally, the technical complexities of fission added another layer of challenges. Accomplishing a controlled chain reaction, where atoms would split in a manner, proved to be an immense undertaking. Early experiments often resulted in reactions that jeopardized project success and endangered the safety of the scientists involved.

Resource limitations further exacerbated these challenges. Despite funding provided by the U.S. Government, rare materials such as enriched uranium and plutonium were required for the project's progress. Acquiring quantities of these materials posed logistical nightmares necessitating covert operations and intricate supply chains.

Furthermore, human interactions introduced another dimension to these challenges. The Manhattan Project brought together a group of scientists, each with their unique approaches, theories, and egos. Managing these dynamics, fostering collaboration, and ensuring everyone worked toward a shared objective was quite challenging. Dr. Oppenheimer led the way by skillfully handling the different personalities and talents, ensuring that individual brilliance contributed to collective achievements.

However, despite the difficulties, the Manhattan Project was also a story of triumphs. Every obstacle overcome, every successful experiment conducted, and every breakthrough achieved showcased the resilience and creativity of the community. The project symbolized hope in a war-torn world, demonstrating the potential of endeavors even when faced with insurmountable odds.

The legacy of the Manhattan Project extends beyond developing atomic weapons; it also offers valuable lessons in perseverance, collaboration, and an unwavering pursuit of knowledge. It serves as a reminder that challenges can be conquered through determination, innovation, and collaborative efforts.

The Ethical Dimension:

The ethical dilemmas surrounding the Manhattan Project were as complex and deep as the hurdles it aimed to overcome. For scientists involved, pursuing knowledge was a noble quest, an endeavor to unravel the mysteries of the universe. However, creating a bomb as the ultimate goal of the Manhattan Project introduced a moral complexity that couldn't be dismissed.

As the project advanced and the energy potential became clearer, numerous scientists began grappling with the consequences of their work. They stood at the threshold of introducing a force that could either revolutionize energy and industry or bring destruction. The dual nature of this potential did not evade them.

Prominent individuals such as Robert Oppenheimer and Leo Szilard, both heavily involved in the project, exemplified this struggle. Despite Oppenheimer's role in realizing the atomic bomb, he later expressed deep remorse, famously quoting from the Bhagavad Gita; "Now I am become Death, destroyer of worlds." His contemplation captured the anguish experienced by colleagues—a recognition of opening Pandora's box.

Leo Szilard, a physicist and significant contributor to the project, was among those who earliest grasped its potential implications. He argued for oversight of atomic energy to prevent a disastrous arms race. His efforts reached a climax with the creation of the Szilard Petition, a document urging President Truman to consider the moral implications of deploying the atomic bomb against Japan without any prior warning. Although several scientists involved in the project signed the petition, it never went to the President.

The ethical dimension of the Manhattan Project extended beyond the inner circle of scientists. Once people became aware of the existence of this bomb, they grappled with a mixture of wonder, fear, and moral ambiguity. The bombings in Hiroshima and Nagasaki further intensified these emotions, leading to contemplation about the ethical limits tied to scientific progress.

In some respects, the Manhattan Project acted as a crucible that compelled society to confront its moral responsibilities amidst technological advancements. It raised questions about science's role in our world, scientist's duties toward humanity, and finding an equilibrium between progress and ethical accountability. These questions that arose during the age continue to resonate even today, serving as reminders of how deeply the Manhattan Project impacted our collective conscience.

To conclude, the community mobilization for this project demonstrated remarkable collaboration power. It demonstrated the power of working with different people, coming together to achieve something that seemed impossible. As we continue, we will explore the contributions of important individuals, revealing the personal narratives that lie at the foundation of this extraordinary undertaking.

KEY FIGURES: OPPENHEIMER'S, FERMI, GROVES, AND OTHERS

J. Robert Oppenheimer's: The Scientific Director:

The path that led J. Robert Oppenheimer to become the director of the Manhattan Project was as complex as the project itself. Oppenheimer was born in 1904 in New York City, and from an age, he displayed a deep passion for literature and science. His exceptional intellect became evident as he made advancements in theoretical physics even before reaching adulthood.

After studying at Harvard and at the University of Göttingen in Germany, Oppenheimer was greatly influenced by the European scientific community. During these years, he developed a strong interest in quantum mechanics, which was still an emerging field at that time. Collaborating with Max Born, a figure in quantum mechanics, further solidified his reputation as a rising star in physics.

However, Oppenheimer's brilliance extended beyond his expertise. As a polymath, he explored Eastern philosophy and French literature. This diverse intellectual background allowed him to approach challenges uniquely with analytical rigor and creative insight.

When selecting the director for the Manhattan Project, appointing Oppenheimer seemed like a natural choice due to his remarkable qualifications and aptitude.

His profound grasp of physics and ability to convey intricate concepts effectively made him an invaluable asset. However, what truly distinguished him was his leadership style. Oppenheimer firmly believed in the power of collaboration, fostering an environment where scientists from different backgrounds could unite, exchange ideas, and work toward a shared objective. This interdisciplinary approach played a role in surmounting the project's most formidable challenges.

Nonetheless, Oppenheimer was fully aware of the implications associated with the project. He frequently engaged in introspection and grappled with the moral and ethical dimensions of developing a weapon capable of mass destruction. A poignant reflection of this conflict is encapsulated in his famous quote from the Bhagavad Gita upon witnessing the first successful test of the atomic bomb; "Now I am become Death, the destroyer of worlds."

In the years following the Manhattan Project, Oppenheimer left behind a legacy characterized by acclaim and controversy. While he garnered recognition for his contributions, he also faced scrutiny for his political beliefs and affiliations. There is no denying his indelible impact on the realm of physics and his instrumental role in shaping historical trajectories.

By delving into the character of Oppenheimer, we not only gain insights into the scientific aspects of the Manhattan Project but also uncover the human elements behind this monumental undertaking. Oppenheimer's serves as an example of the complexities inherent in genius embodying the aspirations, challenges, and dilemmas faced during an era teetering on the edge of the atomic age.

If you're interested in exploring more about Oppenheimer's, I invite you to check out my other book titled **"Oppenheimer's Beyond the Blast,"** which offers a deep exploration into J. Robert Oppenheimer'ss life and enduring legacy at:

https://www.amazon.com/dp/B0CF47FMBK

Enrico Fermi: The Pioneer of Nuclear Reactions:

Enrico Fermi, often hailed as one of the brilliant physicists of the 20th century, possessed a remarkable combination of theoretical insight and experimental expertise. He was born in Rome, Italy, where his early fascination with physics became evident. His natural talent for comprehending scientific concepts was complemented by an insatiable curiosity that drove him to explore the frontiers of established physics.

When he moved to the United States in the 1930s, it represented not only a professional transition but also a personal one. Escaping from Mussolini's regime, Fermi sought an environment where his research could thrive without political limitations. The United States offered him that sanctuary. He quickly became an indispensable part of its scientific community.

Although Fermi made contributions across various branches of physics, his work on nuclear reactions would secure his place in scientific history. He was the person to successfully achieve a controlled nuclear chain reaction—a groundbreaking accomplishment fraught with challenges. This experiment took place beneath the football stands at the University of Chicago. It served as a testament to Fermi's meticulous approach and experimental brilliance. The reactor, Chicago Pile 1, consisted of graphite bricks and uranium; however, its successful operation marked the beginning of a new era in nuclear physics.

Fermi had an understanding of neutron physics. He recognized the potential of neutrons to trigger nuclear fission and conducted a series of experiments to validate this theory. His groundbreaking work on neutron moderation, where he used materials like graphite and water to slow down neutrons, shaped the design of nuclear reactors. Today, Fermi's elucidation of this principle remains at the core of reactor designs.

In addition to his contributions, Fermis's legacy is defined by his mentor and educator role. He possessed an ability to simplify complex concepts, making them accessible to both students and colleagues. Many of those he mentored went on to make advancements in physics, which speaks volumes about Fermi's impact as a teacher.

However, Fermi faced dilemmas during his involvement in the Manhattan Project. Like scientists during that era, he grappled with the ethical implications of his work. The technology he helped pioneer had the potential for good but also unimaginable destruction. This contradiction—the promise of energy juxtaposed with the threat of nuclear weapons—was something that deeply occupied Fermi's thoughts.

After the war, Fermi continued his particle physics and quantum theory research, exploring frontiers in these fields. Fermi's remarkable achievements in the field garnered him honors, notably the 1938 Nobel Prize in Physics. However, what truly stands out about Fermi is his curious nature as a scientist, always driven to venture into uncharted territories.

When contemplating Fermi's lasting impact, it's impossible not to be awed by the extent and diversity of his contributions. He wasn't merely a trailblazer in reactions; he possessed an extraordinary vision that revolutionized our comprehension of the atomic realm.

General Leslie Groves: The Military Strategist:

General Leslie Groves played a role in the Manhattan Project as a military figure and as the linchpin that held everything together. His responsibilities went beyond tasks and were far from ordinary. Groves faced the challenge of overseeing a scientifically groundbreaking and politically sensitive project.

With his background in the U.S. Army Corps of Engineers, Groves brought expertise. Having previously overseen the construction of the Pentagon, he was no stranger to managing large-scale endeavors. This experience proved essential as he navigated through the logistics of the Manhattan Project. From securing research facilities and testing sites to ensuring a steady supply of uranium and plutonium, Groves had countless responsibilities.

However, perhaps one of his challenges was maintaining a delicate balance between the scientific community and the military establishment involved in the project. The Manhattan Project united minds with their ideas, egos, and visions for success. Groves had to ensure that this diverse group worked harmoniously toward a shared objective. His interactions with Dr. J. Robert Oppenheimer serve as an example of this juggling act. While Groves and Oppenheimer often held differing opinions, Groves acknowledged Oppenheimer's brilliance. He ensured he had the freedom and resources to lead the scientific community effectively.

In addition to managing logistics and personnel, Groves understood the project's broader implications. He recognized that the atomic bomb wasn't a weapon but a tool for diplomacy, a means to establish geopolitical dominance. This awareness influenced his decision-making process, from selecting test sites to interacting with leaders.

Groves was unwavering in his commitment to maintaining project secrecy. He implemented strict security measures in an era without today's surveillance technology. He understood that the success of the Manhattan Project depended not only on scientific advancements but also on safeguarding these breakthroughs from prying eyes.

Looking back, General Leslie Groves played a role in the Manhattan Project as a conductor leading a symphony of science, strategy, and confidentiality. His leadership ensured that the project stayed on track despite challenges and ultimately created a weapon that would forever alter history.

Other Notable Figures:

Apart from the trio of Oppenheimer, Fermi, and Groves, the Manhattan Project benefitted from the contributions of numerous brilliant minds, each with their unique expertise and perspectives.

Richard Feynman, a physicist, brought a fresh and innovative approach to problem-solving. His work at Los Alamos primarily focused on the aspects of nuclear fission. Feynman's ability to simplify problems and unconventional methods often led to breakthroughs, making him an invaluable asset to the team. Later in his career, he went on to win the Nobel Prize in

Physics. Became one of the most celebrated scientists of the 20th century.

Niels Bohr, a figure in atomic physics, played a dual role. His profound understanding of structure and quantum mechanics provided crucial insights into the scientific challenges faced by the project. Additionally, due to his knowledge of Europe's dynamics, Bohr offered advice on the geopolitical implications of nuclear weapons while emphasizing the importance of international cooperation in a post-war era.

Edward Teller, widely recognized as "the father of the hydrogen bomb," was another significant figure involved in this endeavor. While Teller made contributions to the Manhattan Project, he is perhaps more famously known for his strong advocacy for developing the hydrogen bomb in the years that followed World War II. His bold vision often put him at odds with his colleagues. There's no denying his undeniable influence on shaping nuclear research in the United States.

Klaus Fuchs, a physicist from Germany, played a crucial role in the project, particularly in the field of implosion mechanics. Unfortunately, his legacy is tarnished by his admission of being a spy for the Soviet Union. He confessed to sharing information about the atomic bomb with them.

John von Neumann was a polymath who contributed extensively to fields such as pure mathematics and economics. His valuable insights greatly influenced the implosion technique in creating the "Fat Man" bomb. His mathematical models and computational skills played a role in solving some of the project's most complex challenges.

The Manhattan Project was a melting pot that brought together diverse cultures, ideologies, and scientific disciplines. Scientists worldwide, many fleeing persecution in their home countries, came together with a shared objective. Their collective efforts extended beyond building a bomb; it was an endeavor to pool humanity's collective knowledge toward achieving a common albeit controversial goal.

The collective efforts of these individuals and others highlight the Manhattan Project's collaborative essence. It serves as a testament to the accomplishments that humanity can attain when united by a shared goal, even in daunting obstacles and moral quandaries.

The success of the Manhattan Project can be credited to the combined efforts of its figures. Oppenheimer's visionary leadership, Fermi's groundbreaking experiments, and Grove's strategic oversight contributed to bringing the project to fruition. The stories of these individuals are marked by their passion, dedication, and collaboration, serving as a testament to the human spirit. As we look back on their contributions, we gain an understanding and admiration for the diverse personalities and expertise that shaped the Manhattan Project.

FUNDING AND SUPPORT: THE ROLE OF THE U.S. GOVERNMENT

The Imperative of Governmental Support:

The Manhattan Project was not a scientific endeavor; it held immense strategic importance due to its wide-ranging implications. Taking place during World War II, when nations were grappling with the challenges of a conflict, the race to harness atomic energy gained immense significance. The U.S. government's involvement in the project went beyond funding and logistics; it reflected the project's crucial role in shaping the broader geopolitical landscape.

The urgency of the situation was undeniable. As the Axis powers expanded their territories and influence, the Allies found themselves in a race against time. They recognized that atomic energy held immense potential as a power source and weapon. Understanding the nature of this technology, the U.S. Government swiftly threw its support behind the project, signaling its commitment to innovation and scientific progress despite daunting obstacles.

Furthermore, the government's participation highlighted that collaboration was at the core of the Manhattan Project. While it brought together some of society's brilliant minds from scientific circles, it also required coordination across various government agencies, military divisions, and international allies.

The government played a role in facilitating the collaborative efforts involved in this complex dance. They provided unwavering support, ensuring that bureaucratic obstacles were minimized and the project gained momentum.

The government's assistance proved crucial in navigating the moral dilemmas that arose during the project. The creation of the bomb posed not only scientific challenges but also profound ethical quandaries. The potential devastation it could cause as well. The government's involvement ensured that these ethical considerations were thoroughly discussed.

Essentially, the U.S. government's backing of the Manhattan Project is a testament to its significance. It demonstrated an understanding of how this initiative could reshape dynamics, and by being actively involved, it ensured that appropriate checks and balances were implemented to realize its potential impact.

The Economic Landscape and Allocation of Funds:

The 1940s posed an economic challenge for the United States. On one hand, the country was recovering from the effects of the Great Depression, a period marked by high unemployment, slow economic growth, and financial uncertainty. On the other hand, the demands of World War II had led to a boost in industrial production, turning the U.S. Into an important contributor to global war efforts. This increased production brought about job opportunities and stimulated economic progress. However, it also meant that financial resources were strained due to the needs of a global conflict.

In this context, deciding to allocate funds to the Manhattan Project was a strategic decision and a bold move from an economic standpoint. The secretive nature of the project meant that its financial details were kept confidential. Nevertheless, estimates suggest that approximately $2 billion (equivalent to over $28 billion today when adjusted for inflation) had been spent on this endeavor by the war's end.

This allocation was substantial considering wartime initiatives that required funding as well. Numerous investments were being made across different fronts, from constructing battleships to developing aircraft. However, recognizing the impact of an atomic bomb as a decisive tool in ending the war and shaping post-war geopolitics made it invaluable. The justification for this perspective was the financial investment involved.

The funding was not solely designated for research purposes. It encompassed a range of needs, including constructing extensive facilities like those in Oak Ridge and Hanford, procuring raw materials, paying salaries to a large workforce, and developing infrastructure to support the project's extensive operations. Each dollar had to be spent to ensure smooth progress without financial setbacks.

Furthermore, the government's decision to finance the project also invested in the nation's future. Beyond its military applications, officials recognized the potential of atomic energy for peaceful endeavors. This long-term vision further emphasized the significance of the commitment.

In essence, examining the landscape of the 1940s and how funds were allocated to the Manhattan Project provides an intriguing exploration of priorities, foresight, and strategic investment. Despite facing conflict and economic challenges at that time, the U.S. Government acknowledged the transformative potential of atomic bombs. It was prepared to allocate significant resources to make it a reality. This financial commitment, scientific brilliance, and unwavering determination ultimately led to the project's successful completion.

The Role of the U.S. Army Corps of Engineers:

The United States Army Corps of Engineers, commonly associated with works and infrastructure development, found itself at the center of one of the most secretive and significant projects of the 20th century. Their involvement in the Manhattan Project was not a bureaucratic procedure; it was crucial in ensuring its success.

General Leslie Groves, a ranking officer in the Corps, was appointed to oversee the Manhattan Project. His leadership style, characterized by attention to detail and an unwavering dedication to the mission, set the tone for how the project operated. Groves understood that blending scientific innovation with military precision was vital for success.

Under his guidance, the Corps took on the challenge of selecting suitable sites for research and production facilities. Locations such as Oak Ridge in Tennessee, Hanford in Washington, and Los Alamos in New Mexico were chosen not because they were remote but because they met various project requirements. Each site had its specific purpose; Oak Ridge focused on uranium enrichment, Hanford on plutonium production, and Los Alamos became a central hub for bomb design and assembly.

The logistical obstacles were immense. Each location necessitated cutting-edge facilities constructed from scratch in remote and difficult terrains. The Corps took on the responsibility of erecting these facilities while upholding the highest safety and security standards. They orchestrated the transportation of materials, equipment, and personnel to ensure that scientists had everything while keeping the project's goals confidential.

However, managing the aspect proved to be an even bigger challenge. The Corps had to oversee an array of individuals with varying backgrounds. From esteemed scientists to construction workers. Each with their own expectations and work styles. General Groves and his team established an environment where everyone comprehended the project's significance and worked together toward a common objective.

Information control also played a role for the Corps. They implemented a layered information classification system in an era predating encryption and cybersecurity measures. This system guaranteed that while everyone had access to the required information for their assigned tasks, only a select few knew about the project's objectives.

In essence, it was through its involvement that the U.S. Army Corps of Engineers provided support as the backbone of the Manhattan Project. Their proficiency in project management and capability to mobilize resources swiftly guaranteed that the scientific community could concentrate on their areas of expertise, pushing the limits of knowledge and fostering innovation. The triumphant detonation of the bombs over Hiroshima and Nagasaki proves the Corps' unwavering dedication and unmatched competence.

Secrecy, Espionage, and Government Vigilance:

The clandestine nature of the Manhattan Project wasn't a choice; it was necessary. During a time of global tensions, harnessing the atom's power became a scientific pursuit and a strategic imperative. The U.S. Government fully understood that the outcome of this project could tip the scales in World War II, and any potential leaks or acts of espionage would have consequences.

The level of secrecy surrounding the Manhattan Project was unparalleled. Entire towns, such as Oak Ridge in Tennessee and Los Alamos in New Mexico, were constructed from scratch to support this endeavor. They remained off the official maps. These towns housed thousands of workers and their families, unaware of the true nature of their work. They knew they were contributing to the war effort but were unaware of details carefully guarded as top secrets.

However, maintaining secrecy was only one aspect of the challenge at hand. There existed concerns about external threats from Axis powers, particularly Germany, who were also exploring atomic research. The stakes were incredibly high. A race was underway. It wasn't just possible. Expected that attempts at espionage would occur. To address these dangers, the government employed a strategy. Stringent background checks became the practice for anyone remotely associated with the project. Surveillance was. Counterintelligence efforts were bolstered. The Office of Strategic Services (OSS), which later evolved into the CIA, was crucial in monitoring and thwarting potential espionage attempts.

An incident worth noting that highlighted the espionage threat was the apprehension of physicist Klaus Fuchs. Fuchs, a figure in the project, was eventually revealed to be a spy for the Soviet Union, leaking crucial information. His arrest and subsequent trial served as a reminder of the project's vulnerabilities and how far rival nations would go to gain an advantage in the atomic race.

In addition to espionage concerns, ethical implications were also at play as the government grappled with secrecy issues. The scientists and engineers leading the project were often unaware of its objectives. This compartmentalization, deemed necessary for maintaining confidentiality, raised questions about transparency, trustworthiness, and ethical considerations when working on such an immense undertaking without a complete understanding of its consequences.

Looking back, the elaborate choreography of secrecy, espionage, and vigilance during the Manhattan Project truly showcases the intricacies of the era. It was a time characterized by contradictions. The quest for knowledge veiled in confidentiality, the potential for power overshadowed by great responsibility, and the desire for peace entangled with the looming threat of unprecedented devastation.

Collaboration with Allied Nations:

The Manhattan Project, though primarily an American initiative, involved collaboration from around the world, reflecting the significance of the atomic age. The immense scale and implications of harnessing energy went beyond national borders, necessitating cooperation among nations with a shared objective.

The United Kingdom, with its emerging atomic research program referred to as "Tube Alloys," had made notable advancements in this field. However, wartime challenges, such as resources and the risk of German bombings, hindered progress. Recognizing the benefits of working together, the U.K. And the U.S. Entered a formal agreement known as the Quebec Agreement in 1943. This agreement facilitated the exchange of research findings, expertise, and resources between both countries. Several British scientists, including renowned physicist Klaus Fuchs, joined forces with the Manhattan Project and made invaluable contributions.

Canada played a role in this endeavor due to its abundant uranium deposits. The vast mines in Canada's Northwest Territories became a source of raw materials for atomic bombs. In addition to supplying resources, Canada also hosted research facilities such as Chalk River Laboratories in Ontario, which became a center for nuclear research, complementing efforts at sites like Los Alamos and other locations within the United States.

The collaboration faced its share of difficulties. Variances in research methods, security protocols, and interpersonal dynamics among scientists occasionally presented obstacles. However, the shared understanding of urgency and acknowledgment of the project's significance ensured these hurdles were overcome.

The international aspect of the Manhattan Project emphasized the implications of the atomic bomb. It wasn't a weapon for warfare but a tool that would shape international relations, diplomacy, and global security for many years. The collaborative nature demonstrated during the Manhattan Project laid a foundation for nuclear agreements and organizations on an international level, emphasizing the importance of collective responsibility in this new atomic era.

Ultimately, the collaboration between allied nations in the Manhattan Project illustrated how interconnected our world had become in the century. It highlighted that countries could set aside their differences and unite toward a common objective by harnessing their collective abilities and intelligence when faced with challenges.

The Manhattan Project serves as a testament to humanity's unwavering determination, collaboration, and innovation. Set against the backdrop of a world grappling with the shadows of war and the emergence of global powers, this endeavor emerged as a beacon of hope and a symbol of our remarkable capabilities. It united minds, strategic foresight, and unwavering support to achieve a shared goal.

Significant shifts and turmoil marked the geopolitical landscape of the 20th century as fascism cast a dark shadow over global peace. In this era defined by upheaval and the looming specter of another world war, the Manhattan Project took center stage. It was not merely a response to these challenges but also a proactive step to ensure that democratic nations maintained control in the balance of power.

The mobilization of the community was truly extraordinary. Renowned physicists, chemists, and engineers gathered their knowledge and expertise. This collaborative spirit was embodied by figures such as Oppenheimer, Fermi, and Groves, whose contributions were crucial in guiding this project to success. Their stories were filled with passion, conflicts, and cooperation—adding a human element to this grand scientific endeavor. However, the project's success cannot be solely attributed to the brilliance of its participants. The involvement of the U.S. Government played a role in providing both financial support and necessary infrastructure with unwavering oversight. Despite challenges, they allocated significant funds and implemented stringent security measures.

The project's global significance was further highlighted through collaborations. Partnerships with countries like the United Kingdom and Canada facilitated the exchange of knowledge, resources, and expertise. These collaborations showcased how interconnected the world was during the age as we worked together toward shared goals and mutual benefits.

By reflecting on this chapter, we can understand the Manhattan Project. It wasn't a historical event; it served as a catalyst for transformative change that profoundly reshaped our world. As we continue through chapters, we will delve deeper into this era's intricacies, shedding light on various aspects that defined the atomic age and left an enduring impact on humanity.

Chapter 5: Secret Cities - The Heartbeat of the Manhattan Project

Throughout the history of the century, the Manhattan Project serves as a remarkable testament to human creativity, collaboration, and an unwavering pursuit of knowledge. While we are well aware of their accomplishments and role in ending World War II, little is known about the extraordinary cities at the heart of this ambitious endeavor. These were not cities; they were hubs of innovation meticulously constructed from scratch, shrouded in secrecy, and inhabited by some of the brightest minds of that era.

The Manhattan Project was more than a series of laboratory experiments; it was a massive undertaking that relied on entire communities working together to achieve its goals. Los Alamos, Oak Ridge, and Hanford communities were established in locations far from prying eyes and potential threats. Their very existence was kept under wraps and remained off most maps.

What can we say about life within these covert cities? How did they come into being? What challenges did their residents encounter? Beyond the scientific advancements, there is a captivating collection of stories waiting to be shared: tales of ordinary life amidst extraordinary global events, tales of collaboration and conflict, and the immense difficulties faced in creating a weapon that could end the war but also raise profound ethical dilemmas.

This chapter will delve into the heart of the Manhattan Project, exploring the establishment and daily life in these cities. We'll uncover the collaborations and discuss the constant presence of espionage. Through accounts, meticulous archival research, and expert insights, we aim to paint a vivid picture of these exceptional urban centers and their pivotal role in one of history's most significant scientific endeavors.

Join us as we embark on a journey in time to unearth the stories behind Los Alamos, Oak Ridge, and Hanford. Together, we will explore the pulse that drove the Manhattan Project forward.

After setting the stage with an introduction that enlightens us about the significance of this project and its covert cities, it becomes imperative to dig deeper into their broader context and consequential implications. These cities not only played a crucial role in achieving project goals but also served as microcosms reflecting larger societal dynamics encompassing politics and ethics.

The Manhattan Project was essentially a race against time. The world was caught amid conflict, and the stakes were incredibly high. The project went beyond simply harnessing the power of the atom; it was about ensuring that the Allies achieved this milestone before their adversaries. In this situation, secret cities emerged as hubs of innovation, where the urgency of war intersected with scientific frontiers.

Selecting often rugged locations for these cities wasn't a matter of chance. The nature of the experiments and materials involved called for isolation for security and safety considerations. However, this isolation came with its set of challenges. Constructing state-of-the-art facilities in areas often with limited resources was truly remarkable from a logistical standpoint. These cities had to be largely self-sufficient due to their secrecy and wartime supply challenges.

Global implications weren't far from anyone's mind, even within these isolated enclaves. The scientists and workers in these cities were keenly aware that their successes and failures would extend beyond the boundaries of their labs and workshops. This awareness added a sense of gravity to their endeavors, transforming these cities into centers of scientific activity and arenas for profound contemplation and discussion.

The Manhattan Project brought together physicists, chemists, engineers, and military personnel from different backgrounds, making the cities involved truly diverse melting pots. This diversity had its advantages and disadvantages. On one hand, it encouraged innovation and the exchange of ideas. On the other hand, it required effective communication and collaboration across different fields—an already difficult task made even more challenging given the high-pressure environment.

Additionally, the project's secrecy presented its set of difficulties. Although crucial for security reasons, keeping information compartmentalized meant that many individuals involved in the project understood its broader goals and implications. This lack of perspective could sometimes lead to frustration and anxiety. The unknown factors and the pressures of war created a psychological atmosphere within these cities.

In essence, the secret cities of the Manhattan Project went beyond being physical locations; they symbolized a global transformation. They encompassed an era's hopes, fears, challenges, and aspirations. As we explore the intricacies of the Manhattan Project in the following chapters, it is important to remember that these cities are not merely backdrops for our story—significant participants in the unfolding drama of the atomic age. We should consider the context within which these cities exist.

ESTABLISHMENT OF LOS ALAMOS, OAK RIDGE, AND HANFORD

Strategic Selection of Locations:

The careful choice of Los Alamos, Oak Ridge, and Hanford sites was a combination of foresight, geographical advantage, and practical logistics. Each location was selected not only for its immediate benefits but also for its potential to support the long-term goals of the Manhattan Project.

Los Alamos, situated on the mesas of New Mexico, was more than just a remote outpost. Its elevated position offered an advantage by providing a wide view of the surrounding areas, crucial for security and surveillance. The stability of the region's geology played a role in its selection. Given the nature of the experiments, choosing a location safe from seismic activities was essential. New Mexico's dry climate reduced the risk of moisture-related issues in experiments – a seemingly small detail important for the project's success.

The choice of Oak Ridge in Tennessee went beyond its landscapes. The geological composition rich in rock made it favorable for underground construction – an aspect worth considering when building bunkers or storage facilities. The winding path of the Clinch River as it flows through Oak Ridge not only provided a water source but also created natural boundaries within the city. This made separating stages of uranium processing easier, which was crucial for safety reasons.

The decision to locate Hanford near the Columbia River in Washington was not for convenience. Detailed studies were conducted on the river's flow rate, volume, and temperature before finalizing the location. These factors were essential for cooling the reactors. Additionally, the soil composition around Hanford, which had silts and loams, allowed for rapid construction without extensive foundational work.

Apart from these geographical and logistical advantages, the socio-political environment of these regions also influenced their selection. Although these areas had some population, they were not urban centers, reducing the risk of information leaks. The local communities were patriotic and supportive of efforts, making them more accepting of any disruptions and need for secrecy from the project.

Overall, choosing these sites demonstrated planning at its finest. It showcased how meticulous and forward-thinking the Manhattan Project was in pursuing its objective.

Infrastructure and Rapid Development:

The transformation of Los Alamos, Oak Ridge, and Hanford from landscapes to bustling scientific innovation centers was truly remarkable. The urgent demands of the Manhattan Project necessitated swift action, leading to the creation of infrastructure.

In Los Alamos, the changes were evident and tangible. Starting with a boys' ranch school as a base, an extensive complex of cutting-edge research facilities quickly emerged. The rapid construction showcased the dedication and resourcefulness of the engineers and workers involved. They faced challenges posed by the terrain while ensuring the facilities were functional and secure. Specialized zones called "Technical Areas" were designed to meet research requirements and equipped with state-of-the-art instruments, often custom-built on-site for atomic research purposes.

Oak Ridge buzzed with activity across its landscape. The gaseous diffusion plants, featuring networks of pipes and chambers, stood as engineering marvels. Of significance was the K-25 plant—an embodiment of human ambition—stretching over a mile in length and holding the title of the world's largest building during its time. Constructing such a facility within a remarkably short timeframe was an extraordinary accomplishment.

Engineers faced the challenge of devising construction techniques on the spot, often having to devise improvised solutions for unexpected obstacles. The calutrons, which were used for separating uranium, were truly remarkable. These immense machines, with their arrangements of magnets and electrodes, posed both technical difficulties and showcased exceptional design.

The transformation of Hanford was equally awe-inspiring. With its imposing complex internal machinery, the B Reactor stood as a symbol of innovation. Building the reactor demanded not only vast quantities of materials but also a deep understanding of nuclear physics principles. The reactor's design had to ensure conditions for nuclear reactions while incorporating safety measures to safeguard workers and the environment. The chemical separation plants, with their networks of tanks and pipes, demonstrated remarkable feats in chemical engineering. Extracting plutonium from irradiated fuel rods involved a process that required precise control over temperature, pressure, and chemical concentrations.

However, it wasn't the large-scale infrastructure that impressed; the cities also boasted various supporting facilities ranging from power plants to water treatment centers. Every aspect of the city's infrastructure was meticulously executed, with attention to the smallest details. Acquiring and moving the materials needed, ranging from concrete to specialized scientific equipment, was incredibly difficult.

In essence, the speedy development of the infrastructure in Los Alamos, Oak Ridge, and Hanford was a combination of engineering skills, logistical expertise, and pure human determination. The obstacles were enormous. The outcomes speak for themselves. These cities, constructed from scratch within a few years, are remarkable testaments to what humans can accomplish when united by a shared objective.

Challenges and Innovations:

Establishing the cities was more than just constructing buildings or setting up laboratories; it explored unexplored realms of science, engineering, and human perseverance. The Manhattan Project encountered a multitude of challenges. The solutions that emerged from these challenges were truly groundbreaking.

In Los Alamos, the high-altitude environment offered seclusion. It also posed unique scientific obstacles. For instance, experiments relying on pressure had to be adjusted due to the altitude. Being in a location meant obtaining materials and specialized equipment was a logistical challenge. To overcome this, a robust internal manufacturing and repair system was established. Scientists and engineers at Los Alamos often had to think on their feet. Come up with creative solutions on the spot. This culture of improvisation led to discoveries that would have been unlikely in a more traditional setting.

Oak Ridge faced its distinct set of hurdles. The gaseous diffusion process used for uranium enrichment at Oak Ridge was an untested method on such a large scale. The process involved using barriers with pores that allowed lighter uranium isotopes to pass through more easily than heavier ones.

Creating these barriers with precision and durability was an enormous undertaking. Initially, the barriers were prone to malfunctions, resulting in disruptions. However, dedicated research efforts led to the development of barriers that greatly improved the efficiency of the enrichment process. Due to the large-scale operations at Oak Ridge, minor inefficiencies could result in significant resource wastage. This necessitated constant. Optimization of processes, which eventually led to some of the earliest computerized process control systems.

At Hanford, there were both environmental challenges to overcome. The reactors at Hanford were unlike anything ever built before. They operated at power levels higher than existing reactors, posing substantial engineering hurdles in heat management. Custom-designed cooling systems had to be created from scratch. Their effectiveness was crucial for ensuring safe reactor operation. While advantageous for water supply purposes, the proximity to the Columbia River also presented challenges. The constant concern was preventing contamination from reaching the river. Water treatment and monitoring systems were developed to address this issue to ensure that any water returned to the river met rigorous safety standards.

The difficulties encountered while setting up the cities were more than just obstacles. They acted as motivators for creativity and ingenuity. They compelled scientists and engineers to explore approaches, question established practices, and enter uncharted territory. The breakthroughs that emerged from these challenges not only guaranteed the triumph of the Manhattan Project but also paved the way for countless technological progressions in the future.

Creating Los Alamos, Oak Ridge, and Hanford was an endeavor marked by innovative engineering, swift progress, and continuous inventiveness. These towns are a testament to creativity and the unwavering commitment to achieving a goal despite daunting obstacles.

DAILY LIFE IN THESE SECRET CITIES

The Social Fabric:

Creating Los Alamos, Oak Ridge, and Hanford was an endeavor marked by innovative engineering, rapid progress, and constant ingenuity. These cities are a testament to creativity and the unwavering pursuit of excellence.

The social dynamics within the boundaries of Los Alamos, Oak Ridge, and Hanford were unlike any American town during that period. The urgency of the war and the secretive nature of their mission fostered a sense of unity and common purpose among the residents. This shared objective and the backgrounds of those living there gave rise to a unique social atmosphere.

Many scientists hailed from institutions worldwide and had international backgrounds. They were accustomed to engaging in debates upholding academic rigor and leading cosmopolitan lifestyles. In contrast, many workers and support staff came from various regions within the United States with diverse cultural and socioeconomic backgrounds. This juxtaposition of scientists alongside everyday workers in such proximity was unparalleled.

Social gatherings became melting pots where ideas converged from different cultures. A physicist from Harvard might engage in discussions about literature with a machinist from the Midwest. Share a dance with a secretary from the South. These interactions arose out of necessity and proximity while breaking down social barriers.

Furthermore, not having extended family members or old friends around meant the residents had to establish new relationships. Neighbors became like family, supporting each other through the difficulties of living in a city. Celebrations for births, weddings, and other significant events often involved the entire community.

The shared experiences of these cities further strengthened the sense of community. Power outages, security drills, and other safety measures were occurrences in daily life. These shared experiences, both challenging and filled with moments of lightness, created bonds that endured throughout people's lives.

However, this knit community also faced complexities. Constant surveillance and the need for discretion made trust a valuable commodity. While friendships were formed and fostered, they were also tested due to the line between personal confidence and classified information.

Despite these challenges, or perhaps because of them, the social fabric within these secret cities remained strong and resilient. It stood a testament to his remarkable ability to establish connections and build communities even in extraordinary circumstances.

Cultural and Recreational Pursuits:

In the cities, cultural and recreational activities played a vital role. They provided a needed balance to the intense atmosphere and heavy responsibilities borne by the residents. Despite their focus on scientific endeavors, these cities also became vibrant centers of cultural exchange and creativity, benefiting from the diverse backgrounds of their inhabitants.

Makeshift theaters, often set up in community halls or open spaces, offered more than entertainment. They served as platforms for residents to express themselves, share stories from their experiences, and forge a collective cultural identity. Amateur actors embraced roles that allowed them to momentarily escape from their routines while audiences found solace in the narratives brought to life on stage. These performances encompassed a range of genres—from Shakespearean plays to contemporary dramas—and subtly reflected the spirit of the times by offering subtle commentary on global events and personal circumstances.

Movie screenings provided not only an escape but also glimpses into the outside world. In an environment where information was limited, films became a means for residents to stay connected with happenings and evolving cultures. Discussions following these screenings were occurrences as residents delved into plotlines, characters, and underlying themes—often drawing parallels with their unique situations.

Music, with its captivating appeal that knows no boundaries, surpassed the challenges of secrecy and the trials of life. Spontaneous jam sessions drew scientists, workers, and their families together to create beautiful melodies. These gatherings went beyond musical events; they symbolized the indomitable human spirit's ability to discover joy and solace even in difficult circumstances. Classical music enthusiasts often collaborated with jazz lovers, resulting in a fusion of styles and genres that perfectly reflected the mix of cultures in these cities.

Sports beyond their benefits played a crucial role in fostering community spirit. Baseball and Basketball courts transformed into arenas where hierarchies became irrelevant. You could witness a scientist pitching to a factory worker, united by their shared love for the game. Tournaments were organized with teams representing departments or neighborhoods within the cities, nurturing healthy competition and camaraderie.

In essence, these cities' cultural and recreational pursuits were not mere distractions; they were vital threads woven into the fabric of daily life. They provided needed moments of relief from hardships while offering opportunities for self-expression and creating platforms for building strong communities. Amid the Manhattan Project, these endeavors stood out, showcasing the people's strength, ingenuity, and unwavering determination.

Education and Schools:

Education in the cities was a unique experience shaped by the extraordinary circumstances these communities operated under. The schools aimed to offer a curriculum, but they couldn't help but be influenced by the intellectual atmosphere surrounding them.

The faculty at these schools in Los Alamos often consisted of spouses of scientists or educators who were intentionally recruited for this purpose. As a result, the quality of education was exceptionally high. Students were introduced to concepts early, and teaching methods often incorporated innovative approaches based on the latest education research.

Furthermore, the diverse backgrounds of families residing in these cities added value to the educational journey. With scientists and workers hailing from parts of the country and even overseas, students experienced rich cultures, traditions, and perspectives. This diversity was seamlessly integrated into the curriculum, fostering a comprehensive and global approach to education.

Although field trips were limited due to the nature of these cities, every effort was made to design them for maximum educational benefit. Visits to on-site laboratories or production facilities offered students supervised glimpses into cutting-edge science and technology. These experiences, although wrapped in secrecy, sparked curiosity and fascination in minds.

The cities also had programs and workshops as part of their educational offerings. Being close to some of the minds of that era, it was not uncommon to have guest lectures by scientists on non-classified subjects. These sessions gave students insights into scientific fields, promoting an atmosphere of questioning and critical thinking.

However, academics weren't the focus. The importance of development ensured that arts, music, and physical education received equal attention. School plays, art exhibitions, and musical performances became community events eagerly attended by residents. The schools turned into centers of activity that provided a sense of normalcy amidst extraordinary circumstances.

Nonetheless, challenges persisted. The changing population dynamics due to scientists and workers coming in and leaving based on project requirements meant that student populations often fluctuated. Establishing an educational experience amidst such a movement demanded adaptability from both educators and students.

In essence, education in the Manhattan Project's cities mirrored the broader community's values and priorities. It was an endeavor to find a middle ground between the immediate needs of the present and the long-term aspirations for a future after the war. The educational experience left behind by this project, similar to the Manhattan Project itself, is multi-dimensional, reflecting the intricacies and difficulties of that era.

The Challenges of Secrecy:

Maintaining secrecy within the cities of the Manhattan Project presented numerous challenges that deeply affected the lives of its residents. These cities were built on the foundation of discretion, considering the global consequences of their work. While crucial for security, this veil of secrecy had significant personal, social, and psychological impacts on those living within.

The weight of uncertainty was tangible for individuals. Despite understanding the necessity for discretion, living with knowledge or complete ignorance about the broader context of their work took a toll. This was particularly true for those not to the project's main objectives. They found themselves contributing to a mission whose ultimate purpose eluded them.

This environment also fostered a social dynamic. Trust became both invaluable and potentially risky. Friendships and relationships are often formed in this crucible of shared secrecy with agreements and mutual respect for conversational boundaries. However, it also bred suspicion. The fear of leaks or espionage meant that residents were cautious around newcomers or those who didn't fit into established patterns. The delicate balance between trust and suspicion created a social dynamic where camaraderie and caution coexisted.

Furthermore, it is crucial to acknowledge the impact of such an environment. The inability to share work experiences with loved ones, the self-imposed restraint during gatherings, and the constant awareness of surveillance led to a sense of isolation for many individuals. The isolation of these cities amplified this feeling, deliberately cut off from the outside world out of necessity.

Nevertheless, amidst these challenges, the indomitable human spirit prevailed. People devised coping mechanisms by finding solace in shared activities, humor, and knowing their sacrifices served a purpose. Over time, a silent bond formed among residents forged through shared secrets and mutual respect for their mission.

In retrospect, the secrecy challenges faced within the cities of the Manhattan Project provide insight into humanity's adaptability. They highlight how far individuals are willing to go to protect a mission and make sacrifices while navigating through lives veiled in secrecy.

Life in the cities of the Manhattan Project was a fascinating study in contrasts. On the one hand, there was groundbreaking work that consumed the scientists and workers. On the other hand, a lively community thrives with cultural events, educational opportunities, and social interactions. It was a life characterized by sacrifice, resilience, and adaptability, where ordinary moments intertwined seamlessly with ones. These cities left behind not only the legacy of creating the atomic bomb but also embodied an exceptional social experiment that showcased humanity's ability to adapt, innovate, and persevere.

SCIENTIFIC COLLABORATIONS AND CHALLENGES

The Confluence of Minds:

The success of the Manhattan Project wasn't solely a result of the resources invested or the cutting-edge technologies utilized. At its core, the coming of brilliant individuals from various backgrounds propelled it forward. This mix of intellect and expertise represented the scientific community converging in secret cities across the United States.

Many key figures involved in the project were immigrants who had fled Europe's turmoil and tyranny. Their journeys to America were stories of resilience and determination. Take Enrico Fermi, a physicist who left his homeland due to anti-Semitic laws imposed by the fascist regime, which affected his Jewish wife. Likewise, Hungarian physicist Edward Teller, often called "the father of the hydrogen bomb, " left Europe to escape the growing influence of Nazism. These scientists were uprooted from their homes, bringing their unparalleled expertise and a deep-seated commitment to combat fascism and totalitarianism.

However, this combination of minds also meant that the Manhattan Project was a melting pot of varying opinions, approaches, and philosophies. The European scientists, many of whom had collaborated closely within academic circles, often approached problem-solving differently than their American counterparts. Their experiences in rigorous and politically charged European institutions made them skeptical and inclined toward rigorous debates.

In contrast, American scientists trained in practical and application-oriented U.S. Institutions tended to prioritize finding immediate and practical solutions. Although this difference sometimes caused tension, it became one of the project's strengths. The combination of the scientist's theoretical expertise and the practical skills of their American colleagues created a vibrant environment where ideas were consistently challenged, refined, and improved upon.

The social dynamics within the cities also reflected this merging of cultures. European traditions, cuisines, and celebrations seamlessly integrated into the fabric of places like Los Alamos. Informal get-togethers became occurrences where scientists from different countries would share their customs, music, and stories. These interactions offered a much-needed break from their demanding work and fostered a sense of camaraderie and mutual respect.

The Manhattan Project, despite being primarily American, was an international endeavor. People from different countries came together, each bringing their perspectives and expertise, which played a crucial role in its success. This blending of cultures, ideas, and philosophies sped up the project's scientific progress and had a positive impact. It created a lasting legacy of cooperation and mutual respect beyond borders.

The Interdisciplinary Nature of the Project:

The Manhattan Project faced strengths and significant challenges due to its interdisciplinary nature. The project brought together experts from scientific fields to address the complex issues it presented. However, this diversity also meant that individuals had to step out of their comfort zones, communicate across disciplines, and often reconsider established methodologies.

Leading the project were physicists who explored the new realm of nuclear physics. Their primary focus was on comprehending the principles of fission and its potential applications in theory. However, translating these theories into use required the collaboration of chemists and metallurgists. They handled and processed radioactive materials, many of which had never been produced in substantial quantities. Their challenges encompassed scientific aspects and logistical concerns like safely producing, transporting, and storing these materials through innovative techniques and equipment.

Engineers were also treading territory as they worked on designing reactors and other project facilities. This engineering challenge was unlike any ones they had encountered before.

Close collaboration with physicists was essential for understanding requirements while working alongside chemists to ensure safe material handling practices. The design process remained dynamic, with revisions based on experimental outcomes and emerging scientific insights.

Furthermore, the interdisciplinary nature of the project went beyond the scientific fields. Biologists and medical professionals were brought in to examine how radiation affects the body, leading to groundbreaking research in radiobiology. Mathematicians and early computer scientists played a role in analyzing data and running simulations using basic computing machines and manual calculations.

This convergence of disciplines also sparked a cross-fertilization of ideas. Techniques and methodologies from one field found applications in another. For example, biologists used statistical methods for studying populations adapted for quality control in production processes. Similarly, advancements in metallurgy influenced reactor design and vice versa.

However, this blending of disciplines was not without its challenges. Each field had its established methods, terminologies, and priorities. Initial collaborations faced misunderstandings and communication gaps. Scientists and engineers had to invest time learning the fundamentals of disciplines by attending lectures and engaging in discussions outside their areas of expertise. Over time, a distinctive culture emerged within the project that valued knowledge and fostered a spirit of continual learning.

In essence, the Manhattan Project represented a scientific triumph and an achievement born out of collaboration. It demonstrated the power of studies, where specialists from various areas collaborate to inspire one another and jointly explore new frontiers.

The Pressure of Time:

The urgency surrounding the Manhattan Project was unmistakable as every passing moment seemed to echo the pace of global events. With World War II raging across continents, the race to atomic energy symbolized the broader struggle for supremacy both on the battlefield and in scientific advancements.

Those at the forefront of the Manhattan Project felt this race against time most profoundly. The enormity of their undertaking and the complexities of nuclear science meant that every breakthrough came with great effort and after countless hours of experimentation and careful thought. The grim reality of war loomed large, serving as a reminder of what was at stake. Every delay or setback wasn't an obstacle to overcome and a potential advantage given to their adversaries.

However, within this crucible of pressure, the true resilience and ingenuity of those involved in the project shone through. Confronted with scientific frontiers and burdened by global expectations, teams often worked tirelessly around the clock. Laboratories buzzed with activity during late hours as scientists and engineers fueled by determination mixed with caffeine strived to solve each new challenge.

Despite its stressful nature, this environment also nurtured a unique camaraderie among all participants. Shared hardships led to shared victories, and the collective moments of success and failure forged connections that would endure a lifetime. The dining halls and recreational spaces of Los Alamos, Oak Ridge, and Hanford were not just places for relaxation; they also became hubs for brainstorming sessions. It was not uncommon for breakthroughs to arise from conversations during meals or coffee breaks.

However, the intense pressure also took its toll. The mental and physical exhaustion was evident as many participants in the project later recalled the strain they experienced. The knowledge that their work could potentially end the war was motivation and an added layer of responsibility. Every. Calculation carried with it the weight of countless lives.

Looking back, we see that the time constraints that characterized the Manhattan Project are a testament to resilience. It highlights how individuals and teams can push themselves beyond their limits when driven by a purpose, even in the face of seemingly insurmountable challenges.

Ethical Dilemmas and Scientific Responsibility.

The Manhattan Project, with its scientific accomplishments, also brought about complex ethical dilemmas that many of the participating scientists grappled with. As they became increasingly aware of the implications of their work, the moral weight of their contributions began to weigh on their consciences.

For scientists involved in the project, their initial motivation stemmed from a genuine desire to safeguard the world against the threat posed by Nazi Germany. The genuine concern that the Axis powers might develop a bomb first was a tangible and urgent worry. This sense of urgency, along with a sense of patriotic duty, compelled many to contribute their expertise to the project.

However, as the war in Europe ended and attention shifted toward the front, a shift in ethical considerations emerged. The primary adversary that had initially motivated scientists—Nazi

Germany—had been defeated. This change prompted introspection within the scientific community. Was it justified to use a bomb against Japan when they were already on the verge of surrender?

Prominent figures like J. Robert Oppenheimer, often known as "the father of the atomic bomb," grappled with profound moral conflicts. Oppenheimer's initial enthusiasm for the project diminished as he confronted the potential of this weapon they were creating. After the bombings of Hiroshima and Nagasaki, he famously referred to a quote from the Bhagavad Gita stating, "I have now become Death, the destroyer of worlds."

The ethical debates extended beyond the use of the bomb. Scientists started considering the long-term consequences of their work. The advent of the age meant that humanity now possessed the capability to self-destruct. The knowledge that was utilized to end a war had the potential to lead to a more devastating conflict in the future.

Due to the secrecy surrounding the Manhattan Project, many participants were unaware of strategic decisions. This lack of transparency complicated ethical considerations. Scientists, often isolated from maneuvers, had to reconcile their contributions with policymaker's choices.

Consequently, the legacy of the Manhattan Project has a nature. On one hand, it stands as a testament to creativity and cooperation. On the other hand, it serves as a poignant reminder of our moral obligations accompanying scientific discoveries. The ethical dilemmas confronted by Manhattan Project scientists continue to resonate today as we navigate through scientific advancements and their impact on humanity.

The Manhattan Project was driven by the era's political landscape, the diverse expertise required, and the moral considerations surrounding their breakthroughs. It's important to recognize that beyond creating the bomb, this collaboration is a testament to the incredible accomplishments humans can achieve when working together toward a shared goal, even in the face of seemingly impossible obstacles.

ESPIONAGE AND SECURITY CONCERNS

The Threat Landscape:

The significance of the Manhattan Project in history was well understood by the world powers of that time. When the United States began this undertaking, there was a buzz within the global intelligence community filled with whispers, speculations, and covert operations. The nature of the project itself, which had the potential to reshape the landscape, made it a magnet for espionage activities.

Although the Axis powers were the primary adversaries during World War II, a threat to the Manhattan Project arose from a different source: the Soviet Union. Despite being allies in their fight against Nazi Germany, an ideological divide existed between the capitalist West and the communist East. The Soviets, led by Joseph Stalin, were keenly aware of how possessing weapons could provide them with strategic advantages. This realization prompted efforts by Soviet intelligence agencies to uncover and infiltrate the secrecy surrounding the Manhattan Project.

Under Lavrentiy Beria's guidance, NKVD established a network of operatives and informants across America. Their main objective was to gather information about progress on designing and potentially deploying bombs. Additionally, GRU (military intelligence) supported these endeavors by focusing on understanding the tactical and strategic implications of such weapons.

The espionage landscape became more complex due to the presence of individuals to communism within the United States and the wider scientific community. Many intellectuals during that time, disillusioned by the Great Depression and the rise of fascism, saw communism as an alternative to what they perceived as capitalism's failures. This alignment of beliefs and a desire to prevent America from having a nuclear monopoly after the war motivated certain individuals to share classified information with the Soviets.

However, it wasn't ideology that drove espionage. The Soviet intelligence apparatus was skilled at exploiting vulnerabilities, whether financial, emotional, or ideological. Through tactics such as blackmailing, ideological persuasion, and covert operations, they gathered a constant stream of information from within the heart of the Manhattan Project.

This influx of intelligence had far-reaching consequences. Equipped with knowledge about atomic bomb design and production processes, the Soviets expedited their nuclear program. The cloak-and-dagger activities of the 1940s laid the foundation for a dance characterized by mutual mistrust in the Cold War era—proxy conflicts and an ever-present fear of nuclear annihilation.

Looking back on those days, espionage activities within the Manhattan Project serve as a reminder of how science, ideology, and geopolitics intertwine. When pursuing knowledge is entangled with aspirations and worldwide tactics, it creates a complex web of collaboration, rivalry, and discord. The era of power initiated by the groundbreaking Manhattan Project is a testament to our inexhaustible capabilities and inherent susceptibilities.

Notable Espionage Cases:

Several espionage cases stand out during this period:

1. Klaus Fuchs:

Klaus Fuchs, a name that would forever be linked to one of the significant espionage cases of the 20th century, was a mysterious figure. He was born in Germany, and a dedication to anti-fascist causes defined his early life. As the Nazis gained power, Fuchs, a communist, was at odds with the regime. His political beliefs compelled him to leave Germany and seek refuge first in France and later in Britain, where he eventually became a citizen.

In Britain, Fuchs's abilities as a physicist did not go unnoticed. He quickly became involved in the atomic research program. As World War II progressed and the Manhattan Project took shape, he was among a group of British scientists sent to collaborate on this groundbreaking endeavor in the United States. Working at Los Alamos, Fuchs had access to classified information concerning the design and production of the atomic bomb.

However, beneath his appearance as a dedicated scientist lay a man torn between conflicting ideological loyalties. Fuchs's unwavering commitment to communism remained steadfast even as he participated in projects related to the development of weapons. To him, these bombs were not just weapons; they represented instruments of influence.
In his mind, it was crucial to maintain a balance of power, and having one country hold a monopoly over such a weapon could upset this equilibrium. This belief, combined with his

connections to the communist network, made him an ideal target for Soviet intelligence recruitment.

His handler, Alexander Feklisov, described Fuchs as a man driven not by money or coercion but by a genuine conviction in the cause. Their meetings took place discreetly in locations and involved the exchange of a wealth of information. Detailed blueprints, production methods, and even theoretical frameworks were quietly shared, all of which proved valuable to the Soviets.

The extent and depth of the information that Fuchs provided were truly remarkable. It wasn't just data; Fuchs offered insights, explanations, and clarifications to ensure that the information was received and understood. This nuanced comprehension greatly expedited the nuclear programs' progress and allowed them to test their first atomic bomb by 1949—several years earlier than anticipated by Western estimates.

Fuchss espionage activities went undetected until the 1940s. The breakthrough did not come from British intelligence agencies but rather from the Venona project—a U.S. Initiative aimed at decrypting Soviet communications. Once his activities were exposed through this project, Fuchs confessed everything while providing details about his motivations and the full extent of his espionage endeavors. The trial and subsequent imprisonment of Klaus Fuchs became widely known, reminding everyone of the risks involved in projects.

The case of Klaus Fuchs highlights the interplay between ideology, science, and geopolitics during the Atomic Age. Fuchs, a physicist who was also a committed communist and spy, represents that era's intricate nature and contradictions.

2. Theodore Hall:

Theodore Hall, a brilliant physicist, remains a mysterious figure in the history of espionage surrounding the Manhattan Project. He was born in New York City in 1925 to parents, and his exceptional talent in physics became evident at an early age. At 18, he made significant contributions to the Manhattan Project at Los Alamos, specifically focusing on implosion designs and other crucial aspects of the atomic bomb.

While his scientific achievements were remarkable, it was his activities that later propelled him into the realms of espionage lore. Unlike many of his peers, Hall's decision to share secrets with the Soviets wasn't motivated by financial gain or coercion alone. Instead, it combined ideology, youthful idealism, and genuine concern for establishing a balanced post-war global order.

Hall's political beliefs took shape at Harvard University when he encountered ideologies and became involved in the broader anti-fascist movement. The emergence of fascism in Europe and the atrocities witnessed during World War II further solidified his conviction that there needed to be a counterbalance to American power. According to his perspective, sharing information with the Soviets was a means of maintaining a balance of power in the world after the war, preventing any single nation from gaining excessive influence.

Under the alias "Youngster," Hall began engaging in espionage activities in 1944. He established contact with Lona Cohen, an operative who played a crucial role in the Soviet spy network within the United States. Through this connection, Hall provided insights into bomb design, production processes, and potential use. The information he shared proved valuable to the Soviets, saving them years of research and discovery.

Despite the nature and importance of his espionage work, Hall managed to avoid detection for several decades. It wasn't until the 1990s, when intercepted communications were decoded (known as Venona intercepts), that his role as a spy became known. By then, Hall had already relocated to the United Kingdom and embarked on a successful scientific research career.

Throughout his life, Hall remained unapologetic for his actions. During interviews, he frequently believed that sharing secrets was necessary for global stability. He saw the bomb as a weapon and a symbolic representation of broader geopolitical dynamics during that era.

The story of Theodore Hall highlights the mix of reasons that led people to become spies. It goes beyond missions and political maneuvering, serving as a powerful reminder of the human factors that shape history, including our intricate emotions, weaknesses, and aspirations.

3. David Greenglass:

David Greenglass's involvement in the espionage activities related to the Manhattan Project is a captivating story that weaves together family ties, beliefs, and the high stakes of Cold War politics. While not among the echelons of scientists and researchers entrusted with the project's most classified information, Greenglass, a machinist at Los Alamos, had access to crucial details about the bomb's design and production.

Greenglass's journey into espionage was influenced by his brother-in-law, Julius Rosenberg, who held communist convictions and was deeply involved in spying to provide classified American information to the Soviets. Their shared leanings and family connections made Greenglass an ideal candidate for recruitment into Rosenberg's spy network.

The information provided by Greenglass held value. He shared sketches and intricate details about the bomb's design, particularly focusing on the implosion-type weapon tested at the Trinity site in 1945. By combining this information with intelligence from sources, the Soviets comprehensively understood how the bomb was designed and operated.

However, in the 1950s, an unexpected twist unfolded in Greenglass's espionage saga. As concerns over communism intensified during the Red Scare era in America, scrutiny fell upon spy networks like Julius Rosenberg. In 1950, Klaus Fuchs, a figure in the espionage network, was arrested and admitted his involvement. This led investigators to Harry Gold, a courier with connections to Greenglass.

When faced with evidence and the possibility of severe punishment, Greenglass made a deal with the authorities. In exchange for a harsh sentence, he agreed to provide testimony that implicated his sister, Ethel Rosenberg, and her husband, Julius, in the spying activities. His testimony played a role in convicting the Rosenbergs, particularly when he claimed that Ethel had typed up the stolen nuclear secrets. The decision to execute them in 1953 remains controversial today.

The Greenglass case highlights the web of motivations behind espionage. Some individuals were driven by conviction and genuinely believed in the communist cause and achieving a balance of power after World War II. Others were influenced by family ties. For many, survival instincts precede loyalty and conviction when confronted with overwhelming state power.

David Greenglass spent ten years in prison for his involvement in espionage activities. He spent the rest of his days living under an identity after his release. It serves as a reminder of the emotional toll and ethical dilemmas that come with the secretive realm of Cold War spying.

Counterintelligence Measures:

The efforts of the Manhattan Project counterintelligence were not a reaction to an external threat but a proactive and intricate network of operations created to protect one of the most important scientific endeavors of the 20th century. Given the scale of the project and its global implications, it became a prime target for espionage. Consequently, intelligence agencies in the United States took on an approach to ensure the security of the project.

The Counter Intelligence Corps (CIC) led these efforts, which consisted of intelligence officers and newly recruited agents. Their monumental task was guaranteeing that thousands of scientists, engineers, and workers spread across cities remained uncompromised. The CIC employed operations for this purpose. One such operation was "Operation Peppermint," specifically designed to identify and counter any sabotage attempts by German forces, especially considering rumors about Axis powers potentially using radioactive poisons.

Background checks, now procedures, were an innovative and crucial tool used by the CIC. Everyone involved in the project, from scientists to janitorial staff members, underwent thorough scrutiny. These checks extended beyond criminal records; they delved into personal lives to identify vulnerabilities that foreign agents could exploit. Friendships, associations, financial situations, and romantic relationships fell within the scope of the CIC's responsibilities.

Surveillance played a role as well. The CIC frequently utilized wiretaps to monitor conversations of individuals classified as high-risk or showing suspicious behavior. Although this might be seen as intrusive by today's standards, it was deemed necessary at the time to safeguard security.

Mail censorship served a purpose. It helped identify any direct communication attempts with foreign agents and acted as a preventive measure against unintentional leaks. Letters containing information, even if shared innocently, were intercepted and either edited or sometimes not delivered at all.

Collaborating with the Office of Strategic Services (OSS) brought an international perspective to counterintelligence operations. While the CIC focused on threats, the OSS expanded its efforts outward to gather intelligence on foreign espionage networks targeting their mission. Their joint operations extended beyond U.S. Borders and often involved intelligence agencies, particularly British MI6. Together, they worked tirelessly to infiltrate and dismantle espionage rings using tactics like agents and misinformation campaigns.

One noteworthy achievement from these combined efforts was a success in neutralizing the "Lucy" spy ring in Switzerland that had connections reaching into Nazi Germany.
During World War II, the United States and British intelligence agencies used a tactic to deceive German efforts and gain valuable insights into their intelligence system. They accomplished this by providing controlled information to the enemy through a channel.

Counterintelligence during that time was not focused on detection and prevention; it also placed great importance on education. The leaders of the Manhattan Project recognized that the best way to defend against espionage was to have a workforce. They regularly conducted briefings educating their staff about the significance of discretion, the dangers of conversations, and the various tactics foreign agents employ to extract sensitive information.

Looking back, it is evident that although extensive counterintelligence measures were implemented during the Manhattan Project and often proved successful, they were not foolproof. Subsequent revelations regarding espionage activities revealed that with stringent precautions in place, there were limitations. Nevertheless, these efforts laid the groundwork for counterintelligence practices by emphasizing a comprehensive approach combining detection, prevention, and education.

The Impact of Espionage:

The consequences of espionage during the era of the Manhattan Project went beyond just helping the Soviet nuclear program advance quickly. The leaked intelligence, though focused on matters, had significant geopolitical effects that reshaped the world order after World War II and influenced international relations for much of the 20th century.

The early detonation of the atomic bomb in 1949, partly made possible by information obtained from spies involved in the Manhattan Project, disrupted the expected balance of power on a global scale. The United States, which had anticipated a period of superiority for a few years, suddenly found itself on equal footing. This unexpected development heightened suspicions between nations and deepened the divide between the capitalist West and the communist East.

The subsequent arms race was not about who had more weapons; it became a symbolic competition showcasing scientific expertise, industrial capabilities, and national determination. Each new advancement, whether it was hydrogen bombs or intercontinental ballistic missiles, held both significance and political messages.

Furthermore, these espionage revelations affected international scientific collaborations. The prominent spirit of open exchange and cooperation within the scientific community was scrutinized. The realization that colleagues we trust could share secrets with nations resulted in tighter information controls, stricter vetting processes, and an overall atmosphere of suspicion within international scientific communities.

During this period, McCarthyism emerged in the United States as a campaign targeting alleged communists within the government and other institutions. While McCarthyism had causes and expressions, instances of espionage within the Manhattan Project contributed to fears of extensive communist infiltration. Careers were. Lives are disrupted based on mere suspicions and associations.

On a scale, these intelligence breaches highlighted the challenges of maintaining confidentiality in an interconnected world. They underscored the vulnerabilities in large-scale collaborative endeavors and the difficulties in safeguarding crucial information from determined adversaries.

In the years following, as more information about espionage during the Manhattan Project surfaced, the Cold War narrative was reevaluated—the simplistic portrayal of the U.S. As a victim of unscrupulous Soviet spying, it gave way to a more nuanced understanding. It became clear that both superpowers engaged in intelligence games and counterintelligence efforts, each striving for an advantage.

The Manhattan Project's main impact lies in introducing the age, but it is important to recognize that the espionage activities connected to it had wide-ranging effects. They influenced relations, shaped policies at home, and made a lasting impression on the scientific community. Even though these events took place in the mid-20th century, their reverberations can still be felt in present-day conversations surrounding proliferation, international collaboration, and balancing transparency and safety.

The events involving espionage during the Manhattan Project demonstrate how science, politics, and ideology were intricately connected. Although the scientific accomplishments of the project are unquestionable, the presence of espionage reminds us of the geopolitical context at that time. Pursuing dominance was a demonstration of scientific ability and a high-stakes endeavor involving intelligence operations, counterintelligence efforts, and global strategic planning.

The Manhattan Project, with its vast scope and profound implications, is often distilled into its scientific and military achievements. However, the heart and soul of this monumental endeavor can be found in the secret cities of Los Alamos, Oak Ridge, and Hanford. These cities, built from the ground up in remote locations, became the nexus of innovation, collaboration, and reflection during one of history's most tumultuous periods.

The establishment of these cities was a marvel of engineering and logistics. Los Alamos, perched amidst the mesas of New Mexico, became the crucible where nuclear research and atomic design took shape. With its sprawling facilities in Tennessee, Oak Ridge played a pivotal role in the intricate process of uranium enrichment. Meanwhile, Hanford, along the banks of the Columbia River in Washington, stood as a testament to the challenges and triumphs of plutonium production.

Life within these cities was a study in contrasts. On the one hand, there was the routine of daily life, with families settling into new homes, children attending schools, and communities coming together for social and cultural events. On the other hand, there was the ever-present shadow of the project's immense purpose, with scientists and workers navigating the challenges of groundbreaking research, often without a full understanding of the broader picture.

Collaboration was the lifeblood of these cities. The convergence of brilliant minds from diverse disciplines led to an unprecedented cross-pollination of ideas. Physicists, chemists, engineers, and many others worked tirelessly, often against technical challenges and the weight of wartime urgency. Yet, even amidst this hive of activity, the cities were not immune to the undercurrents of espionage and security concerns, with the very secrecy that protected them also poses its own set of challenges.

However, beyond the scientific and logistical achievements, the secret cities also became arenas for profound ethical and philosophical reflections. The transformative power of the atomic bomb and its potential for destruction and progress sparked intense debates and introspections. The stories of Hiroshima's survivors, the global reactions to the bombings, and the ensuing philosophical discussions on using such a weapon brought to the fore the ethical quandaries of the atomic age.

In retrospect, the secret cities stand as a microcosm of the broader challenges and triumphs of the Manhattan Project. They encapsulate the spirit of an era where innovation met determination, the boundaries of science were pushed, and humanity grappled with the implications of its creations. As we explore the atomic age, the legacy of Los Alamos, Oak Ridge, and Hanford serves as a poignant reminder of the intricate interplay of science, society, and ethics in shaping the course of history.

CHAPTER 6: THE TECHNICAL ODYSSEY - CRAFTING THE BOMB

The beginning of the century marked a significant period of scientific breakthroughs that reshaped our understanding of the universe. Among these discoveries, nuclear physics emerged as a field offering incredible potential and unprecedented dangers. The atomic bomb, which resulted from this exploration, is a testament to human innovation's dual nature: our ability to create and the immense power we possess to destroy.

The development of the bomb was not a straightforward path. It was a convergence of physics, practical engineering, and urgent geopolitical circumstances. As nations grappled with the landscape of World War II, the race to harness atomic energy took center stage. Behind doors, brilliant physicists and dedicated engineers worked in secrecy, united by a singular objective: to design an incredibly destructive weapon.

At the core of this endeavor lay the principle of fission—a process where an atom nucleus splits into two smaller nuclei when struck by a neutron—releasing an enormous amount of energy. Initially confined to physics discussions, this discovery eventually found practical application in creating atomic bombs. However, transitioning from theory to reality presented challenges along the way.

How can someone control such a powerful reaction? Is it possible to harness the energy in a predictable manner?

Beyond the obstacles, there were remarkable engineering accomplishments. Creating a bomb involved more than comprehending fission; it required designing a device that could trigger, maintain, and regulate this reaction under specific conditions. It entailed miniaturization, precision, and dependability. Every element needed design and testing, from the detonation mechanism to material selection.

However, this technical journey extended beyond physics and engineering. It intertwined with geopolitics, ethics, and the very essence of society. The atomic bomb was not only a scientific marvel but also presented profound ethical dilemmas. By tapping into the power of the atom, humanity has possibilities for both unparalleled progress and unimaginable destruction.

This chapter delves deeply into the web of creating the atomic bomb. From theoretical foundations in nuclear physics to astonishing engineering achievements that brought about its realization, we embark on a journey that explores the intersection of science, engineering, and history. Through this exploration, we aim to provide an understanding of the technical voyage behind one of the most significant and controversial inventions of the 20th century.

THE INTRICATE PHYSICS BEHIND THE BOMB

The Genesis of Nuclear Physics:

The late 19th century was a time of change in the field of physics. During this period, there was a shift in our understanding of matter and energy. The concept of the atom, previously believed to be the unit of matter that couldn't be divided, started to reveal its hidden secrets.

Ernest Rutherford, widely known as the "father of physics," played a crucial role during this transformative period. His groundbreaking gold foil experiment in 1909 proved to be a moment. Initially, alpha particles were expected to easily pass through gold foil based on the prevalent "plum pudding" model of the atom. However, contrary to expectations, some particles were even bounced back. This surprising outcome led to the realization that atoms possess a central nucleus containing most of their mass and positive charge. This discovery paved the way for the model of the atom, where electrons orbit around this nucleus.

Around this time frame, Marie Curie's pioneering research on radioactivity provided valuable insights into spontaneous particle emission from certain elements. Her discoveries of radium and polonium and her investigations into their properties unveiled our understanding of radioactive decay. This phenomenon is when unstable atomic nuclei release energy and serve as a foundation for comprehending controlled nuclear reactions.

In the 1900s, Niels Bohr dedicated his research to exploring the mysterious world of quantum physics. His atomic model, which he introduced in 1913, proposed that electrons revolve around the nucleus at energy levels. Although this model would later undergo refinements, it laid the groundwork for studying quantum mechanics – a field for understanding how particles within the nucleus behave.

These remarkable discoveries made in the 20th century were only scratching the surface. As scientists delved deeper into their investigations, they started unraveling the forces holding together the nucleus, leading to the identification of what is now known as the strong nuclear force. Simultaneously, they realized that protons and neutrons made up the core of an atom nucleus. This revelation explored how these particles interact with one another – sometimes fusing and occasionally breaking apart with tremendous energy release.

However, progressing from these breakthroughs to harnessing atomic power through devices like nuclear weapons was far from a straightforward journey. It demanded a combination of insights, experimental validations, and technological innovations. The origin of physics indeed paved a path forward, yet it was paved with obstacles, debates, and moments of sudden realization or "aha" moments. With each step taken along this path, humanity moved closer to unlocking both potential and potential risks associated with harnessing atomic energy.

Fission - The Heart of the Reaction:

The discovery of fission was a groundbreaking phenomenon that revolves around the intricate movements of subatomic particles inside the nucleus. As we explore this process further, we realize it's not merely about an atom splitting; it involves an interplay of forces, particles, and energy.

At this level, the nucleus comprises tightly bound protons and neutrons held together by the strong nuclear force. This force acts as a glue, ensuring the nucleus remains intact despite the forces between positively charged protons. However, it disturbs this delicate balance when an external neutron collides with this nucleus in heavier elements like uranium or plutonium. This disturbance adds energy. Causes rearrangements within the nucleus, making it unstable and leading to its division into two or more smaller nuclei.

The term 'fission' is fittingly derived from the word 'fissus' meaning 'split.'. Indeed, split it does. However, this splitting isn't random. The resulting fragments, known as daughter nuclei, often consist of isotopes of lighter elements. Additionally, during fission, extra neutrons are released into the surroundings. These generated neutrons are highly energetic and capable of triggering further fissions if they encounter other fissile nuclei.

The concept of chain reactions forms the foundation for a series of reactions.

However, the fascination with fission extends beyond the division of the atomic nucleus. The combined mass of the resulting fragments is slightly smaller than the mass of the parent nucleus. This small amount of missing mass has been transformed into energy, as Einstein's theory of relativity suggested. This energy appears as both the energy possessed by the fragments produced from fission and as emitted radiation accounting for the significant release of energy during a fission event.

Fission follows nature. Not every collision between a neutron and a fissile nucleus leads to fission. The probability of fission, known as 'fission cross section,' varies depending on factors such as the type of nucleus, neutron energy, and other considerations. This probabilistic characteristic adds another layer of complexity to designing an atomic bomb.

While it may appear that fission is simply an atom-splitting process, it is actually an intricate and nuanced phenomenon governed by quantum mechanics and relativity laws. Its discovery and subsequent utilization in developing bombs have brought about a significant shift in our comprehension of the universe and our place within it.

Chain Reactions and Critical Mass:

The concept of chain reactions in fission can be likened to a series of falling dominos, where one falling domino triggers the sequential fall of many others. This analogy holds true in the world but with much more profound and powerful consequences.

When a fissile atom undergoes fission, it doesn't just divide into two smaller nuclei and releases additional neutrons. These moving neutrons can then collide with other nearby fissile atoms, causing them to undergo fission. This sets off a chain reaction, where each fission event generates fissions, exponentially increasing the number of reactions and the energy released.

However, maintaining this cascade is not straightforward. For a chain reaction to sustain itself, there needs to be a balance. On average, each fission event should lead to at least one more fission. If each event triggers subsequent fissions, the reaction can become uncontrollable rapidly. Conversely, if it leads to than one subsequent fission, on average, the reaction will gradually fade away.

This equilibrium is intricately connected to the concept of mass. The term refers not only to the amount of fissile material but also to its arrangement and purity. For example, if uranium is spread thinly, it may not undergo a chain reaction. However, when the same amount of uranium is arranged in a shape or configuration, it can become "critical."

The surrounding environment also plays a role in this process. Materials that reflect neutrons into the core of the material can reduce the necessary critical mass. On the other hand, materials that absorb or allow neutrons to escape can increase it.

Additionally, the concept of "super criticality" is significant to atomic bombs. In this case, the fissile material is rapidly assembled into a configuration that becomes not critical but supercritical, resulting in an explosive and rapid chain reaction. Achieving this state without occurrences was one of the significant challenges faced by scientists during the Manhattan Project.

Managing chain reactions and critical mass involves balancing physics, geometry, and material science with care. The ability of scientists and engineers from that era to harness and control such a force stands as a testament to their meticulousness and ingenuity.

Neutrons - The Unsung Heroes:

While much attention is often given to the known components of the atomic bomb, it is crucial to examine the role of neutrons in the entire process closely. These subatomic particles lack charge and are vital in initiating and sustaining the chain reactions that fuel atomic explosions.

Neutrons act as silent facilitators in the realm of atoms, where discussions usually revolve around protons and electrons due to their charges. Their lack of charge allows them to bypass repulsion from positively charged nuclei, making them ideal candidates for triggering fission. Inside a nucleus, a neutron can destabilize it, resulting in atom splitting and energy release.

However, neutrons go beyond initiating fission. The fission process releases neutrons that can cause further fissions in neighboring atoms. This cascading effect forms the core of the chain reaction that gives bombs their devastating power. The efficiency of this chain reaction depends greatly on the energy and speed of these neutrons.

With high kinetic energy, fast neutrons can swiftly induce fissions, accelerating the chain reaction process. However, there are situations where it can be advantageous to slow down these particles, known as neutrons, transforming them into what we call neutrons. Certain substances called moderators, such as water or graphite, are employed to achieve this. Slowing down the movement of neutrons enhances the likelihood of triggering fission reactions, particularly in specific nuclear reactors.

Nevertheless, not all neutrons contribute to the chain reaction. Some manage to escape from the material without inducing fissions. It becomes crucial to redirect these escaping neutrons back into the material to maximize the efficiency of the chain reaction process. This is where neutron reflectors made from materials like beryllium or tungsten come into play. They effectively bounce back these neutrons, ensuring they actively sustain the ongoing chain reaction.

In essence, while fissile substances like uranium or plutonium often grab attention in news headlines, the behavior of neutrons acts as conductors in this symphony. Their controlled and harnessed actions determine the tempo and magnitude of reactions—a remarkable role for these unsung heroes in our atomic age.

The Energy Equation:

Albert Einstein's famous equation, $E=mc^2$, goes beyond being a mathematical formula; it holds deep insights into the nature of our universe. At its core, this equation reveals that energy and mass are not entities but interconnected aspects of the same fundamental principle. This concept becomes particularly significant when we explore the world of atoms.

Upon delving into the realm, we discover that the combined masses of protons and neutrons within a nucleus do not precisely match the overall mass of that nucleus. This intriguing disparity, known as the " defect," is crucial in understanding the immense energy released during nuclear reactions. It is important to note that this missing mass has not vanished;

instead, it transforms energy, effectively bonding and stabilizing the nucleus. This energy is aptly referred to as "binding energy."

During fission processes, the resulting smaller nuclei possess greater binding energies than their original state within a single nucleus. The difference in binding energies manifests itself as energy and radiation when released. Considering that even a minuscule mass can yield energy due to Einstein's equation (where c represents the speed of light—a truly significant value), one can fully grasp its tremendous potential.

The immense power of the bomb stems from its ability to harness the difference in energy on a large scale. Although each fission event releases an amount of energy, when multiplied by the vast number of atoms in a few kilograms of fissile material, it leads to an enormous release of energy. This understanding was crucial for the scientists involved in the Manhattan Project. They were not splitting atoms but tapping into the fundamental relationship between energy and mass in our universe.

Nuclear reactions have a greater efficiency in converting energy compared to chemical reactions. In reactions like burning coal or gasoline, the energy changes involve the outer electron shells of atoms. Conversely, nuclear reactions occur within the nucleus where forces and energies are significantly higher. This distinction makes nuclear energy a game changer, for better or worse, in history.

The exploration of the physics behind the bomb reveals a fascinating world where tiny particles possess tremendous power and fundamental principles shape the destinies of nations. From investigations into atomic structure to the profound implications of Einstein's energy-mass relationship, the science underlying the bomb is inspiring and humbling. As we delve into the complexities of fission, chain reactions, and the crucial role of neutrons, it becomes clear that the atomic bomb is not merely a weapon but a testament to human creativity and the vast domain of nuclear physics. This comprehension sets the stage for chapters where engineering marvels intersect with these scientific discoveries to create a device that would forever change history.

ENGINEERING CHALLENGES AND INNOVATIONS

The Precision Imperative:

The success of the bomb relied on numerous factors, but none were as crucial as precision. It wasn't a technical requirement for the bomb's components to synchronize; it was the key to determining whether the bomb would achieve its intended destructive power or fail to work.

In the realm of detonation, even microseconds made a difference. The distinction between an explosion and a failed one could be as small as a fraction of a second. This was particularly significant considering the implosion needed to bring the bomb core to its critical mass. A slight delay in any part of the shell could hinder the core from reaching necessary compression, rendering the bomb ineffective.

Engineers and scientists delved into intricate details of detonation science to attain precision. They delved into understanding how shockwaves propagate, studying their movement through materials and finding ways to synchronize them to converge simultaneously. These efforts led to advancements like lensed explosives, where various explosive materials were shaped to focus shockwaves inward and ensure compression of the bomb's core.

Flawless triggering mechanisms were essential. Traditional detonators, although effective, for explosives lacked the precision required for an atomic detonation. This meant that new accurate detonation technologies had to be developed. Engineers experimented with mechanical and even optical triggering systems to find the perfect balance between reliability and precision.

However, precision wasn't focused on timing; it also involved measurement. The Manhattan Project team needed to know the precise quantities and specifications of the materials they were working with. This led to advancements in measurement technologies ranging from sensitive scales capable of measuring materials down to the microgram level to advanced spectroscopy techniques that could analyze material compositions with unparalleled accuracy.

The quest for precision also extended to assembling the bomb. Due to the tolerances required, even the slightest misalignment or manufacturing flaw could jeopardize the bomb's functionality. As a result, rigorous quality control protocols were established where every component, regardless of size, underwent inspection and testing before being integrated into the final assembly.

In essence, striving for precision was not merely a challenge but a philosophical approach that influenced every aspect of the Manhattan Project. It highlighted their attention to detail, unwavering commitment to perfection, and relentless pursuit of excellence, defining both the project and its outcomes.

Material Challenges: From Theory to Reality:

The shift from concepts to practical engineering solutions posed many material obstacles. The atomic bomb, beyond being a device, exemplified the marvels of material science. Each component, alloy, and wire had a role to fulfill, chosen meticulously through extensive research and testing.

Numerous factors influenced the selection of materials. For instance, the bomb casing had to possess both resilience against the strains of high altitude drops and pliability for symmetrical implosion during detonation. While conventional materials offered durability, they did not always provide the precision or specific properties required. Consequently, extensive efforts were made to develop alloys that could strike an ideal balance between strength, malleability, and longevity.

In addition to the casing challenges, internal components presented their hurdles. The detonators necessitated materials to endure initial explosive shockwaves while ensuring precise triggering of the nuclear chain reaction at just the right moment. Even slight delays could lead to explosions or, worse—a complete failure.

Furthermore, radioactive materials themselves posed challenges. Uranium and plutonium, components of the bomb, were also highly reactive and corrosive. Scientists had to find materials that wouldn't degrade or react with these elements to store and handle them safely. This required exploration in the fields of chemistry and metallurgy, resulting in the development of specialized containers capable of securely housing these radioactive substances.

Although often overlooked in the picture, the wiring and electrical components also played a crucial role. They needed to be resistant to interference to ensure that external factors did not disrupt the bomb's detonation sequence. This was particularly important considering the bomb would be transported by aircraft surrounded by electronic equipment and signals.

Due to temperatures experienced during flight and explosion, every material used had to possess a high melting point and excellent thermal resistance. Even a minor failure, like a wire or bolt, could potentially jeopardize the entire mission.

In essence, each material challenge encountered during the Manhattan Project was like solving a puzzle that demanded innovation, research, and unwavering determination. The solutions devised were often groundbreaking—a testament to the project's dedication to excellence and relentless pursuit of perfection.

Through experiments, mistakes, and ongoing improvement, the project brought ideas to life, creating a weapon showcasing advancements in material science and nuclear physics.

Safety Mechanisms: Walking the Tightrope:

The immense power and volatility of the bomb meant that even the smallest mistake could have disastrous consequences. The Manhattan Project team was deeply concerned about ensuring the safety of the bomb throughout its development, testing, transportation, and eventual use. This challenge extended beyond considerations; it also had psychological implications. The team understood that they were dealing with a force of obliterating entire cities, and this realization heavily influenced their decision-making processes and designs.

During the stages of development, one of the primary concerns was preventing accidental detonations during experimentation and assembly. Special precautions had to be taken when handling the bomb's core material. Even a brief moment of assembly resulting in a supercritical mass could trigger a nuclear explosion. To address this risk, engineers developed tools and procedures for handling and assembling the various components of the bomb. These measures ensured that the core pieces would fit together controlled, minimizing any chances of criticality.

As the project progressed toward deployment, new challenges emerged. Now, it was necessary to transport the bomb over distances, often by air, to its intended drop location. This introduced risks such as potential crashes or fires.

Engineers faced the challenge of designing protective systems to safeguard the bomb's core against external shocks and impacts. These systems were often layered, with each layer having a function, such as absorbing shocks or resisting fire.

Another important consideration was ensuring the bomb would only explode at the intended time and location, and achieving this involved developing mechanisms for arming and timing. These safe mechanisms were designed to default to a safe state in case of malfunctions. The arming process typically involves deliberate steps to prevent accidental or unauthorized activation.

In addition to safety measures, there was also a focus on procedural safety. Stringent protocols were established for every stage of the bomb's life cycle, from assembly to deployment. These protocols underwent testing and refinement, accounting for every possible scenario. Regular mock drills and simulations ensured that all personnel involved were well-trained in safety procedures and capable of responding to emergencies.

The safety mechanisms employed in bombs combined advanced engineering with meticulous planning and adherence to strict protocols.

Every possible threat was recognized, examined, and reduced, guaranteeing that the explosive device remained manageable throughout its lifespan. This unwavering dedication to safety emphasized the seriousness of the endeavor and the immense obligation borne by those participating.

Miniaturization: The Compact Powerhouse:

Making things smaller wasn't a technical challenge but an important strategic goal. It was crucial to have a way to deliver the bomb to its intended target, and that meant finding a size that could fit into the aircraft of that time, particularly the B-29 Superfortress, which was selected for this mission. The size and weight of the bomb directly affected its range, accuracy, and the safety of the crew delivering it.

It was quite an achievement to achieve this design—every tiny measurement. Every bit of weight shed made a difference. They had to reevaluate methods and materials used in explosives and weapons. New alloys that could provide strength and resilience while keeping weight to a minimum were explored. The internal components underwent iterations, from neutron reflectors to detonation circuits, to achieve significant size reductions.

But miniaturization wasn't just about making things smaller but maximizing performance within those reduced dimensions. The core of the bomb, which contained the material, needed to retain its integrity and functionality even as its dimensions decreased. This led them to develop geometric designs to still achieve critical mass even in a compact form.

The electrical systems also presented their unique challenges. The engineers faced challenges when it came to fitting the wiring switches and circuits into the limited space of the bomb while maintaining reliability. They implemented redundancies as a safety measure so that if one system failed, backups were in place to ensure the bomb's functionality.

The miniaturization process wasn't done in isolation from considerations. Integrating safety mechanisms into the design was a crucial aspect that couldn't compromise their effectiveness. Similarly, they had to maintain precision requirements for detonation even as they reduced the size of components.

Achieving miniaturization involves finding a balance between compromise and innovation. Every decision and design change had far-reaching implications for the overall architecture of the bomb. The engineer's resourcefulness and determination were evident in their ability to successfully meet their miniaturization goals without compromising power or reliability. Their efforts transformed the bomb from a mere laboratory experiment into a deployable weapon of significant impact.

Collaborative Synergy: The Confluence of Disciplines:

The success of the Manhattan Project was not solely due to the brilliance of individuals. Rather, the combined efforts of a diverse group of experts. This collaborative environment created an intellectual ecosystem where ideas from different disciplines influenced and enhanced one another, leading to innovative solutions beyond traditional boundaries.

Within the project laboratories, brainstorming sessions became hubs of creativity. A chemist's understanding of material properties could inspire a physicist to reconsider a reaction mechanism. Similarly, an engineer's insights into limitations could prompt a metallurgist to explore new alloy compositions. This dynamic interplay accelerated problem-solving as challenges were approached from different perspectives, increasing the likelihood of finding effective solutions.

Furthermore, the interdisciplinary nature of the project facilitated knowledge transfer. Discoveries made in one domain were rapidly shared and applied in others. For example, advancements in physics directly influenced the design and calibration of instruments used by chemists and engineers. This fluid exchange of knowledge ensured that all team members remained at the cutting edge in their fields, enabling unprecedented progress for the project.

The spirit of collaboration extended beyond engineering challenges alone. The holistic approach also benefited the administrative aspects of the project. Economists, experts in logistics, and administrators collaborated closely with scientists to ensure that resources ranging from materials to human resources were allocated optimally. This collaboration ensured the smooth functioning of the project's machinery spread across multiple locations in the country.

However, beyond the outcomes and advancements, the cooperative spirit of the Manhattan Project left a lasting legacy. It emphasized the significance of teamwork when dealing with complex challenges. It demonstrated that when diverse minds come together with a shared purpose, they can accomplish impossible feats. This important lesson learned from the crucible of the Manhattan Project remains relevant today, reminding us of the limitless possibilities that emerge when we break down barriers and collaborate.

In the interplay between science and engineering that gave rise to the atomic bomb, the numerous challenges faced were not merely obstacles but catalysts for innovative thinking. The Manhattan Project, with its array of experts from various fields, is a testament to the remarkable power of collaborative synergy. Through their efforts, theoretical concepts were transformed into tangible realities, pushing the limits of what was considered achievable. This journey, characterized by experimentation and interdisciplinary collaboration, revolutionized warfare and redefined the essence of collaborative scientific pursuit. As we contemplate the engineering wonders of the bomb, we are reminded of the limitless potential that arises when diverse minds come together in pursuit of a shared objective.

THE ROLE OF RAW MATERIALS: URANIUM AND PLUTONIUM

Uranium: The Natural Element:

With its gray appearance, Uranium has been a part of Earth's composition since the planet was formed. It's not just found on Earth; this element scatters throughout the universe when stars explode in supernovae. This heavy element is created through heat and pressure during cosmic explosions and eventually reaches our planet.

In the past, uranium was mainly valued for its ability to create colors when it oxidizes. This made it highly sought after as a pigment for glass and ceramics. Even ancient Roman artisans used uranium oxide to produce glassware with green hues, unaware of its radioactive properties or the future importance of this element in unlocking atomic power.

The name "uranium" is a tribute to Uranus, the discovered planet at that time. German chemist Martin Heinrich Klaproth named it in honor of Uranus when he isolated the element in 1789. However, it wasn't until the 19th century that scientists understood its unique characteristics. The discovery of radioactivity by Henri Becquerel in 1896 using uranium salts marked a new chapter in scientific exploration.

Most of an atom's mass resides within its nucleus at the center. The nucleus of uranium contains protons and neutrons with electrons orbiting around it. Uranium's nucleus is known for its instability, which makes it prone to changes or decay. This instability is a characteristic of materials and the energy source scientists and engineers aim to harness.

Uranium's isotopic composition adds complexity to its properties. Isotopes are atoms of the element with different numbers of neutrons but the same number of protons. U 235 is particularly interesting for energy production and weaponization among these isotopes due to its ability to sustain a chain reaction. However, extracting quantities of this rare isotope for practical use poses significant challenges.

The journey of uranium from its origins in space to its impact on shaping the century demonstrates how intertwined science, history, and geopolitics are. Once valued for its beauty, this element now plays a role in discussions about power dynamics, ethics, and the future of humanity.

Uranium Enrichment: From Ore to Weapon:

The uranium enrichment process, which played a role in developing atomic bombs, was not just about increasing the percentage of U235. It involved an interplay of chemistry, physics, and engineering. To transform raw uranium ore into weapon-grade material, scientists needed an understanding of its properties and innovative techniques to manipulate its isotopic composition.

When uranium is extracted from the Earth, it mostly exists as uranium oxide. This raw ore is converted through chemical processes into a compound called yellowcake, mainly of uranium oxide. The next step involves converting yellowcake into uranium hexafluoride—a more suitable compound for enrichment purposes.

The selection of uranium hexafluoride was not arbitrary; it had properties that made it ideal for separation processes. For example, it becomes gaseous at low temperatures and has a molecular structure that allows for clear differentiation between isotopes—facilitating their separation.

Enrichment posed challenges. One such challenge was the difference in mass between U 235 and U 238, making their separation incredibly intricate. Additionally, the equipment required for enrichment had to withstand the nature of uranium hexafluoride and operate with high precision over extended periods.

The electromagnetic separation method employed at the Y 12 plant involved calutrons that were a remarkable display of engineering precision. These calutrons, shaped like the letter 'Ds, utilized magnetic fields to alter the paths of ionized uranium. Due to the difference in mass between U 235 and U 238, their paths diverged just enough to allow for separate collection. Although this process was effective, it required operators who meticulously fine-tuned the equipment to achieve optimal separation.

On the other hand, gaseous diffusion relied on the principle of effusion. The rate at which gases pass through a barrier is inversely proportional to the square root of their molar masses. Given the mass distinction between U 235 and U 238, numerous stages were necessary to achieve substantial enrichment. The K 25 plant in Oak Ridge was dedicated to this method and spanned over a mile. It housed cascades of barriers through which uranium hexafluoride was continuously pumped, gradually increasing its U 235 content.

Despite their contrasting approaches, both methods exemplified the lengths scientists and engineers went to harness uranium's potential. The challenges they encountered. From isotope separation techniques to awe-inspiring engineering feats. Underscored the immense efforts that contributed to the success of the Manhattan Project.

Plutonium: The Man-Made Marvel:

Plutonium, with its silver color and radioactive properties, is a testament to humans' ingenuity when it comes to creating new elements. Unlike uranium, which has been present in the Earth since its formation, plutonium is primarily a man-made element synthesized in laboratories and reactors. It is the result of intervention in the natural decay processes of atomic particles.

The story of how plutonium was discovered is closely intertwined with the narrative of scientific progress during the 20th century. In the 1930s and early 1940s, while physicists around the world were unraveling the mysteries of atomic nuclei, a team led by Dr. Glenn T. Seaborg at the University of California Berkeley stumbled upon plutonium. They created this element by bombarding uranium with deuterons, thus synthesizing an element that had not been identified before. They named it after Pluto, which was then considered our system's ninth planet, following the tradition of naming elements after planets (such as uranium after Uranus and neptunium after Neptune).

What made plutonium truly remarkable was its ability to undergo fission and release amounts of energy in the process. This characteristic made it a potential candidate for use in weapons. However, producing plutonium for such weapons was no easy task.

Scientists turned to reactors since natural decay processes did not produce the required quantities.

Specifically designed for this purpose, the reactors at the Hanford Site had a singular objective: converting as much U 238 into Pu 239 as possible. The process was complex. Uranium rods were inserted into the reactors, where they underwent neutron bombardment. As neutrons were absorbed by U 238, they transformed into Pu 239. However, this formed plutonium remained trapped within the irradiated uranium rods. Extracting it necessitated chemical procedures to separate plutonium from remaining uranium and other fission byproducts.

Plutonium discovery played a role in weaponization and had broader implications for nuclear science. It opened up possibilities for types of nuclear reactors where plutonium could serve as fuel, presenting a more efficient energy source than traditional uranium reactors. Furthermore, the techniques developed for plutonium separation and purification found applications in other nuclear research and industry areas.

The journey of plutonium, starting from its discovery in a Berkeley laboratory and culminating in its role during World War II, epitomizes the dual-edged nature of scientific progress. It demonstrated the progress achieved in nuclear physics and chemistry while drawing attention to the complex moral and philosophical questions raised by these advancements.

The Dual Path: Diversifying the Approach:

The decision to pursue both uranium and plutonium pathways wasn't just driven by curiosity and the geopolitical climate of the time. During World War II, with international rivalries and fears of Axis powers racing toward nuclear capabilities, diversifying the approach was like hedging bets on multiple horses in a race. Nuclear science was still being. Scaling laboratory successes to industrial levels presented immense challenges. By advancing on both fronts, the United States aimed to increase its chances of success. If one pathway faced obstacles, they had another option.

This dual-path approach facilitated a cross-pollination of ideas. Scientists and engineers working on uranium shared insights with those focusing on plutonium and vice versa. This collaborative environment allowed diverse teams to tackle problems from different perspectives, fostering innovation. It wasn't uncommon for breakthroughs in one pathway to inspire solutions in the other.

Each material's choice of weapon design also considered its properties and challenges.

The design of uranium, for example, was simpler in concept. It required precise execution. The explosion could be less effective or even fail if the sub-critical masses were not aligned correctly or brought together with a delay. On the other hand, plutonium design relied on a symmetrical compression of the core to achieve supercriticality. This meant that innovative explosive lens designs and synchronization of detonation were necessary.

Beyond the aspects, having a dual path strategy had implications for managing resources, logistics, and even countermeasures against espionage. By having facilities like Oak Ridge for uranium and Hanford for plutonium, the Manhattan Project effectively spread out its operations. This reduced the risk of sabotage or espionage at one critical location and allowed for parallel processing to speed up the overall timeline.

Looking back, diversifying their approach was a decision. It demonstrated the foresight of the project's leaders, their ability to adapt to situations, and their unwavering commitment to achieving their goals. The intertwined journeys of these pathways serve as evidence of how scientific rigor, engineering expertise, and strategic insight came together in defining the Manhattan Project.

The Manhattan Project was an endeavor that relied heavily on uranium and plutonium. These two materials played roles in the development of atomic weapons, and their discovery, processing, and application showcased the remarkable scientific and engineering achievements of that time. The project's approach, which involved planning and technical expertise, demonstrated its ability to adapt and persevere. Reflecting on the transformation of these elements, from ores to powerful weapons, reminds us of the intricate processes and groundbreaking advancements that marked the beginning of the nuclear age.

THE DESIGNS: LITTLE BOY AND FAT MAN

The Evolution of Bomb Design:

The development of the bomb during the Manhattan Project was a complex and intricate process, driven by a combination of scientific curiosity, engineering expertise, and the urgent needs of a world at war. In its stages, the project brought together some of the brightest minds from various fields, each contributing unique perspectives. The goal was not merely to create a bomb but to design a weapon that could effectively and reliably function within the limitations of time and resources.

Initial discussions primarily focused on aspects. Physicists drawing on the advancements in nuclear research engaged in debates about the fundamental principles that would form the basis of the bomb. They grappled with questions surrounding fissions nature, how sub-critical masses behaved, and what conditions were necessary to initiate a chain reaction. These discussions held significance as they laid the foundation for forthcoming challenges.

Simultaneously, engineers and metallurgists tackled considerations related to bomb design. Among their primary concerns were selecting materials, understanding detonation mechanics, and addressing miniaturization hurdles. The Manhattan Project was rooted in advanced physics and showcased remarkable feats of engineering. The design of the bomb had to take into account factors, including the properties of the fissile material and the environmental conditions during detonation.

As the project progressed, there was an interaction between theory and practice. Theoretical models were tested, improved, and sometimes discarded based on results. Various setups provided valuable data, from small-scale tests to larger mock detonations. These experiments were not without risks. The project faced its fair share of setbacks and failures. However, each failure was a lesson that motivated the team to innovate and adapt.

Collaboration played a role in this evolutionary process. The Manhattan Project brought together scientists and engineers from backgrounds and nationalities, creating a melting pot of ideas. This diversity proved to be a strength as it allowed for an exchange of ideas and approaches. Debates were common during each design iteration as they underwent scrutiny, challenges, and refinements.

External factors also influenced the evolution of bomb design. Intelligence reports detailing advancements in nuclear research added a sense of urgency. There was concern that the Axis powers might develop an atomic bomb before anyone else, which could drastically alter the course of the war. The geopolitical situation at that time made the design process more complex, requiring the team to decide priorities and compromises.

Looking back, the development of bomb designs during the Manhattan Project demonstrated resilience, creativity, and teamwork. It highlighted how diverse groups can come together to overcome obstacles and reach a shared objective. The creation of "Little Boy" and "Fat Man" was not solely a result of engineering brilliance; it was the culmination of a collective effort shaped by the challenges and necessities of a rapidly changing world.

"Little Boy": The Gun-Type Design:

The design of "Little Boy" as a gun-type mechanism combined scientific innovation and wartime necessity. Despite its straightforward name, the intricacies and considerations behind this design were far from simple.

At its core, the gun-type mechanism used explosives to propel two sub-critical masses of uranium 235 toward each other. The collision of these masses would create a mass, initiating the desired chain reaction. This concept was rooted in the properties of uranium 235. Although fissile and capable of sustaining a chain reaction, it required a quantity or arrangement to do so effectively. The challenge lay in assembling this supercritical configuration before the chain reaction could commence, thus ensuring maximum output.

Uranium 235 was chosen due to its nuclear properties. Unlike its abundant counterpart, uranium 238, even small amounts of uranium 235 could sustain a chain reaction. However, procuring pure uranium 235 posed difficulties. With around 0.7% occurring naturally within uranium deposits, an extensive and resource-intensive enrichment process became necessary to produce the quantities needed for the bomb.

The simplicity of the design proved advantageous yet brought forth its set of challenges.
The speed at which the two masses of uranium needed to be brought was extremely important. A delay or misalignment during the collision could result in a "predetonation," where the chain reaction starts before everything is properly assembled, leading to a lower yield. Engineers ensured that the conventional explosives and gun mechanisms worked seamlessly to address this concern.

Another crucial consideration was the safety of the bomb. Since the mechanism involved firing one piece of material into another, there were genuine worries about accidental detonations. This led to the development of safety measures guaranteeing that the bomb would only detonate when it received the correct sequence of arm signals.

In addition to aspects, developing "Little Boy" was also a race against time. Intelligence reports indicated that Nazi Germany was also pursuing an atomic bomb project, and there was a fear that they might succeed first. This sense of urgency motivated and pressured scientists and engineers working on the Manhattan Project. However, it also meant that there wasn't time for extensive testing. In fact, due to their confidence in its design, "Little Boy" was deployed in combat without testing—a decision highlighting how high stakes things were during that era.

Looking back, "Little Boy" serves as a testament to the difficulties and moral quandaries of the years of atomic warfare. Its creation, based on principles and driven by the necessities of war, provides a deep understanding of the complexities of utilizing nuclear energy for military objectives.

"Fat Man": The Implosion-Type Design:

The "Fat Man" design imploded upon detonation was an example of engineering and scientific innovation. It represented a departure from the more straightforward "Little Boy" design, which relied on a gun-type mechanism. The implosion-type design of "Fat Man" was driven by the properties of plutonium 239.

Plutonium 239, a produced element in nuclear reactors, initially showed promise as a material for the bomb due to its rapid fission capabilities. However, it presented challenges that couldn't be addressed by the gun-type design. For instance, plutonium had a spontaneous fission rate compared to uranium 235, making it prone to premature detonation if approached with a gun-type method.

Scientists and engineers devised the implosion mechanism to utilize the power of plutonium effectively. Of linearly bringing together two sub-critical masses as in a gun-type approach, they aimed to compress a single sub-critical mass of plutonium 239 into a supercritical state using symmetrically placed conventional explosives.

Achieving implosion posed significant challenges. The explosives needed to be shaped into specialized forms called "lenses." This ensured that the detonation waves converged simultaneously on the plutonium core from all directions.

This particular technique of focusing waves played a role in the Manhattan Project. It required understanding shockwave physics and precise engineering to ensure that the explosive waves would concentrate accurately on the core.

The core was meticulously crafted as a sphere of plutonium surrounded by a tamper. The tamper had two functions: it reflected escaping neutrons back into the core, enhancing the explosion and adding inertia to the implosion process for maximum compression.

Designing it was just one part of the challenge. Producing plutonium 239 itself was a task. This element had to be generated in reactors by bombarding uranium 238 with neutrons. Once produced, it needed to be separated from other reactor products in specialized facilities, ensuring high purity levels. Maintaining this purity was critical, as any impurities could impact the bomb's performance.

In essence, "Fat Man" represents a collaboration between nuclear physicists, chemists, metallurgists, and engineers who faced unique challenges in their respective fields. Together, they successfully overcame these obstacles and ultimately created a weapon pivotal in ending World War II and shaping 20th-century geopolitics.

Trials and Tribulations: The Trinity Test:

The Trinity Test took place on July 16, 1945, in the Jornada del Muerto desert of New Mexico. It was more than a technical confirmation of the design of "Fat Man"; it was a pivotal moment for the scientists and engineers involved in the Manhattan Project. As the early morning skies were illuminated by the blinding flash of the world's nuclear explosion, they truly comprehended the immense power they had created.

The location for the test was carefully selected to ensure secrecy and minimize collateral damage. Despite these precautions, the explosion force surpassed expectations. A mushroom cloud soared over 40,000 feet into the sky, and the intense heat transformed sand at ground zero into trinitite—a glass substance with a distinctive green hue.

Leading up to this test, there were uncertainties. While scientists had a theoretical understanding of how implosion would work, applying it on such a massive scale remained uncharted territory. There were concerns about its efficiency and even speculation about igniting Earth's atmosphere—although these fears were later proven unfounded. These uncertainties highlight how much unknown territory this team was navigating.

The test had an emotional impact on those involved. Dr. J. Robert Oppenheimer, the director of the Manhattan Project, famously recalled a line from the Hindu scripture called the Bhagavad Gita, stating, "Now I have become Death, the destroyer of worlds." This statement captured the nature of the atomic age; on the one hand, it promised limitless energy, while on the other hand, it cast a dark shadow of unprecedented destruction.

The data collected from the Trinity Test proved to be extremely valuable. It provided insights into how nuclear explosions behave, including details about the initial blast wave and subsequent radioactive fallout. This information played a role in refining the designs for "Little Boy" and "Fat Man," as well as understanding their potential impact if used in warfare.

Beyond its significance, the Trinity Test is a pivotal moment in human history. It marked the beginning of an age that brought about geopolitical tensions during the Cold War and fueled global efforts toward nuclear disarmament. The test symbolized the possibilities and profound dangers of this new nuclear era.

Legacy and Impact:

The impact of "Little Boy" and "Fat Man" extends beyond the immediate aftermath of Hiroshima and Nagasaki. These two bombs, representing ingenuity and destructive potential, have lasting influenced global consciousness. They have shaped relations, policymaking, and public opinion regarding nuclear energy and warfare.

In the years following World War II, these bombings triggered a race for dominance. The Cold War era witnessed the United States and the Soviet Union accumulating nuclear arsenals, each striving for a strategic edge. This competition was not about numbers; it revolved around technological advancements. Both superpowers aimed to develop powerful and sophisticated weapons based on the designs of "Little Boy" and "Fat Man." Subsequent decades saw the emergence of thermonuclear weapons, intercontinental ballistic missiles, and submarine-launched systems.

However, the legacy of these bombs goes beyond weaponry. They spurred efforts toward arms control and disarmament. Realizing the consequences of nuclear warfare led to various treaties and agreements, like the Nuclear Non-Proliferation Treaty (NPT) and the Comprehensive Nuclear Test Ban Treaty (CTBT). These treaties were designed to limit the spread of weapons and encourage the peaceful use of nuclear energy.

Apart from implications, the bombings of Hiroshima and Nagasaki have profoundly impacted culture and society. They have influenced literature, movies, and art, serving as reminders of the devastating consequences of nuclear warfare. Works like John Hersey's "Hiroshima" and Stanley Kubrick's "Dr.

Strangelove" have explored, criticized, and memorialized these bombings, shaping public discussions and awareness.

Furthermore, the ethical debates surrounding these bombings continue to resonate. Was it justified to use bombs to hasten the end of the war? Could civilian casualties have been avoided? These questions don't offer answers but highlight the complex moral landscape left behind by these bombings.

Lastly, the legacy of "Little Boy" and "Fat Man" has significantly impacted perspectives on nuclear energy. The same scientific principles that power nuclear bombs can also be harnessed as a potent energy source for peaceful purposes. However, considering events like Chernobyl and Fukushima, alongside Hiroshima and Nagasaki, has led to a nuanced debate on the role of energy in creating a sustainable future.

The impact of the bombings is far-reaching, affecting various aspects such as international relations, policy-making, culture, ethics, and energy. The tale of "Little Boy" and "Fat Man" serves as a reminder of how scientific advancements can have both positive and negative consequences. They hold the potential for progress but pose a significant risk of destruction.

Throughout the pages of history, inventions have had such a significant impact on human events as "Little Boy" and "Fat Man." These two atomic creations, born out of brilliance and the urgency of wartime, not only reshaped the outcome of World War II but also set the stage for the nuclear era. The intricate designs, challenges faced during their development, and their eventual use in Hiroshima and Nagasaki are representations of humanity's ability to innovate and destroy. As we contemplate their lasting impact, it becomes clear that these designs go beyond weapons; they symbolize profound aspects of the 20th century, encompassing ethical dilemmas, political consequences, and societal struggles that continue to perplex our world. The narrative surrounding "Little Boy" and "Fat Man" is a moving reminder of the responsibilities associated with harnessing the power of energy.

The exploration of physics, as discussed in this chapter, showcases humanity's curiosity and unwavering pursuit of knowledge. The foundations of science were meticulously established from the groundbreaking experiments conducted by Rutherford that reshaped our comprehension of the atom's structure to Marie Curie's pioneering research on radioactivity. These initial discoveries marked the beginning of a much larger story.

The concept of fission, with its potential to release vast amounts of energy from minuscule amounts of matter, emerged as a groundbreaking idea. This process involves splitting an atom nucleus, resulting not only in energy but also in additional neutrons that could trigger chain reactions. However, comprehending this phenomenon was half the battle; harnessing it posed an even greater challenge. The achievement of mass—where a self-sustaining chain reaction occurs—and mastering control over it became crucial in developing atomic bombs.

The engineering marvels that transformed knowledge into functional weapons were equally remarkable. Building these bombs demanded precision, innovation, and a profound understanding of the materials. The selection and intricate processing of materials such as uranium and plutonium played vital roles. Developing the "Little Boy" and "Fat Man" bombs involved overcoming challenges and complexities, representing the culmination of extensive research and development efforts.

However, beyond the engineering aspects, the creation of atomic bombs also triggered deep ethical and philosophical inquiries. The tremendous power of energy presented opportunities for limitless progress and risks of unprecedented devastation. It marked the dawn of an era, the atomic age, which forever transformed society, politics, and ethics.

As we contemplate this chapter in history, it becomes clear that building bombs was not merely a technical triumph; it fundamentally reshaped humanity's relationship with the natural world. The intricate interplay between particles within nuclei, engineering hurdles faced during development, and profound implications associated with harnessing such immense power all contribute to a narrative that continues to shape our global landscape. Moving forward, we carry with us lessons learned from this journey into the heart of the atom — lessons that bring forth challenges and important questions for our collective future.

Chapter 7: Trials and Triumphs

The mere mention of the Manhattan Project evokes a sense of awe, intrigue, and even a touch of unease. It is one of human history's most ambitious and significant undertakings, blending cutting-edge scientific innovation with the urgency of a world engulfed in war. However, beyond the equations, experiments, and technical terminology, it was an expedition driven by the indomitable human spirit—an unwavering pursuit of knowledge even when faced with insurmountable obstacles.

During the 1940s, when World War II cast its grim shadow across nations, a group of scientists embarked on an extraordinary yet covert mission. Their objective was clear but daunting: to harness the power hidden within atoms – a force that had until then merely existed in theoretical physics. Yet their aspirations extended beyond ending a global conflict; their venture sought to redefine what was scientifically attainable.

The Manhattan Project encompassed more than constructing a bomb; it epitomized pushing boundaries and exploring uncharted scientific territories. It was an amalgamation of minds from various disciplines, such as physics, chemistry, engineering, and countless others, who united for a cause greater than themselves. Each individual brings their unique expertise to the table. The stakes were incredibly high. The challenges they faced were numerous. They had to secure materials like uranium and plutonium and understand the complexities of nuclear fission. Each step they took showcased the ingenuity and resilience of human beings.

However, beyond the technical obstacles, there were also moral and ethical dilemmas to contend with. The very nature of this project meant that its success would bring about an era of warfare – a time when humanity's survival would hang in the balance. The scientists involved weren't just battling against time and technical hurdles; they were also grappling with the responsibility resting on their shoulders.

Located amidst New Mexicos mesas and canyons, Los Alamos became a melting pot where science, ambition, and ethics intersected. Here, some of the minds of their generation – from Oppenheimer's to Fermi – worked tirelessly, driven by curiosity, duty, and the looming presence of a world engulfed in war. Every experiment conducted, every calculation made, and every discussion held brought them closer to an awe-inspiring goal.

As we explore the essence of this chapter, we will venture into the hallways of Los Alamos, accompany the scientists on their journey, experience their worries, celebrate their successes, and grapple with the dilemmas they encountered. This is more than a narrative about nuclear weapons and scientific advancements; it's a tale of humanity standing at a critical juncture, making decisions under pressure, and showcasing our resilient nature even in the face of adversity.

THE TRINITY TEST: PREPARATIONS, EXECUTION, AND AFTERMATH

The Genesis of Trinity:

The choice to name the test 'Trinity' went beyond poetic symbolism; it reflected the deep philosophical and existential ponderings that often accompanied the rigorous scientific work of the Manhattan Project. J. Robert Oppenheimer, the director, was not just a physicist but also a man with a profound interest in literature and philosophy. His decision to draw inspiration from John Donne's sonnets when naming the test was indicative of the profound questions raised by the project about existence, creation, and destruction.

John Donne's metaphysical poetry frequently explored themes such as love, mortality, and divinity. These themes resonated with Oppenheimer, particularly as he led a project pushing the boundaries of knowledge and capabilities. The very essence of the Manhattan Project, including its Trinity test, aimed to harness the forces governing our universe. It sought to grasp something, a power previously reserved for nature or God alone.

Oppenheimer's appreciation for literature and philosophy offered him a perspective on this undertaking. While its primary objective undeniably lay in applications, he never lost sight of its profound philosophical implications. The act of creation, whether crafting a poem, constructing a universe, or inventing a bomb, carries great responsibility. The name 'Trinity' served as a reminder of this weighty responsibility.

The threefold nature of the name also mirrored the project's three challenges: the scientific hurdles in comprehending and harnessing atomic energy, the logistical and operational obstacles in translating this understanding into a functional weapon, and the ethical dilemmas surrounding its use.

During moments of tranquility, when from equations and experiments, Oppenheimer might have found solace in Donne's words that often expressed the interconnectedness of all things. The Manhattan Project aimed to unlock the atom's secrets and uncovered connections between science, ethics, and our human essence. In ways, the name 'Trinity' reflected this intricate interplay.

Choosing Ground Zero:

The decision to choose the Alamogordo Bombing and Gunnery Range as the location for the Trinity test was not taken lightly. At a glance, the barren and dry landscape of the Jornada del Muerto desert might have seemed an unconventional choice. However, it was these characteristics that made it an ideal option.

The primary allure of this location was its ability to maintain secrecy during a time when espionage and counterintelligence operations were at their peak, particularly for the Manhattan Project. The isolated desert ensured that domestic and foreign prying eyes would be kept away. Additionally, its vastness meant that any accidental fallout or unforeseen consequences from the test would be confined to minimize harm to populated areas.

Alamogordo's selection wasn't solely based on isolation. The region's geological stability played a role as well. The flat terrain supported by rock layers provided a steady foundation, reducing the risk of seismic disturbances triggered by the explosion. This geological stability ensured not only the safety of the test but also accurate data collection.

Furthermore, another contributing factor in choosing Alamogordo was its existing infrastructure within the Bombing and Gunnery Range. Although primarily used for weapons testing, the range included facilities that could be repurposed or expanded to meet the requirements of the Trinity test. This made the challenges of setting up the test site somewhat easier, allowing the team to focus more on the technical aspects of the test.

However, transforming this desert into a nuclear testing ground came with challenges. The arid conditions presented issues, such as ensuring a reliable water supply and dealing with frequent sandstorms that could disrupt preparations. Additionally, the intense heat during New Summer posed an additional hurdle as temperatures often soared, making demanding work even more strenuous.

Nevertheless, despite these obstacles, the desert quickly became a center of activity. Scientists, engineers, and military personnel converged on this forgotten patch of land, each contributing their expertise to the preparations. Temporary structures emerged throughout. From laboratories for last-minute checks to observation posts for witnessing the test. The serene desert now reverberated with sounds of machinery operating discussions taking place and an underlying sense of anticipation.

The selection of the Jornada del Muerto desert for the Trinity test symbolizes the essence of the Manhattan Project. It showcases a combination of planning, scientific precision, and determination to overcome obstacles. This choice highlights the team's dedication to ensuring their mission's triumph and meticulous approach in every aspect of the project.

The Gadget: Birth of a Behemoth:

The device, although commonly called the Gadget, was far from simple. Its creation involved an amount of labor, meticulous calculations, and groundbreaking innovations. Essentially, the Gadget was a bomb designed to implode, which posed both revolutionary advancements and significant challenges; unlike the gun-type design that relied on an explosion to bring together two sub-critical masses, the implosion-type design required surrounding a sub-critical mass with conventional explosives. When detonated, these explosives compressed the core, causing it to become supercritical and initiate a chain energy reaction.

The selection of plutonium 239 as the core material was not arbitrary. This artificial element produced in reactors was preferred for its ability to sustain a rapid chain reaction necessary for the bomb's explosive power. However, working with plutonium came with its set of challenges. It had isotopes, not all of which were suitable for bomb-making purposes. The team needed exclusively Pu 239 plutonium—a challenging objective given the technological limitations at that time.

The metallurgical obstacles were immense. Plutonium had never been produced in quantities, and its properties were not entirely understood. It was discovered to have crystalline structures, each possessing unique physical properties. The different forms of plutonium presented a challenge. To build the bomb, it was necessary to have plutonium in a state that could be shaped precisely for the core.

Layers of materials surrounded the plutonium core, each with its purpose. Reflectors were used to redirect escaping neutrons into the core while tampering increased compression. Additionally, designed conventional explosives ensured a symmetrical implosion. The timing and synchronization of these explosives were critical; even a tiny difference in timing could result in an outcome.

Assembling the Gadget was a task that required both engineering and delicate precision. In the New Mexico desert, atop a tower, scientists and engineers worked with excitement mixed with apprehension. Every wire, detonator, and screw had its function. There was no margin for error. The Gadget wasn't a bomb; it represented years of dedicated research demonstrating human creativity and marking the beginning of a new era.

Countdown to Destiny:

The atmosphere at the Alamogordo Bombing and Gunnery Range that morning was filled with an intense tension that could be sensed in every breath and heartbeat. Scientists, military personnel, and a few fortunate observers had gathered at vantage points, each searching for a spot that would provide a clear view and some degree of safety. Many had put on welder's glasses in anticipation of the blinding flash expected from the Gadget.

Whispers permeated the air as last-minute checks were carried out. Some scientists meticulously reviewed their instruments to ensure they would capture all the data from the explosion. Others engaged in conversations discussing their speculations about the explosion yield or contemplating the various things that could go wrong. The weight of this moment was tangible. For many, it represented years of work, countless sleepless nights, and countless obstacles overcome. For others, it was an opportunity to witness the power of innovation firsthand while grappling with its ethical implications.

A few kilometers away, within a heavily fortified bunker, significant figures from the Manhattan Project. Including Dr. J. Robert Oppenheimer and General Leslie Groves. Anxiously awaited what was to come.

Each person had played a role in bringing the project to this point, and they all understood the moment's significance. Oppenheimer, being philosophical by nature, contemplated the implications of the test, while Groves, being a military man, was focused on the immediate task at hand.

As the final seconds ticked away, the bustling desert fell into an eerie silence. Samuel Allison's voice as he meticulously counted down each passing second was the only sound that could be heard. His voice remained steady, filled with anticipation as it reverberated across the vast expanse.

Then, in an instant, the peacefulness of New Mexicos desert was shattered. A blinding and searing light flooded the landscape with a brilliance surpassing that of multiple suns. Long and ghostly shadows were cast as shockwaves rippled through the atmosphere, devastating everything in their path.

For those who witnessed this event unfold before them, time seemed to freeze. The initial burst of light was followed by an ascending fireball that transitioned from red to orange and eventually settled into a pale yellow hue. Its shape gradually transformed into what has become synonymous with destruction, the iconic mushroom cloud—the earth. A roar, a mix of indescribable sounds, filled the surroundings.

After the explosion, as the echoes of the blast grew faint and the bright cloud kept rising into the sky, a range of emotions overwhelmed those who witnessed it—happiness, relief, wonderment, and, in some cases, a sense of contemplative sadness. The world had been forever altered, marking the beginning of the era.

Echoes in the Aftermath:

The impact of the Trinity test reached beyond the physical aftermath in the desert. It had psychological and geopolitical effects.

In the hours and days following the test, scientists who had dedicated years to creating the bomb were faced with the magnitude of their accomplishment. A sobering realization overshadowed the initial excitement of success; they had unleashed a devastating power. The test not only confirmed that the atomic bomb was feasible but also raised ethical concerns and moral dilemmas.

Dr. Kenneth Bainbridge, director of the Trinity test, succinctly expressed this sentiment when he said to Oppenheimer, "Now we are all sons of bitches." These words captured the conflict experienced by many involved in the project. They had achieved what was once believed impossible but at a cost.

The global implications were equally significant. Though ending World War II was initially their primary objective, the success of the Trinity test had far-reaching consequences for international geopolitics. The United States now had a weapon of power that would undoubtedly change the balance of power and influence international diplomacy.

Furthermore, this test marked the beginning of a nuclear arms race, a competition between superpowers that lasted for decades and led to a growth in the world's nuclear arsenal. The Cold War emerged from this era characterized by distrust and the constant threat of nuclear destruction, all stemming from that blinding flash in New Mexico that announced the dawn of the atomic age.

On a personal level, the people living in nearby communities were left to grapple with the mysterious explosion and its aftermath, many unaware of what had transpired. Rumors and speculations circulated widely. It would take years before the true nature of the Trinity test was officially acknowledged.

The legacy of the Trinity test is multi-dimensional. It serves as a testament to innovation while symbolizing how scientific progress can be beneficial and dangerous. It stands as a reminder of our profound responsibility when wielding such power. The echoes from that day in July 1945 continue to resonate today, shaping our understanding of science, ethics, and the intricate relationship between progress and accountability.

The Trinity Test was a significant historical moment, representing the beginning of a new era. It highlighted the meeting point between humanity's scientific abilities and the ethical challenges of wielding unprecedented power. The event, from its planned preparations to its awe-inspiring execution and the lasting impact it had, captured the intricate nature of human ambition, innovation, and responsibility. As we look back on the Trinity Test, it serves as a reminder of how crucial it is to strike a delicate balance between our pursuit of knowledge and our responsibility to use it wisely. Today, we can still hear the echoes from that New Mexico desert urging us to remember to learn from our past experiences and navigate the path of progress with caution.

THE DECISION-MAKING PROCESS: MILITARY AND POLITICAL CONSIDERATIONS

The Geopolitical Landscape:

The mid-20th century was a time of changes in global politics. As the 1940s progressed, not only did the world witness the end of a devastating war, but it also experienced a shift in power dynamics. The standing European empires, which had held sway over global affairs for centuries, were losing their influence to emerging superpowers like the United States and the Soviet Union.

Amidst this changing landscape, the Pacific theater of World War II posed a challenge. While Europe saw the rise and fall of the Third Reich and witnessed the retreat of Axis powers, Asia had a different situation. Driven by its ambitions, Japan had established control over vast areas in East and Southeast Asia. Its conquests encompassed territories such as the Philippines,

Indonesia, and significant parts of China. The Japanese Empire was not a military force but also presented an ideological challenge with its Greater East Asia Co-Prosperity Sphere concept.

The United States emerged from the war less devastated than Europe's war-torn lands and stood in a position of strength. Its industrial and economic prowess played a role in supporting the Allied forces during wartime. However, for Americans, there was also a dimension to their conflict with Japan due to the attack on Pearl Harbor. The Pacific War went beyond geopolitical strategy; it was a fight to establish American dominance and safeguard its regional interests.

At the time, the Soviet Union, after enduring the full force of Nazi aggression on the Eastern Front, was solidifying its gains in Europe. The Red Army's advance toward Berlin significantly expanded its influence in Eastern Europe. Although they joined the Pacific War, their presence introduced another aspect to the geopolitical calculations. American policymakers were determined to prevent a war in Asia with substantial Soviet influence.

The end of World War II wasn't about ending hostilities. Evidently, the post-war era would become an arena for competing ideologies. The democratic principles upheld by the United States and its allies were destined to clash with the vision of the Soviet Union. In this struggle, Asia, with its vast populations and resources, became a highly coveted stage.

Therefore, decision-making during the war stages went beyond tactical military considerations alone; it intertwined deeply with America's broader geopolitical aspirations. The atomic bomb, in this situation, served not only as a means to bring the war to a close but also as an instrument for shaping the world after the war.

The Military Perspective:

The military's perspective in the stages of World War II was primarily focused on achieving victory while minimizing the loss of lives. The challenges faced in the Pacific front differed from those in the theater. Japan, known for its ingrained Bushido code, emphasized values such as honor, sacrifice, and unwavering loyalty to the Emperor. Due to this ethos, Japanese soldiers often fought with great determination and resilience, making a ground invasion of the Japanese mainland daunting.

The island hopping campaigns provided insights into Japanese forces' intensity and unwavering defense during fierce battles like Iwo Jima and Okinawa. These battles resulted in casualties for both sides, a stark preview of what an invasion of Japan's home islands might entail. Military analysts projected that Operation Downfall, which involved plans for invading Japan, could potentially lead to over half a million troops losing their lives, with even higher estimated casualties among Japanese forces.

Given this context, the atomic bomb emerged as an alternative to avoid a ground invasion altogether.

The military leaders involved in the Manhattan Project, such as General Leslie Groves and Admiral William Leahy, were fully aware of the stakes involved. They understood that while the atomic bomb had the potential to end the war quickly, it also carried implications. It wasn't about the immediate devastation caused by its explosion; it was also about its impact on the psyche of the Japanese leadership and their people. The hope was that witnessing such a level of destruction far beyond what conventional warfare could achieve would shake Japan's resolve and make them reconsider their position.

However, it is important to note that there were differing opinions within the military. Some influential figures like General Dwight D. Eisenhower expressed reservations about using weapons, especially against civilian targets. They believed that Japan was already close to surrendering and that using weapons might not be necessary.

Nevertheless, there was a prevailing sense of urgency. The longer the war persisted without a resolution, the more the loss of human life there would be. Each passing day meant more lives lost and more families torn apart. More resources are consumed. The atomic bomb, despite its destructive capability, provided a means to resolve the impasse and end a conflict that had already inflicted significant losses on numerous individuals.

The Political Calculus:

The later stages of World War II were not a culmination of military tactics and battles. Still, they also served as a prelude to the geopolitical landscape shaping the latter half of the 20th century. The atomic bomb, while used to end the war, was also a piece in the larger game of international politics.

President Harry S. Truman, who was relatively new to leadership following Franklin D. Roosevelt's passing, was at the forefront during these transformative times. With the United States emerging relatively unharmed from the war's destructions, it was in a position to shape the world after the war. Europe lay in ruins. Established powers were grappling with dealing with its aftermath. This presented both opportunities and challenges for U.S. Leadership.

Under Joseph Stalin's guidance, the Soviet Union rapidly expanded its influence across Eastern Europe. The Red Army played a role in defeating Nazi Germany, and as they liberated nations, they aimed to establish governments aligned with communist ideology. This expansion raised concerns in Washington as cracks began to appear in the wartime alliance between the U.S. And the USSR that had formed out of necessity. The ideological differences between capitalism and communism, which had been put aside during the war, were becoming more prominent.

In this situation, the atomic bomb held significance beyond being a mere weapon; it represented technological and scientific advancement. Demonstrating the ability to harness power would send a clear message to the world about America's leadership in science, technology, and military strength. It was a declaration of intent indicating that the United States was ready to lead the world against the growing influence of communism.

The Potsdam Conference in July 1945 added another layer to this calculation. Truman, Stalin, and British Prime Minister Winston Churchill came together to discuss war arrangements. With knowledge of the Trinity test, Truman approached these negotiations with newfound confidence. The subtle hints about a powerful weapon were not only aimed at Japan but also carried implications for the Soviets—a discreet indication of shifting global power dynamics.

However, this strategy had its drawbacks as well. While it demonstrated superiority, it also sparked an arms race that would define the Cold War era. The choice to use the bomb in Hiroshima and Nagasaki was not made in a vacuum; it was closely connected to broader geopolitical strategies aimed at reshaping the global power dynamics after the war. The consequences of this decision resonated for years, impacting international relations, diplomacy, and even the way warfare is conducted.

The Ethical Quandary:

The ethical considerations surrounding the use of the bomb were incredibly complex, just like the scientific principles that powered this devastating weapon. At the core of this dilemma was a fundamental question: Is it acceptable to achieve a desired outcome by any means necessary? While the main goal was clear. To bring an end to a war as quickly as possible. The methods used involved unleashing a force capable of obliterating entire cities and causing long-lasting harm to survivors.

As the reality of their creation became apparent, many scientists who had worked on the Manhattan Project began expressing their concerns. Initially driven by fear that Nazi Germany might develop a bomb first, their motivations shifted once World War II in Europe ended and Germany was defeated. The bomb was no longer seen as a deterrent against Nazi aggression but as a tool to subdue Japan and potentially demonstrate global power.

Dr. J. Robert Oppenheimer, often called the "father of the bomb," famously quoted from the Bhagavad Gita upon witnessing the Trinity test; "Now I am become Death, the destroyer of worlds." This statement encapsulated the inner conflict experienced by many involved in this endeavor.

They managed to uncover the mysteries of the atom. In doing so, did they also unleash a Pandora's box of ethical dilemmas?

The potential deployment of the bomb in areas raised concerns about distinguishing between combatants and non-combatants during warfare. Conventional ethics in warfare stressed the significance of this distinction. The atomic bomb, by its very nature, blurred those boundaries. The immediate explosion would claim lives among soldiers and civilians, while the subsequent radiation would bring suffering without discrimination.

Looking beyond the consequences, there was an acknowledgment that using such a weapon would establish a precedent. If the United States, a nation that prided itself on its values, chose to employ such destructive power, what would prevent other nations from following suit in future conflicts? The global ramifications were immense. The deployment of bombs could potentially usher in an era where conflicts were no longer defined by battles and strategies but by the constant looming threat of mutual destruction.

The voices expressing dissent were not limited to scientists. Religious leaders, philosophers, and even some military officials questioned the morality behind using such a bomb. They debated advocating for methods like showcasing the bomb's potency on an uninhabited island or a military facility. The idea was that the sheer demonstration of its power would potentially lead to a surrender.

Ultimately, the choice to deploy the bomb was influenced by a combination of factors, with ethical concerns being one aspect of a multifaceted puzzle. Nonetheless, the moral dilemmas associated with this decision still hold significance as a reminder of the weighty responsibilities accompanying scientific and technological progress.

In the final chapters of World War II, the decision to use the atomic bomb stands out as one of the most debated and significant choices. It was a decision made at the crossroads of necessity, political strategy, and ethical dilemmas. While the immediate aim was to expedite the war's end, its consequences extended beyond that moment, shaping global geopolitics, scientific accountability, and our shared human conscience. The multifaceted considerations surrounding this decision highlight leaders' challenges in unprecedented times and underscore their profound moral obligations when making monumental choices.

THE FLIGHT CREWS AND THEIR TRAINING

The Selection Process:

The thorough process of choosing flight crews for the Manhattan Project reflected the importance of its mission. It went beyond identifying skilled pilots; it aimed to find individuals who could bear the weighty responsibility of being part of a mission capable of reshaping history.

Every potential crew member faced scrutiny, extending beyond their flying abilities to encompass personal attributes. Their backgrounds underwent examination, ensuring those selected were free from dissent or unreliability. The military understood that the stakes were too high for any lapses in judgment or loss of focus.

Interviews with officers and peers played a vital role in the selection process. These conversations aimed to assess not only technical expertise but also character, resilience, and the ability to handle stress. Questions often touched upon moral aspects, exploring candidates' perspectives on warfare, the use of powerful weapons, and the potential consequences of their actions.

Simulated flight missions constituted another element in the selection process. These missions went beyond training flights; they were designed to push pilots to their utmost limits. Facing obstacles became common, ranging from sudden equipment malfunctions to intricate navigational challenges. These trials put their problem-solving abilities, adaptability, and composure under pressure to the test.

However, the uncertainty surrounding the mission was the most demanding aspect of the selection process. Candidates were intentionally kept in the dark regarding the nature of their assignment. This veil of secrecy served as an evaluation itself, assessing their capacity to function with information, place trust in their superiors, and remain committed to a mission that held elusive details.

Ultimately, those who successfully emerged were not merely pilots or navigators. They embodied individuals with unwavering dedication, impeccable character, and an innate understanding of their role in ushering in the atomic age. They constituted a few ready to embark on a mission that would undoubtedly be etched into history's records.

Specialized Training Regimen:

The training program for the flight crews involved a combination of military drills and innovative techniques specifically tailored to the unique requirements of the atomic mission. Every aspect of their training was meticulously designed to ensure that the crews would be fully technically and mentally prepared when the critical moment arrived.

Central to this program was the challenge posed by the bomb itself. Unlike bombs, the atomic bomb's size and weight presented distinct aerodynamic challenges. Pilots had to learn to maneuver their aircraft with this added weight during crucial moments like takeoff and release. Simulated exercises using imitation bombs became a part of their training, enabling pilots to become familiar with the altered flight dynamics.

However, it wasn't about handling the aircraft. The precise release of the bomb demanded accuracy in aerial warfare at that time. Bombardiers underwent training sessions to refine their skills and ensure they could hit their targets accurately when it mattered most. They practiced extensively with technology like the Norden bombsight, considered an extraordinary marvel back then as it promised previously unattainable levels of accuracy. Day and night in weather conditions, these bombardiers trained diligently while simulating scenarios similar to what they would encounter over Hiroshima and Nagasaki.

Navigators also encountered their share of challenges. The lengthy journey to Japan over vast stretches of open ocean required flawless navigation skills. Even the tiniest mistake could spell failure for the mission. Navigators underwent a training program covering traditional celestial navigation techniques and the latest electronic navigation tools to prepare for this. They diligently practiced charting courses in scenarios to ensure they could adapt to unexpected obstacles during the mission.

The aircraft, the B-29 Superfortresses, underwent modifications to meet the unique demands of the atomic mission. Engineers and technicians worked closely with flight crews, making adjustments and ensuring the planes were in optimal condition. Crews received training in maintaining and troubleshooting these modifications, equipping them with the skills to tackle any issues that might arise during their mission.

Overall, this specialized training regime took an approach by addressing every conceivable challenge that crews might encounter. It showcased the Manhattan Project's meticulousness, as no aspect was overlooked in its pursuit of ensuring a mission.

Psychological Preparation:

The psychological preparation for the flight crews was just as important as the aspects of their mission. Military leaders and psychologists recognized the nature of their tasks and wanted to provide them with tools that went beyond the usual.

Even though the crews were highly skilled and resilient, they couldn't ignore the weight of delivering a weapon of mass destruction. The secrecy surrounding the mission added more stress to their shoulders. Many of them were separated from their families and loved ones, increasing their strain.

To address these challenges, the military introduced psychological training programs. These programs aimed to prepare the crews for their upcoming mission and ensure their long-term mental well-being. They included workshops on stress management, coping mechanisms, and emotional intelligence as parts of their training routine. Renowned psychologists, some with experience in assisting soldiers returning from war zones, led these sessions, giving them insights into the minds of these individuals.

One significant aspect of this training involved scenario-based role-playing exercises. Crew members were placed in simulated high-pressure situations that mirrored elements of their mission and explored personal dilemmas and ethical challenges. The goal was to enhance their decision-making ability, ensuring they stayed composed in the toughest situations.

Unconventional as it may seem in a context, the crew members were introduced to meditation practices aimed at finding inner tranquility and focus. They participated in guided meditation sessions, practiced breathing exercises, and even tried early forms of visualization techniques. These methods aimed to center their minds, enabling them to approach their mission with clarity and determination.

Recognizing the significance of support, a "buddy system" was established where each crew member had a partner with whom they could share their anxieties, hopes, and fears. This arrangement fostered a sense of camaraderie and mutual assistance, ensuring that no one felt isolated during their journey.

Post-mission debriefings went beyond evaluating the aspects of bombing runs. Psychologists were present to help the crew process their emotions by providing a space for expressing feelings, addressing any guilt or trauma they might be experiencing, and initiating the healing process.

Ultimately, the psychological preparation undergone by these flight crews exemplified the military's mindset.

Recognizing the emotional and ethical aspects of the mission ensured that these courageous individuals were prepared to fulfill their duties and capable of navigating the complex emotional challenges that accompanied them.

Team Dynamics and Cohesion:

The success of any mission, especially one as significant as the atomic bombings, depends not only on the technical expertise of its participants but also on their ability to work together seamlessly. The flight crews involved in the Manhattan Project were a group with various backgrounds, skills, and personalities. However, they had to function as a team built on trust and mutual respect for the mission to be accomplished.

Establishing this unity was no task. Although each crew member was carefully selected for their abilities, ensuring they could work harmoniously required a deliberate effort. The military understood that the dynamics within these crews would be crucial for the mission's triumph. Therefore, fostering a sense of camaraderie and trust became a priority.

Despite receiving training, many crew members had never been part of an operation of such magnitude before. The immense responsibility they carried and the inherent dangers involved in the mission could easily lead to doubt or discord among them. To prevent this from happening, the military organized shared experiences aimed at forging bonds among the crew members. These experiences ranged from survival training in locations to simulated emergency scenarios that pushed them to their limits and compelled them to rely on one another for support and guidance.

Beyond the training sessions, the crew members were encouraged to have informal gatherings. They would gather around campfires, share meals, and engage in activities, creating opportunities to establish deeper connections beyond their military duties. During these moments, they would share stories from their homes, discuss their aspirations, and even reveal fears. These interactions humanized each member in the eyes of their peers.

The leaders within the crews played a role in shaping these dynamics. While being experts in their roles as bombardiers, navigators, and pilots, they were also responsible for ensuring harmony within their teams. They were trained to identify signs of stress or discord and take measures to address them. Promoting communication was vital so that any concerns, doubts, or fears could be dealt with directly.

As the mission approached closer each day, the bonds between the crew members became stronger and more solidified. They were no longer colleagues; they had become brothers in arms who shared a common purpose and held deep trust in one another. This strong cohesion had been nurtured over months of training and shared experiences. It would prove crucial in maintaining composure during high-pressure bombing situations as it ensured that each member executed their role with precision and unwavering dedication.

In the Manhattan Project, the flight crews are a remarkable example of human strength, dedication, and the power of working together. They underwent technical and psychological training to prepare for a mission unmatched in terms of its gravity. However, it was not just their skills and training that defined their journey but also the trust they shared among themselves. These men were carefully chosen for their expertise. Then, they transformed into unified teams ready to carry out a mission that would change the world forever. Their story beautifully combines talent with collective unity, a powerful reminder of the human factor in scientific and military history.

The journey of the Manhattan Project, culminating in the Trinity Test, stands as a testament to human ingenuity, determination, and the relentless pursuit of knowledge. This chapter delved deep into the events, decisions, and reflections that marked this pivotal historical moment.

The Trinity Test, named with poetic resonance drawn from John Donne's profound meditations on existence and divinity, was not just a scientific experiment. It was a moment when humanity touched the essence of creation and destruction. The choice of the Alamogordo Bombing and Gunnery Range in New Mexico for the test was not just for its isolation but also as a canvas upon which this monumental event would be painted. With its vastness and silence, the desert witnessed an explosion that changed the course of history.

The meticulous preparations leading up to the test, from the assembly of the "Gadget" to the final countdown, showcased the convergence of brilliant minds and unwavering resolve. Each individual, whether a scientist, engineer, or soldier, played a role in bringing the vision to fruition. Interrupted with military strategy and political considerations, the decision-making process highlighted the complexities of wielding such unprecedented power.

The flight crews and their rigorous training underscored the gravity of the mission. These were not just routine sorties; they were flights that would deliver a force hitherto unseen by humanity. The dedication and precision of these crews were emblematic of the larger ethos of the project.

Yet, amidst the scientific and technical triumphs, the chapter also sheds light on the profound ethical and moral dilemmas those involved face. The luminous glow of the Trinity explosion illuminated not just the New Mexican desert but also the challenges of wielding such power responsibly. The aftermath of the test, marked by awe and introspection, set the stage for global discussions on the role of nuclear energy, both as a tool of war and a beacon of hope for a future of clean and abundant energy.

In essence, the trials and triumphs of the Manhattan Project and the Trinity Test are not just historical events but reflections on the human spirit's capacity to innovate, aspire, and reflect. As we progress in this narrative, we must carry with us the lessons, reflections, and insights from this chapter, for they lay the foundation for understanding the broader implications of the atomic age.

CHAPTER 8: HIROSHIMA AND NAGASAKI - THE BOMB'S IMPACT

The 20th century witnessed an event that forever changed the course of human history, characterized by rapid technological advancements and geopolitical shifts. In August 1945, Hiroshima and Nagasaki became the epicenters of a display of destructive power. The atomic bombings marked the conclusion of World War II and the dawn of the atomic age, resulting from years of scientific research, political maneuvering, and military strategy.

The decision to utilize weapons was influenced by a complex interplay of various factors. Factors such as the prolonged Pacific War, the desire to avoid an invasion of Japan's mainland, and strategic considerations in shaping post-war geopolitics played a role. However, amidst these broader considerations are the personal stories—stories filled with humanity—of those who experienced life and loss in the aftermath of these bombings.

Let us take a moment to envision Hiroshima on that morning of August 6th, 1945—a bustling city brimming with everyday life. Trams traversed streets adorned with shops and homes, children playing joyfully while families carried out their routines beneath an azure summer sky. In moments, this vibrant feature was irreversibly transformed. A blinding flash, a roar, and an intense wave of heat turned the cityscape into a terrifying scene of utter devastation.

Nagasaki, too, experienced a fate merely three days later. Tucked amidst hills and valleys, this coastal city, with its historical background and cultural significance, was reduced to nothing but ashes. The vibrant streets, the churches, temples, and homes bore the brunt of an atomic inferno.

However, the physical destruction alone does not fully capture the impact of these bombings. The true legacy of Hiroshima and Nagasaki lies in the human toll—the stories of survivors who endured hardships and tales of loss, resilience, and hope. In the aftermath, chaos reigned as Hibakusha (survivors) navigated through unrecognizable landscapes. Overwhelmed hospitals struggled to treat injured individuals while families were torn apart. Society grappled with a terrifying reality that demanded acceptance.

These bombings cast an enduring shadow over geopolitics and ethical considerations. The world wrestled with implications surrounding nuclear warfare—questions regarding morality, necessity, and far-reaching consequences took center stage in international discussions. The essence of warfare, diplomacy, and international relations underwent a transformation when nations gained the capability to obliterate entire cities and civilizations.

This section explores the impacts of the atomic age's beginnings. We will journey through the streets of Hiroshima and Nagasaki by conducting research and presenting a narrative that intertwines the big picture with individual experiences. Along this exploration, we will retrace the footsteps of those who lived through, died in, and survived the aftermath of these bombings. It is important to acknowledge that beyond being stories of destruction, the tales of Hiroshima and Nagasaki embody hope, resilience, and the unwavering human spirit.

THE IMMEDIATE AFTERMATH AND DESTRUCTION

The Unleashing of Unprecedented Power:

The explosion of the bombs over Hiroshima and Nagasaki was not merely a blast; it represented humanity's newfound ability to harness the universe's fundamental building blocks. These bombs, deriving their power from nuclear fission, showcased an unprecedented leap in destructive capabilities.

At the core of these weapons are uranium 235 for the "Little Boy" bomb dropped on Hiroshima and plutonium 239 for the "Fat Man" bomb over Nagasaki. A chain reaction occurs within this core when triggered, causing atomic nuclei to split apart and unleash energy. This energy, previously contained within atoms but now suddenly released, became the power source in these bombs.

The immediate result of this energy release was a burst of gamma rays. These gamma rays, an energy electromagnetic radiation, interacted with air molecules around them, producing a dazzling flash of light. This brilliant flash served as the sign of detonation and could be seen from great distances, even within the confines of Enola Gay—the B-29 bomber that dropped the bomb on Hiroshima.

The radiation released during the explosion was incredibly strong, causing burns to anyone exposed, even if they were some distance away from the center. The intense light briefly etched shadows into objects and people, leaving behind imprints known as nuclear shadows. These haunting remnants can still be seen in places in Hiroshima, serving as a silent testament to the immense power of the bomb.

Apart from the burst of radiation, there was also a rapid expansion of air due to the energy release. This created a ball of gas and plasma that rose quickly into the sky, leaving destruction in its wake and setting the stage for ensuing shockwaves and fires.

The deployment of bomb power went beyond showcasing scientific advancements; it served as a stark reminder of humanity's dual nature. The same principles of physics that allowed us to understand the mysteries of our universe were now being used for one of history's devastating acts of warfare.

The Shockwave's Wrath:

The shockwave that spread out from the center of the explosions in Hiroshima and Nagasaki wasn't a physical power but a clear indication of the immense strength of atomic energy. As it moved across, it interacted with these cities' landscapes, topographies, and structures in ways that emphasized both the indiscriminate and distinct nature of atomic destruction.

In Hiroshima, where the land was relatively flat, there was resistance against the advancing shockwave. Buildings, regardless of their construction or purpose, faced pressures. Wooden structures splintered and shattered, sending debris flying at high speeds. Even concrete buildings, which might have been expected to withstand, often crumbled under the force of the shockwave—walls collapsing inward or being torn away from their foundations. Once symbols of connection and engineering excellence, bridges buckled and twisted so they couldn't be crossed.

Nagasaki presented a situation due to its diverse topography. The city's valleys and hillsides provided pockets of protection in some areas. It has also directed the energy of the shockwave, in others—amplifying its effects. Narrow alleyways turned into wind tunnels that intensified their force and created localized zones with severe destruction. In some areas, hillsides reflected the shockwave, resulting in overlapping pressure zones that caused even greater devastation.

Beyond the physical damage, the impact of the shockwave had other effects that were not easily quantifiable. The sounds accompanying the shockwave. From the loud explosion to the symphony of collapsing buildings, shattering glass, and ensuing fires. It created a cacophony of chaos and despair. Those who survived often described feeling disoriented by these sounds as they added another layer of trauma to an overwhelming experience.

Additionally, as the shockwave passed, it disrupted the air people breathed. Its movement compressed the air, resulting in an intense surge of heat. Combined with fires, this led to updrafts that drew in cooler air from all around, fueling stronger winds that further spread destruction and fanned flames.

In the aftermath of the shockwave path and amidst settling dust and raging fires, city inhabitants were confronted with a drastically transformed landscape. Streets familiar became unrecognizable; landmarks were obliterated; and everyday life was torn apart. The shockwave's brief but powerful impact forever changed the history of Hiroshima, Nagasaki, and, indeed, the world.

The Firestorms:

The firestorms that swept through Hiroshima and Nagasaki after the atomic bombings were not just fires. They were events that completely transformed the cities. These firestorms, born from the heat of the explosions, were like whirlwinds of flames that devoured everything in their path, leaving behind a trail of utter devastation.

When the initial flash of the explosions ignited fires throughout the cities, these individual fires merged on such a scale and with such intensity that they created immense infernos. These weren't your fires; these firestorms caused by atomic blasts had a unique ability to sustain themselves. As they raged, they drew in air from their surroundings, creating powerful winds that further fed the flames. The temperatures within these firestorms reached extremes that even materials known for their resistance to burning, like stone and metal, began to melt or distort under the intense heat.

The firestorm spread rapidly in Hiroshima, where wide boulevards and flat terrain prevailed. The flames moved with force, giving residents very little time to escape. Many who sought shelter in rivers or water tanks discovered that even the water boiled due to the heat providing no relief.

Nagasakis distinct topography. Its valleys and hills influenced how the firestorm behaved in a way. Although the hilly landscape prevented a firestorm like the one witnessed in Hiroshima, it did result in pockets of intense fires. These isolated infernos trapped people in valleys, cutting off escape routes and causing areas of devastating destruction.

Apart from the physical devastation, the firestorms had a profound psychological impact on those who survived. The relentless flames, suffocating heat, and smoke-filled skies created an atmosphere. For survivors of the bombings, known as Hibakusha, the memories of these firestorms remained vivid and haunting long after the initial explosion. The image of their familiar city being consumed by flames, accompanied by sounds of collapsing structures and cries for help from those trapped, left an indelible mark on their memories.

The aftermath of the firestorms presented a scene. Streets that were once bustling with activity now stood lined with remains of buildings and homes. The few structures that managed to withstand were skeletons stripped bare by intense heat, devoid of their outer facades and inner contents. However, perhaps the most heart-wrenching sight was that of the victims themselves. Those who perished in the firestorms often left shadowy imprints etched onto walls or pavements—a haunting reminder of lost lives.

Throughout the history of warfare, the firestorms in Hiroshima and Nagasaki remind us of the immense destructive capabilities of nuclear weapons. It is not just their explosive impact but also their capacity to cause long-lasting and diverse devastation.

The Black Rain:

After the explosions in Hiroshima and Nagasaki, something else haunting occurred: the arrival of the black rain. It wasn't a drizzle like an ordinary rainy day; instead, it was a thick, dark downpour carrying the remains of destroyed buildings, burned plants, and radioactive byproducts from nuclear fission.

The origins of this rainfall can be traced back to the intense heat generated by the atomic explosions. This heat caused a rapid upward movement of dust, soot, and radioactive particles into the atmosphere. As these particles rose higher, they mixed with moisture in the air. They formed heavily saturated rain clouds infused with radiation. Within hours, these clouds released their payload onto the devastated cities below.

For those who survived, many already dealing with injuries and shock from the bombings, the black rain added another layer of horror to their ordeal. When raindrops landed on surfaces, they left behind a dark residue reminiscent of oil. This residue not only served as a grim reminder of the bombings but also posed a significant radiation threat. The rainwater that gathered in puddles turned into radioactive substances, and any water source contaminated by this rain posed a serious risk to people's health.

The impact of the rain on humans was both immediate and long-lasting. People who came directly into contact with the rain experienced severe burns, skin discoloration, and nausea. However, the true consequences of the rain were more insidious. The radioactive contaminants in the rain seeped into the soil. They entered the food chain, affecting generations of Hiroshima and Nagasaki residents. Crops became tainted, fish in water bodies showed increased radiation levels, and even livestock was affected.

In addition to health effects, the black rain also left an enduring mark on the collective consciousness of those who survived the atomic bombings (known as Hibakusha). It symbolized the unseen threat of radiation—a constant reminder of how their world changed forever that day. Stories and testimonies about the rain have become an integral part of Hiroshima and Nagasaki's oral history, passed down through generations as a testament to the lasting impact of nuclear technology.

In records, the black rain is a powerful reminder of the complex consequences of nuclear warfare.

It highlights how everything in life is interconnected – our environment, our choices, and the impact they have. It serves as a reminder for future generations about the wide-ranging consequences of our actions.

The Landscape Transformed:

In the aftermath of the explosions, Hiroshima and Nagasaki were unrecognizable compared to their former selves. The vast expanse of debris and ash that now dominated the landscape told stories of lives lived, memories created, and histories erased. Once lively streets, filled with the laughter of children bustling commerce and the rhythm of city life, now lay silent except for cries from the wounded and mournful wails from those searching for loved ones.

The rivers that flowed through these cities, once hubs of recreation, transportation, and daily rituals, became witnesses to this tragedy. The waters that once sparkled under the summer sun were clouded with ash and debris. Amongst them floated belongings – a child's toy, a woman's kimono, a merchant's ledger – each item silently bearing witness to lives disrupted. The rivers became resting places for many victims as the currents carried their bodies, a sad reminder of the human toll exacted by these bombings.

Open spaces that had previously offered solace from urban life as havens for relaxation and leisure transformed into makeshift relief centers and triage points. In this place, survivors came together to seek help, solace, and updates on their missing loved ones. The green areas, once filled with birds chirping and leaves rustling, now echoed with whispered prayers, cries of pain, and hushed conversations as people tried to comprehend the unfathomable.

The unique blend of Japanese structures and modern buildings that defined the architectural heritage of the cities was utterly devastating. In Hiroshima, the renowned Shukkeien Garden, with its designed landscapes, was left in ruins. In Nagasaki, a portion of the Urakami Cathedral remained standing. Still, its broken facade stood as a stark contrast amidst the widespread destruction—a poignant reminder of the city's rich Christian history.

Nevertheless, amid this scene of desolation, sporadic signs of resilience emerged. Some structures defied the fury unleashed by the explosion and stood partially intact. Charred trees stripped bare began showing signs of growth in the following weeks. These symbols represented both endurance and nature's unwavering determination to regenerate itself. Beacons guiding these cities toward eventual recovery and rebirth.

The altered landscapes of Hiroshima and Nagasaki were more than destroyed areas; they represented the deep emotional, cultural, and historical consequences of the onset of the atomic age. The visible marks left on these cities would forever remind us of the imperative for peace, disarmament, and our shared duty to prevent any occurrence of such devastation.

The immediate aftermath of the bombings in Hiroshima and Nagasaki revealed a scene of immense devastation unlike anything the world had ever witnessed. It went beyond the physical destruction of buildings and landscapes; the true toll was measured in shattered lives, erased histories, and the deep psychological impact on those who survived. The haunting images of these transformed cities serve as a testament to humans' incredible destructive power and highlight the pressing need for reflection, understanding, and a strong commitment to peace. As we continue our journey forward, let us carry these visuals as a poignant reminder of the far-reaching consequences of decisions made in positions of authority.

THE HUMAN COST: STORIES OF SURVIVORS

The Hibakusha: Living Testimonies:

The survivors of the bombings, known as the Hibakusha, represent a powerful symbol of the fragile nature of humanity and the overwhelming impact of technology. Their lives were forever changed by a moment in history offering us a glimpse into personal stories that often go unnoticed amid larger geopolitical discussions.

In the aftermath of the bombings, many Hibakusha experienced a whirlwind of pain, confusion, and disbelief. The familiar landmarks that once defined their cities were instantaneously transformed. However, amidst this chaos, moments of humanity emerged. Strangers lending a helping hand to one another communities uniting to assist, and individuals risking their lives to save others became beacons of hope in an otherwise desolate landscape.

As time passed and days turned into weeks and months, the Hibakusha faced an immense challenge: rebuilding their shattered lives. They had lost not only their families but also their homes and means of livelihood. The physical injuries they sustained were painful. Often overshadowed by the emotional and psychological trauma they endured. Nightmares, flashbacks, and anxiety became part of their existence. The trauma extended beyond experiences; entire communities grappled with shared grief and devastation.

However, in the midst of this suffering, the true resilience of the Hibakusha emerged. They found strength out of necessity and became a source of inspiration for those around them. Many took it upon themselves to record their experiences, ensuring that the world would never forget the consequences of nuclear warfare.

Over time, the Hibakusha also became advocates for peace and disarmament. They traveled across the globe, sharing their stories with leaders, activists, and ordinary people. Their testimonies were raw and impactful, reminding them of the human toll caused by political and military choices. They stood as living proof of war horrors, urging nations to seek peace and diplomacy.

In their years, many Hibakusha expressed a deep-seated desire for their stories to endure and for future generations to learn from their experiences. They hope their testimonies will act as a deterrent—an argument against nuclear weapons. To people, the real significance of Hiroshima and Nagasaki is not just about military events but about how their stories inspire individuals to strive for a peaceful, fair, and empathetic world.

Here are some testimonials that offer insight into the distressing experiences of the Hibakusha and the significant obstacles they encountered following the bombings.

Sumiteru Taniguchi:

"I could feel my skin hanging from my back, arms, and legs. It was so painful that I walked in a crouching position, all the while looking at my burned and tattered back."

Taniguchi was delivering mail in Nagasaki when the bomb fell. He was 1.8 km from ground zero. His back was severely burned, and he spent the next 21 months lying on his stomach.

Sunao Tsuboi:

"Suddenly, a flash of light spread across in front of me, and I was thrown to the ground. I don't know how much time passed before I came to. I found myself pinned under a collapsed building. Somehow, I managed to creep out, and I saw a town on fire."

Tsuboi was going to report for military duty when the bomb fell on Hiroshima. He was 1.2 km from ground zero.

Akiko Takakura:

"The heat was tremendous. And I felt like my body was burning all over. For my burning body, the cold water of the river was as precious as the treasure. Then I left the river, and I walked along the railroad tracks in the direction of my home. On the way, I ran into another friend of mine, Toshiko Sasaki. She was badly burnt, just like myself."

Takakura was 300 meters from ground zero in Hiroshima. She survived despite being so close to the epicenter.

Physical and Psychological Scars:

The bombings of Hiroshima and Nagasaki had far-reaching consequences that extended beyond the immediate devastation. The survivors, known as Hibakusha, were left with psychological scars shaping their lives for years.

The physical impact of the bombings was evident through the injuries sustained by the survivors. In addition to the burns and wounds, the release of radiation from the bombs posed a silent and insidious threat. This radiation deeply penetrated their bodies, causing damage to cells and DNA. As a result, many Hibakusha started experiencing health issues that were previously rare or unheard of. Survivors' prevalence of cancers, including leukemia, was alarmingly high, even among those who initially appeared unharmed by the blast. Furthermore, subsequent generations faced an increased risk of birth defects and other radiation-related illnesses.

In the aftermath of the bombings, healthcare professionals faced challenges understanding and treating these radiation-induced ailments. Many medical practitioners encountered firsthand the effects of radiation exposure for the time and had limited resources and knowledge at their disposal. As a result,

Hibakusha often lived a life characterized by hospital visits, uncertainties about their health condition, and an ever-present fear of latent complications arising from their exposure.

However, the psychological wounds proved to be more difficult to overcome than the physical scars. The impact of the bombings left emotional scars that couldn't be easily erased or pushed aside. Many survivors found themselves plagued by nightmares, flashbacks, and constant anxiety in their day-to-day lives. The immense loss they experienced of family, friends, and the familiar surroundings of their cities weighed heavily on their minds. The memories of that day haunted them with vivid recollections of loved ones lost and the chaotic scenes they witnessed.

The Hibakusha faced challenges due to societal reactions, further exacerbating their psychological distress. Discrimination and isolation were common due to misunderstandings and fears surrounding radiation. They were often met with pity and suspicion, some even encountering difficulties securing employment or finding partners due to misconceptions about radiation effects.

The combination of this stigma and their deeply rooted trauma left many Hibakusha feeling isolated from the rest of the world. While others moved forward, Hiroshima and Nagasaki remained ever-present in their lives, constant reminders of their sacrifices and ongoing struggles. Despite overwhelming adversity, witnessing the resilience and strength demonstrated by the Hibakusha is truly remarkable.

Their incredible journey, filled with emotional obstacles, showcases the unwavering resilience of the human spirit. It demonstrates how, in the most difficult moments, we can discover glimmers of hope that help us persevere.

Stories of Resilience and Advocacy:

In the aftermath of the bombings in Hiroshima and Nagasaki, the survivors known as Hibakusha emerged not just as individuals who had endured immense suffering but also as symbols of hope, resilience, and an unwavering commitment to peace. Their journeys, marked by both psychological scars, were a powerful testament to their indomitable spirit and determination to ensure that the atrocities they experienced would never be forgotten.

One remarkable story among many is that of Sunao Tsuboi. Like other survivors, he faced a future filled with uncertainty after the bombings. Dealing with the lasting effects of radiation exposure, societal prejudice, and haunting memories of that fateful day presented ongoing challenges. However, Sunao chose to transform his experiences into advocacy for peace. He actively engaged with the Hiroshima Peace Memorial Museum, sharing his narrative with visitors from across the globe. His efforts extended beyond Japan's borders well; he traveled extensively and collaborated with other international peace advocates to emphasize the human toll of nuclear warfare and advocate for urgent disarmament.

Setsuko Thurlow's journey from being a schoolgirl in Hiroshima to becoming a champion for peace is equally compelling. Having survived the bombing, Setsuko faced rebuilding her life amidst unimaginable ruins. Her losses were immeasurable; many family members and classmates perished in the blast. Yet these tragedies only ignited her determination further.

After relocating to Canada, she became a critic of nuclear weapons, sharing her journey with diverse audiences, including schoolchildren and policymakers. In recognition of her dedication, she received an invitation to jointly accept the prestigious Nobel Peace Prize on behalf of the International Campaign to Abolish Nuclear Weapons in 2017.

In addition to these individuals, numerous other survivors of nuclear bombings (known as Hibakusha) have played crucial roles in advocating for peace. Organizations like Nihon Hidankyo and the Japan Confederation of A and H Bomb Sufferers Organizations have brought survivors together, offering them a platform to share their stories and amplifying their call for peace. Led by Hibakusha themselves, these organizations have been at the forefront of movements against testing, fighting for comprehensive healthcare for survivors and ensuring that the memories of Hiroshima and Nagasaki are preserved for future generations.

The advocacy efforts by Hibakusha go beyond recounting past events; they passionately urge us to consider the future. Their stories serve as reminders of the devastating consequences that stem from decisions made in positions of power. They challenge us to question the essence of war and conflict, inspiring us to strive toward a world where peace is not just an abstract concept but a tangible reality we live by.

Their remarkable capacity to turn their hardships into a worldwide crusade for harmony is a powerful testament to the indomitable spirit of humanity. Within their narratives, we encounter stories of survival and discover a guiding path toward creating a more empathetic and benevolent society.

A Legacy of Memory and Hope:

The impact of the Hibakusha goes beyond the confines of Hiroshima and Nagasaki, resonating deeply within the consciousness of humanity. Their stories, rooted in August

1945, hold universal significance as they explore themes of remembrance, optimism, and our shared human existence.

Remembrance for the Hibakusha is more than recalling past occurrences; it is a living testament to the indomitable spirit of humanity. Each survivor's narrative is a patchwork of moments — some heart-wrenching, others uplifting — that create a depiction of life in the aftermath of unimaginable devastation. These memories serve as a bridge between generations, ensuring that the lessons learned from Hiroshima and Nagasaki remain in our memory.

However, mere recollection alone cannot suffice. The Hibakusha recognized that to honor those who lost their lives, they had to transform their experiences into a catalyst for positive change. This unwavering determination to make a difference and ensure that their suffering was not in vain, it lies at the core of the Hibakusha's legacy—a legacy filled with hope.

For the Hibakusha, hope is not merely a wish but an active pursuit. Their tireless dedication to advocating for disarmament, reaching out to younger generations, and their unwavering determination to create a world where the horrors of atomic warfare are confined to history's pages is evident. They firmly believe in the potential of action, recognizing that ordinary individuals can come together and shape history.

This blending of memory and hope has given birth to initiatives aimed at preserving the enduring legacy of the Hibakusha. Museums, peace parks, and memorial ceremonies serve as poignant reminders of the past and carry a forward message of unity and optimism—educational programs within Japan. Globally, ensure that future generations continue to be inspired and educated by the stories of the Hibakusha.

The influence of the Hibakusha's legacy extends beyond accounts into art, literature, and popular culture. Films, novels, and artworks inspired by their experiences have resonated with audiences, amplifying their message of peace and hope. Although these artistic endeavors differ in form and narrative style, they all share a respect for the spirit of Hibakusha while being committed to ensuring that their legacy lives on. Ultimately, the legacy of the Hibakusha stands as a testament to how memories coupled with hope can bring about transformations.

In times of despair, it serves as a gentle reminder that the resilience and strength of the human spirit have the power to radiate brightly, guiding us toward a brighter and more optimistic tomorrow.

Few historical events have had such an impact as the bombings of Hiroshima and Nagasaki. The stories of the survivors, known as the Hibakusha, serve as reminders of the human toll of war and the significant consequences of decisions made by those in positions of authority. These accounts are not just records from the past; they also hold lessons for the present and future generations. As we contemplate their experiences, we are reminded of how fragile life is, how resilient humanity can be, and how crucial it is to strive for a world where peace triumphs over conflict. The legacy left by the Hibakusha serves as proof that memories and hope can bring about transformation, inspiring us to work toward a future rid of the shadow cast by nuclear warfare.

THE WORLD'S REACTION

Global Shockwaves:

The immediate aftermath of the bombings of Hiroshima and Nagasaki caused shockwaves of surprise, disbelief, and deep contemplation worldwide. The world, already exhausted by the prolonged horrors of World War II, now faced a weapon that went beyond warfare, challenging the essence of human morality and technological accountability.

Leaders in capitals across the globe scrambled to comprehend the implications of this groundbreaking weapon. Diplomats, military strategists, and intelligence agencies sought to grasp its immediate tactical consequences and the long-term geopolitical shifts brought about by the dawn of the atomic age. The balance of power, already unsettled due to war outcomes, was further complicated by a weapon that had the potential to render conventional military strength obsolete.

For people everywhere, these bombings were a jarring wake-up call. Conversations in cafes, tea houses in Shanghai, and homes in Cairo alike revolved around the events unfolding in Japan. The atomic bomb became a symbol that evoked both awe and horror. People marveled at its marvel while wrestling with ethical concerns regarding its use. The line between achievement and moral responsibility blurred as debates transcended national boundaries.

The global media played a role in shaping these discussions. News footage in movie theaters depicted the devastation, exposing the horrors of atomic warfare to people worldwide. Photos capturing the mushroom cloud, which would later become a symbol of the 20th century, were featured on newspaper front pages forever, etching the frightening power of the bomb into the collective consciousness.

However, amidst the shock and disbelief, there was also a moment of deep introspection. Religious leaders, ranging from those in the Vatican to monasteries nestled in the Himalayas, sought to offer spiritual guidance. Sermons and teachings that followed often delved into themes such as vulnerability, responsibilities associated with power, and fostering peace and understanding in an increasingly complex global landscape.

Educational institutions were not immune to the impact caused by these bombings either. In universities and research centers, profound reflection ensued regarding science's societal role. Scientists who had witnessed nuclear physics evolve from its stages now grappled with ethical considerations tied to their work. The age-old debate surrounding knowledge and discovery suddenly took on a renewed sense of urgency.

Ultimately, it becomes clear that the atomic bombings of Hiroshima and Nagasaki reverberated beyond just ending a war or ushering in a new era of technology. It was a time when people came together to think deeply about the state of humanity. It served as a reminder of how progress can have both positive and negative consequences and how the fates of all nations are interconnected in this era of atomic advancements.

Allied Celebrations and Controversies:

In the aftermath of the bombings, people in the Allied nations felt a sense of relief. The atomic bomb, a result of scientific efforts and vast resources, had achieved its intended purpose. The lasting war that caused immense loss of life seemed on the verge of ending. In cities like New York and London, there were expressions of joy as citizens celebrated what they saw as the approaching conclusion to the deadliest conflict in human history.

However, beneath this show of celebration, there existed a complex mix of emotions and discussions. Military strategists and politicians publicly praised the bombings as a measure but privately grappled with their implications. President Harry Truman, who authorized the bombings, faced commendation and criticism. While many applauded him for taking action to end the war, others within his administration expressed concerns about its morality.

Within the military community, there were differing opinions. Some top generals and admirals believed bombing was crucial in Japan's surrender, while others remained uncertain. Admiral William Leahy, Trumans Chief of Staff, famously commented that the bombings had no impact on how the war unfolded and criticized them as "barbaric."

The scientific community, including individuals who were part of the Manhattan Project, faced their own ethical dilemmas. J. Robert Oppenheimer, often called the "father of the bomb," famously quoted a line from the Bhagavad Gita upon witnessing the first successful test saying, "Now I am become Death, the destroyer of worlds." The immense responsibility of creating such a weapon weighed heavily on numerous scientists, prompting some, like Oppenheimer himself, to advocate for international control over atomic energy to prevent future conflicts.

Initially, public opinion largely supported the bombings due to media portrayals and official statements. However, as people became aware of the extent of human suffering in Hiroshima and Nagasaki, many began questioning whether these bombings were a proportionate response. Journalists and Red Cross workers relayed accounts of destruction that painted a deeply distressing picture. As a result, there was introspection and debate among members of the public.

Religious institutions and churches played a role in shaping moral discussions surrounding the bombings. While some religious leaders justified them as evil to bring an end to war, others condemned them as grave sins. Leaders' sermons, op-eds, and public statements brought a deeper perspective to the moral discussion, highlighting the importance of forgiveness, repentance, and the value of human life.

The Allied reaction to the bombings was anything but uniform. It encompassed a range of emotions, debates, and soul-searching moments that revealed the difficulties in reconciling war demands with our innate sense of morality.

The Global Ethical Debate.

The ethical debate that unfolded worldwide following the bombings of Hiroshima and Nagasaki went beyond the aftermath of these events. It delved into contemplation about the very essence of warfare, human morality, and the responsibilities that come with scientific advancements.

At the core of this debate lay a question: Is it justifiable to achieve a desired end at any cost? While the bombings may have hastened the conclusion of World War II, they exacted a toll on human lives. This dilemma compelled society to confront the equilibrium between military objectives and the inherent worth of every human being. The atomic bomb, with its destructive power, blurred distinctions between combatants and civilians, challenging established conventions of warfare.

Religious leaders from faiths contributed their perspectives to these discussions. For instance, the Vatican expressed concerns about the bombings as it emphasized respect for life and moral imperatives for peace. Buddhist monks in Japan and other places contemplated life's impermanence. It was reflected in karmic implications arising from such widespread devastation.

Academic institutions became points for these deliberations. Universities hosted debates where scholars from diverse fields—from physics to philosophy, actively participated. The scientific community found itself at a juncture in these discussions. Many scientists who played a role in the development of nuclear technology, including those involved in the Manhattan Project, grappled with feelings of guilt and responsibility. Prominent figures like J. Robert Oppenheimer, often called the "father of the bomb, " expressed deep ambivalence about their involvement in the bombings. Oppenheimer's quote from the Bhagavad Gita – "Now I am become Death, the destroyer of worlds" – captured the internal conflict that many experienced.

Literature and artistic expression also played a crucial role in shaping ethical discussions. Through novels, poems, and plays, writers explored the impact of these bombings by touching upon themes such as loss, guilt, and redemption. These creative works allowed individuals to process their trauma and engage in introspection.

Furthermore, grassroots movements advocating for peace and disarmament gained traction. Regular citizens, deeply affected by the horrors witnessed at Hiroshima and Nagasaki, organized rallies, marches, and campaigns to voice their opposition against weapons. These movements highlighted a yearning for a world free from the grim threat of nuclear destruction.

Ultimately, the ethical debate surrounding Hiroshima and Nagasaki went beyond being an immediate response to a historical event. It evolved into contemplating humanity's values, perceptions of conflict, and moral considerations regarding technological advancements. The bombings reminded us how interconnected we all are and our collective duty to create a future built on peace and mutual respect.

The Birth of Nuclear Diplomacy:

The atomic bombings of Hiroshima and Nagasaki not only marked the end of World War II but also signaled the beginning of a new era in global relations. The immense power unleashed by the bomb profoundly changed the dynamics of international politics, introducing unimaginable complexities to leaders.

Following the bombings, the United States emerged as the possessor of nuclear weapons, a capability unmatched by any other nation. This unique position bestowed both power and tremendous responsibility upon American policymakers. However, they were well aware that their monopoly on weapons would be short-lived. The race to develop capabilities had already commenced, with the Soviet Union taking a leading role among the Allied powers.

In 1949, the Soviets successfully conducted their atomic bomb test, ending America's nuclear monopoly and setting in motion an arms race that would shape much of the 20th century. The Cold War emerged as a result characterized by differences between Western capitalist nations and Eastern communist countries. Central to this conflict was a threat of nuclear devastation—a situation where the stakes had never been higher.

Realizing the danger posed by an uncontrolled arms race, leaders on both sides embarked on efforts to engage in dialogue and foster cooperation. However, these initial attempts were marred by suspicion and mistrust. However, the Cuban Missile Crisis that occurred in 1962, when the world was on the verge of nuclear war, served as a reminder of the crucial importance of effective diplomatic channels.

This sense of urgency led to the creation of a hotline between Washington and Moscow, enabling direct communication between the leaders of these two superpowers. It may have been a step, but it significantly reduced the risk of unintended nuclear conflict.

As time went on, the intricacies surrounding diplomacy became more complex. Various nations began seeking nuclear capabilities, each with its own strategic and geopolitical factors to consider. Israel, India, Pakistan, and North Korea introduced dynamics into an already intricate web of nuclear diplomacy.

Efforts to control and limit proliferation took center stage in global diplomatic endeavors. The signing of the Treaty on the Non-Proliferation of Nuclear Weapons (NPT) in 1968 marked a milestone. Its primary objectives were preventing the spread of nuclear weapons, promoting disarmament initiatives, and facilitating peaceful utilization of nuclear energy. While critics voiced concerns and implementation challenges arose over time, it represented a commitment toward creating a world free from the threat posed by nuclear conflicts.

In parallel with these endeavors were initiatives aimed at reducing arms proliferation. Treaties such as the Strategic Arms Limitation Talks (SALT) and the Strategic Arms Reduction Treaty (START) were implemented to limit the number of weapons powerful nations possess. Although these agreements were often contentious and faced challenges, they demonstrated a shared understanding of the importance of preventing a large-scale nuclear conflict.

The impact of Hiroshima and Nagasaki goes beyond the devastation they caused. These bombings triggered an effort to navigate the complexities of the atomic age, striving to strike a delicate balance between national security interests and the collective pursuit of peace. Over decades, through negotiations, treaties, and dialogues, countries worldwide aimed to ensure that the horrors witnessed in 1945 would serve as a sad lesson never to be repeated.

The bombings of Hiroshima and Nagasaki weren't significant events in the history of warfare, but they also triggered a profound shift in global consciousness. The world's reaction was a mix of shock, introspection, and a strong determination to prevent such devastation from happening again. From bustling city streets to prestigious arenas, the events of August 1945 had a deep impact. They emphasized how fragile our shared existence is and highlighted the need for collective action when faced with unmatched power. As nations grappled with the era's dawn, these bombings were a stark reminder of the immense responsibilities of possessing such formidable capabilities. With all its aspects, the world's response stands as proof of humanity's unwavering hope for a future free from the looming threat of nuclear annihilation.

Chapter 9: Humanity at the Crossroads - Ethical Dilemmas of the Atomic Age

On the morning of August 6, 1945, a significant event occurred that forever changed the course of history. When the atomic bomb was detonated over Hiroshima, it marked the beginning of an era bringing immense power and complex ethical debates. This pivotal moment, followed shortly by the bombing of Nagasaki, brought together years of scientific progress and sparked a global moral discussion that still resonates today.

The atomic age introduced energy possibilities and unimaginable destruction, forcing humanity to confront its moral compass. It raised questions about right or wrong and when actions can be justified ethically. Can wiping out cities and instantly taking thousands of lives be morally acceptable? If so, under what circumstances?

The decision to use the bomb was not made in isolation. It emerged from geopolitics, military strategies, and ethical considerations. World War II ravaged for six years, causing millions of casualties and devastated many parts of Europe and Asia. Ending the war became paramount for Allied leadership, who saw the bomb as a way to achieve that goal.
At what price?

The immediate aftermath of the bombings made the human toll of the atomic age painfully clear. The images of Hiroshima and Nagasaki cities reduced to ruins, with survivors carrying radiation scars, served as a reminder of the devastating power of nuclear weapons. These haunting visuals, set against a world celebrating the end of a conflict, presented a moral dilemma. Was the cost of peace high?

As the world grappled with the consequences of these bombings, a broader ethical debate began to emerge. Warfare itself had transformed. Battles were no longer limited to battlefields; entire cities and their civilian populations now faced potential threats. The rules and conventions that had governed warfare for centuries became obsolete in light of this danger.

Beyond warfare's scope, the atomic age raised ethical concerns. The same scientific advancements that brought bombs also offered boundless energy possibilities—a world liberated from reliance on fossil fuels. How could humanity harness this potential while safeguarding against its destructive capabilities?

The bombings of Hiroshima and Nagasaki marked the conclusion of World War II and signaled the start of a new era in human history. Ethical challenges and the constant interplay between power and responsibility define this era. As we explore this period further, we will be prompted to contemplate the consequences of the atomic age to examine our individual beliefs and values and confront the ethical dilemmas that persistently shape our world.

THE AMERICAN PERSPECTIVE, HIROSHIMA'S LENS, AND THE GLOBAL ETHICAL QUANDARY

The American Perspective:

In the stages of World War II, as Europe began its slow recovery from the devastating aftermath, the situation in the Pacific theater remained highly volatile. After achieving victory in Europe, the United States shifted its focus to the Pacific region, where the Japanese Empire, although weakened, continued to resist with determination. The battles that took place were incredibly intense. American leaders understood well the potential human toll a ground invasion of Japan could bring. The memories of Iwo Jima and Okinawa, where American forces faced opposition, were still fresh in their minds.

President Harry S. Truman assumed office following Franklin D. Roosevelt's passing and was confronted with an enormously consequential decision. The Manhattan Project, initiated during Roosevelt's term, had successfully developed a bomb. An unprecedentedly powerful weapon that presented Truman with a military option capable of swiftly ending the war. However, making this decision was far from simple.

While there were military advantages to using such a bomb, profound ethical considerations were also. The United States, built on principles of freedom and justice, now contemplates using a weapon of obliterating entire cities within seconds. Truman and his advisors were acutely aware of the gravity accompanying this decision.

Prominent individuals within the government discussed the advantages and ethical considerations of utilizing the atomic bomb. Secretary of War Henry Stimson acknowledged its potential to end the war and expressed concerns about its long-term impact on international relations and the moral precedent it would establish. J. Robert Oppenheimer, a scientist in the Manhattan Project, famously uttered these words after witnessing the Trinity test; "Now I have become Death, the destroyer of worlds." This statement reflects the moral and philosophical dilemmas those who participated in this project faced.

Apart from considering military and ethical factors, America also had its eyes on a post-war world. Relations with the Soviet Union, once allies in defeating Nazi Germany, were starting to strain. The ideological divide between the West and the communist East grew wider, creating a new geopolitical rivalry. In this context, deploying weapons wasn't just about ending the war; it also served as a strategic asset during the emerging Cold War era. Demonstrating its power was as much about shaping war geopolitics as it was about compelling Japan to surrender.

However, despite its implications, whether or not to use atomic bombs remains one of history's most heavily debated moments in American history. It encompasses the difficulties that leaders encounter during times of conflict when military requirements, geopolitical tactics, and ethical obligations intersect in an intricate web. Examining the viewpoint on the bombings of Hiroshima and Nagasaki provides insight into the essence of a nation wrestling with the gravity of its choices and the extensive ramifications they bring forth.

Strategic Imperatives.

The choice to use the bomb was based on various strategic considerations. After experiencing the atrocities of World War II, the United States aimed to end the conflict. The fierceness of resistance in battles like Iwo Jima and Okinawa highlighted the challenges that an invasion of Japan would present. Such an invasion would probably lead to Allied losses. From a perspective, the atomic bomb provided a way to hasten Japan's surrender.

The Ethical Debate Within.

However, there was no complete agreement on the decision among the influential people in American positions of authority. A few important individuals, including scientists involved in the Manhattan Project, voiced concerns. They raised doubts about employing a weapon of this nature against civilian populations, particularly considering that Japan's surrender appeared to be near. The internal discussion was fervent and mirrored the wider ethical challenges brought forth by the nuclear era.

Post-War Geopolitics.

Apart from the goal of ending the war, the United States had a keen understanding of the geopolitical situation that would follow. The Soviet Union, a friend, was swiftly becoming a possible foe. The demonstration of atomic bomb power was not intended for Emperor Hirohito but also served as a message to Stalin. In the days of the Cold War, this bomb represented America's dominance in technology and military prowess.

Hiroshima's Lens:

Hiroshima, a thriving city, became the epicenter of a pivotal moment in the 20th century. The transformation of this hub into a desolate landscape provides a unique perspective on the atomic age's profound human and ethical implications.

In the aftermath of the bomb's detonation, chaos and confusion prevailed. A mushroom-shaped cloud hung ominously over the city, casting its shadow on its inhabitants. Streets that were once bustling with life now echoed with haunting silence punctuated only by cries of pain from the injured and mournful wails of those grieving for their lost loved ones. Landmarks that defined the city's identity, cultural centers, and historical sites were reduced to rubble, serving as reminders of the bomb's devastating force.

However, amidst this devastation emerged stories of resilience and hope. The survivors of the bombing, known as Hibakusha, became living witnesses to that day. Their experiences varied from horror at ground zero to enduring long-term effects caused by radiation exposure. These personal accounts offer insights into the human toll exacted by atomic bombs. These stories, often characterized by a blend of suffering, grief, and an unyielding spirit, offer insight into the difficulties faced by the survivors in the aftermath of the bombing – both in the days and over the long term.

One particular account follows a mother's search for her missing child amidst the debris, holding onto hope that he may still be alive. Another narrative tells of a man who, despite suffering severe burns himself, bravely aided in rescuing others trapped beneath collapsed buildings. These personal stories shed light on immense pain and loss and highlight the resilience and determination of Hiroshimas residents.

Throughout time, Hiroshima has become a symbol of peace and disarmament efforts. The city's remarkable transformation from a place of devastation to a beacon of hope and harmony is truly extraordinary. The Hiroshima Peace Memorial Park is a reminder of this commitment – with its iconic Genbaku Dome serving as an enduring testament to ensure that humanity never forgets the horrors of nuclear warfare. Every year, thousands of visitors from around the globe travel to Hiroshima to pay their respects and to join in advocating for a world free from nuclear weapons.

The educational endeavors in Hiroshima, which aim to nurture a culture centered around peace and disarmament, have received recognition. Educational institutions at all levels, including schools, universities, and research centers in the city, have integrated peace education into their programs. This integration ensures that the forthcoming generations are well-prepared to carry forward Hiroshima's enduring legacy.

Essentially, Hiroshima provides a perspective on the atomic era. It serves as a lens through which we can witness the emotions experienced by a city ravaged by nuclear warfare and observe the resilience displayed by its residents. It highlights their dedication to creating a world free from nuclear weapons and committed to peace. Viewing history through this lens reminds us of our ethical responsibilities regarding scientific and technological advancements. It becomes our duty to ensure that such horrific events are never repeated.

Immediate Aftermath.

The explosion that occurred above Hiroshima released a raging fire, swiftly destroying the city and burning its residents alive. Those who survived the impact were confronted with the terrifying consequences of radiation sickness, severe burns, and a city reduced to ruins. The immediate aftermath presented a landscape of complete devastation, serving as a chilling reminder of the immense destructive force wielded by the atomic era.

Hibakusha - Voices of the Survivors.

The individuals who survived the bombing, called Hibakusha, carried both physical and emotional wounds from the devastating event. Their accounts, filled with stories of grief, strength, and optimism, provide an understanding of the immense toll caused by the atomic bomb. Passed down from one generation to another, these narratives serve as a reminder of the importance of disarmament and the pursuit of peace.

Hiroshima as a Symbol.

Throughout the years, Hiroshima has risen above its history and become a worldwide emblem of peace and disarmament. The city's dedication to ensuring that the atrocities caused by the bomb are always remembered is seen in its memorials, museums, and peace efforts. Hiroshima's transformation from destruction to rebuilding and its advocacy for peace is a shining light of hope in a world facing the era's complexities.

The Global Ethical Quandary:

The bombings of Hiroshima and Nagasaki were not only the end of World War II but also a turning point that made people worldwide reflect deeply. It was a realization that humanity now possessed the power to destroy itself completely, sparking discussions on ethics, philosophy, and politics.

Even countries away from the immediate battlegrounds found themselves grappling with the moral implications of these bombings. The immense devastation caused by these attacks, both in terms of casualties and long-term environmental and health consequences, raised questions about the fundamental principles of international warfare. Were we entering an era where a total war without distinction between combatants and civilians was becoming normal? Were these bombings seen as an exception—a tragic yet necessary action to bring an end to one of the most devastating conflicts in human history?

Within academic circles, these bombings ignited intense debates. Ethicists and philosophers analyzed this event from moral perspectives. Utilitarians argued whether such bombings could be justified if they saved lives by preventing warfare. On the other hand, deontologists questioned whether this act was inherently immoral regardless of its outcomes. These debates went beyond intellectual exercises; they influenced policymakers, activists, and society.

The peace movement that gained momentum after the war was, in many ways, a direct response to the bombings. Activists, including survivors and war veterans, tirelessly advocated for disarmament and global peace. Their efforts resulted in treaties and agreements to reduce nuclear arms and promote peace.

However, the ethical dilemma extended beyond disarmament. The same technology that enabled the bomb also held the potential for clean and abundant energy. Many argue that nuclear power could solve our growing energy needs. This raised another set of debates: Could humanity harness the positive aspects of nuclear energy while acknowledging its association with such a destructive weapon? If so, what measures were necessary to prevent potential misuse?

The bombings had an impact on global geopolitics. In this new era, nations recognized that possessing capabilities was essential for being considered a global power. This realization sparked a race among nations to develop their atomic arsenals. This race played a significant role in shaping the Cold War and its doctrine of mutually assured destruction.

The world now finds itself in a balance with the looming threat of nuclear destruction.

The age and its ethical implications have become recurring themes throughout literature, art, and cinema. From timeless literature to blockbuster films, the bombings and their aftermath have been explored, analyzed, and immortalized. These creative expressions reflect society's conscience as we grapple with the moral dilemmas brought about by the atomic age.

The global ethical dilemma presented by the bombings in Hiroshima and Nagasaki is complex. It forces us to contemplate the nature of warfare, question those in positions of power, and ponder the ethical consequences of scientific and technological advancements. As we venture further into the century, these lessons remain relevant as they remind us of the profound ethical responsibilities accompanying power and knowledge.

The World Reacts.

The bombings of Hiroshima and Nagasaki sparked a range of responses worldwide. While some people saw it as a measure to end a devastating war, others strongly criticized it as a clear violation of humanitarian principles. The ethical arguments weren't limited to political or academic circles; they resonated with the general public, resulting in widespread protests and demands for disarmament.

The Philosophical Debate.

Philosophers and ethicists played a role in the worldwide discussion on ethics. The deployment of the atomic bomb sparked moral inquiries questioning long-standing ideas about fair warfare, proportionality, and the protection of civilians. The conversation was passionate, with influential figures from philosophical backgrounds sharing their perspectives on the ethical consequences of living in the nuclear era.

The Legacy of Hiroshima and Nagasaki.

The bombings had a lasting impact on the landscape worldwide. They acted as a reminder of how human creativity can lead to destruction and the ethical obligations that accompany it. The influence of Hiroshima and Nagasaki still shapes efforts toward disarmament agreements on arms control and moral discussions concerning the application of force in international affairs.

As we ponder the intricacies and moral dilemmas of the atomic age, it becomes clear that the events of Hiroshima and Nagasaki have deeply affected humanity as a whole. The American perspective, driven by needs and geopolitical considerations, aimed to end a devastating conflict. However, within this context, there was a strong recognition of the moral weight of using such a weapon, leading to intense internal discussions and reflections.

The haunting images of Hiroshima and Nagasaki cities reduced to ruins with survivors bearing the emotional scars of radiation serve as powerful reminders of the human toll caused by this momentous decision. The voices of the Hibakusha survivors reverberate through time, sharing stories of loss, resilience, and hope. Their narratives stand alongside Hiroshima's transformation into a symbol promoting peace and disarmament—a testament to the city's unwavering commitment to ensuring that the horrors inflicted by atomic bombs are never forgotten.

However, the ethical ramifications resulting from these bombings extend beyond just their immediate aftermath. The international community grappled with profound moral dilemmas, from leaders to ordinary citizens. These events challenged established norms in warfare on a global scale and sparked intense philosophical debates while giving rise to a robust movement advocating for global peace. The era of power brought about a mix of potential and peril, compelling nations to confront their moral compass and leading to a delicate balance of power during the Cold War period.

In the realm of culture, the atomic age found its way into literature, art, and cinema as an expression of society's effort to grapple with the moral dilemmas presented by this era. These creative endeavors not only served as a critique of the bombings but also shed light on the broader ethical challenges stemming from scientific and technological progress.

In essence, the events that unfolded in Hiroshima and Nagasaki and the global responses encapsulate the profound ethical dilemmas faced in the 20th century. They prompt us to contemplate about power dynamics, knowledge-related responsibilities, and moral obligations tied to our actions. As we navigate today's world, these lessons from history remain relevant and urge us to proceed with caution, empathy, and a strong sense of responsibility.

CHAPTER 10: REFLECTIONS UNDER HIROSHIMA'S SKIES

The morning of August 6, 1945, began in Hiroshima like any other. The sun's gentle rays illuminated the city with shades of gold and amber. Little did the people know that within a few hours, their lives would be forever changed by an unprecedented event. By the end of that day, Hiroshima would become a symbol not for its culture or contributions to society but as the epicenter of a catastrophic event – the world's first atomic bombings.

These bombings were not merely actions; they marked a significant turning point that resulted from years of scientific research, political maneuvering, and wartime necessities. However, beyond their strategic implications, they also raised profound ethical, moral, and philosophical questions that puzzle humanity today.

Take a moment to imagine how different our world was before that August morning. The Second World War had ravaged continents for six years – Europe, Asia, and even parts of the Pacific were engulfed in its destructive flames. Nations were brought to their knees; countless lives were lost; cities lay in ruins.
Against the backdrop of a global conflict, a secretive scientific project was quietly emerging, aiming to unlock the fundamental elements of the universe. Known as the Manhattan Project, it operated in the shadows and held the promise of harnessing the immense power hidden within atoms.

The successful detonation of a bomb was not merely a testament to human intelligence and scientific expertise; it demonstrated our ability to wield powers previously considered godlike. In that blinding flash over Hiroshima, humanity, for the time, harnessed star-like energy. However, this newfound capability came with responsibility, forcing the world to confront profound implications.

The immediate aftermath of these bombings presented a scene of devastation. Cities that had stood for centuries were wiped out within seconds. Tens of thousands lost their lives instantly while countless others grappled with the lasting effects of radiation exposure. The very fabric of these societies was torn apart, leaving behind a legacy marked by pain, trauma, and profound loss.

Nevertheless, beyond destruction, these bombings triggered global reflection, debate, and deep introspection on an unprecedented scale. Nations, leaders, intellectuals, and everyday people grappled with the ethical implications of deploying such a weapon. Was it a measure to expedite the end of a brutal war? Was it an unnecessary display of power, an act of arrogance that disregarded moral boundaries?

We will explore these inquiries and more as we delve into this chapter. We will embark on a journey through the corridors of power from the revered halls of Washington to the streets of Hiroshima. We will listen to the voices of leaders, ordinary citizens, scientists and soldiers, survivors and witnesses. Through their narratives, contemplations, and insights, we will strive to comprehend the impact that the atomic bombings had on human psychology and global awareness.

The bombings of Hiroshima and Nagasaki are not merely occurrences; they stand as enduring symbols representing the complexities and challenges of the atomic age. They remind us how scientific progress can enlighten us and bring devastation. As we reflect upon these events, we are compelled to ask ourselves: What lessons have we gained? More importantly, how can we ensure that similar tragedies never recur in Hiroshima or Nagasaki?

GLOBAL RESPONSES TO THE BOMBINGS

The Immediate Aftermath: Shockwaves Beyond Ground Zero:

In the hours and days following the bombings, the world faced a reality that felt almost surreal. The atomic explosions over Hiroshima and Nagasaki weren't just events; they signaled the dawn of a new era, and their effects reached far beyond their immediate locations.

Radio broadcasts, which served as a news source, then interrupted regular programming to provide updates from Japan. Families gathered around their radios, hanging onto every word, trying to grasp what had happened. The descriptions of cities vanishing from existence due to a single bomb's unprecedented destruction sent chills down listeners' spines worldwide.

Newspapers in cities worldwide printed special editions with front pages dominated by images of mushroom clouds. An iconic symbol that would forever be associated with the nuclear age. Journalists who had witnessed firsthand the horrors of World War II struggled to find words to depict such devastation. The language used in discussing warfare had to expand; terms like "ground zero," " fallout," and "atomic shadows" entered public consciousness.

Beyond media responses, spontaneous gatherings took place in public squares and places of worship as people grappled with what had occurred. People gathered together not much to discuss the geopolitical consequences but to mourn, find comfort, and grapple with the deep questions that arose from the bombings. Candlelit vigils were organized in cities ranging from Paris to Buenos Aires as individuals from diverse backgrounds and beliefs came together in their shared sorrow and disbelief.

Even educational institutions were profoundly affected. There was a significant reevaluation within universities and research organizations among scientists specializing in physics. Many scientists had previously believed that their work contributed positively to humanity. However, the bombings compelled them to reconsider the aspects of scientific research. Conversations within lecture halls and academic publications began shifting focus from the technicalities of fission toward pondering the moral responsibilities of those who possess such knowledge.

Economically speaking, these bombings sent shockwaves throughout markets. The realization that warfare had entered an era caused fluctuations in stock exchanges worldwide. Industries associated with defense and wartime production prepared for changes as they anticipated a shift toward prioritizing research and defense over traditional warfare mechanisms.

These bombings reshaped things. Embassies and consulates received an influx of communications as nations sought to comprehend the impact of these events on geopolitics. The dynamics of warfare, diplomacy, and international relations shifted when the atomic bomb occurred.

In the aftermath of the bombings in Hiroshima and Nagasaki, there was a period of reflection, sorrow, and evaluation. A new kind of power has been introduced to the world. This power carried obligations and difficulties. The events that unfolded in

August 1945 would have a lasting impact on awareness, influencing the trajectory of history for many years after that.

The Allies: Justification and Internal Debate:

The immediate aftermath of the bombings gave rise to a whirlwind of emotions and debates among the Allied camp. While the public portrayal of the Allied leadership showed unity in advocating for the bombings as a measure to end the war and save lives behind closed doors, things were more complex.

President Harry S. Truman, who authorized the bombings, initially had limited knowledge of the extent of the Manhattan Project when he assumed office after President Roosevelt's passing. After being briefed on it, he grappled with the decision before him. Although he firmly believed that dropping the bombs would prevent a land invasion of Japan and save lives, he was also keenly aware of the moral dilemma of such a powerful weapon. His subsequent defense of his decision was rooted in this belief; however, it's noteworthy that Truman later expressed remorse, indicating a struggle over his choice.

Within ranks, there were dissenting opinions. Several ranking officers like General Dwight D. Eisenhower and Admiral William D. Leahy voiced reservations about using atomic bombs. In particular, Eisenhower believed that Japan was already on the brink of surrender and saw no necessity for dropping them. Leahy expressed the view, stating that dropping the atomic bomb on Hiroshima and Nagasaki did not provide any significant help in Japan's defeat during the war.

The scientific community, which played a role in developing the bomb, had differing opinions. Many scientists, including some who were involved in the Manhattan Project, were deeply disturbed by the bombs used on populations. Dr. J. Robert Oppenheimer, often called the "father of the bomb," famously said, "Now I have become Death, the destroyer of worlds," reflecting his profound inner turmoil and moral conflict regarding its deployment.

Apart from scientific circles, these bombings triggered heated discussions among theologians, ethicists, and ordinary people. Churches across Allied nations grappled with the implications of such bombings. While some denominations outright condemned them, others tried to reconcile these actions with their broader objective of ending the war.

The British response was also complex. Prime Minister Clement Attlee, who had recently taken office, supported the bombings as an evil to end the war. However, reservations existed within segments of British authorities. Many people within the intelligence communities in Britain were already aware of the details of the Manhattan Project. They had contemplated the implications of atomic warfare long before Hiroshima and Nagasaki.

Essentially, although the Allied leadership justified the bombings as a way to hasten the war's end, they sparked debates and introspection beyond military and political considerations. The ethical, moral, and humanitarian aspects of this decision became topics of discussion, exposing deep-seated conflicts and reservations among those in positions of power.

The Soviet Perspective: Cold War Foreshadowing:

The bombings of Hiroshima and Nagasaki had an impact beyond the end of World War II. For the Soviet Union, they marked the start of an era in global politics. While the world was grappling with the consequences of these bombings, leaders in Moscow were already anticipating the long-term implications of America's newfound nuclear capability.

Stalin, being a strategist, understood that these bombings were not just about Japan; they were also a display of American power and a clear message to the world, especially to the Soviet Union. The fact that the United States had developed and used such a weapon twice in secret emphasized how crucial it was for the USSR to catch up in this nuclear arms race.

This realization was further intensified by the timing of the Soviet Union's declaration of war on Japan. Just before Hiroshima was bombed, the Soviets launched an offensive against Japanese forces in Manchuria. Although their swift conquest demonstrated military strength, it was overshadowed by subsequent atomic bombings. It was evident that the power of weapons could overshadow traditional military achievements.

The bombings also had diplomatic consequences. The Potsdam Conference, which occurred before the bombings, involved discussions among the Allies about the post-war order. However, with the introduction of atomic bombs, these discussions were fundamentally altered. The Soviets, confident in their position as one of the world's superpowers, now found themselves strategically disadvantaged. The "balance of power" was. The Soviets became acutely aware of their newfound vulnerability.

This feeling of vulnerability prompted the Soviet Union to take action. They made developing their atomic bomb a top priority. Their espionage network, which had already infiltrated the Manhattan Project, expanded rapidly—allowing them to acquire nuclear technology swiftly. There was a sense of urgency; four years after Hiroshima and Nagasaki in 1949, the USSR successfully conducted its first atomic test.

However, beyond fueling an arms race, these bombings also set the stage for a battle that would shape the Cold War. The

United States and the USSR. Once allies against Nazi Germany. Now, they found themselves at odds with conflicting visions for a war world. The bombings gave the USSR material for propaganda portraying the U.S. As aggressors ready to unleash devastating weapons on innocent civilians. This narrative was used to gather support both within the country and among nations in the developing world, positioning the USSR as a defender against aggression.

In essence, the atomic bombings of Hiroshima and Nagasaki were moments that drastically influenced the Soviet Union's strategic, diplomatic, and ideological paths. They triggered the Cold War, laying the groundwork for decades of rivalry, espionage, and proxy conflicts. The dark shadows cast by the mushroom clouds over Japan spread far and wide, reaching the cold corridors of power in the Kremlin and shaping global history throughout much of the latter half of the 20th century.

Asia's Response: Sympathy, Fear, and a New Geopolitical Reality:

Asia, with its various cultures, histories, and political landscapes, was pivotal following the atomic bombings. The continent had played a role in World War II, experiencing occupation, resistance movements, and the devastating impacts of warfare. The bombings of Hiroshima and Nagasaki added another layer of complexity to Asia's war narrative.

In China, which had endured years of occupation by Japanese forces, there was an undeniable sense of relief that the war would soon come to an end. The Chinese people had witnessed atrocities like the Nanjing Massacre. Initially, the bombings were a form of retribution. However, as the true scale of devastation caused by bombs became apparent, a more nuanced perspective emerged. Chinese intellectuals and leaders started expressing sympathy for Japanese citizens affected by these events. They distinguished between the actions carried out by the Japanese military and the suffering endured by innocent civilians. These sentiments were reflected in writings from Chinese figures who called for Asian solidarity in response to Western technological dominance.

India was on the verge of gaining independence from colonial rule during this time and responded with a blend of empathy and introspection. Influential leaders such as Mahatma Gandhi and Jawaharlal Nehru expressed sadness for the victims of these bombings. Nehru specifically expressed concerns about the future of humanity in the age and emphasized the importance of global disarmament. The bombings also had an impact on India's perspective on weapons. Initially, India advocated for disarmament. Eventually, it felt compelled to develop its nuclear arsenal due to geopolitical pressures.

Asian nations, many of which had firsthand experience with Japanese occupation, experienced mixed emotions. Countries like Indonesia and the Philippines were relieved that the war was coming to an end but also apprehensive about the power dynamics. The atomic bombings highlighted the significance of aligning with global powers, resulting in significant shifts in regional geopolitics.

Japan, being at the center of the atomic attacks, underwent a profound transformation. Beyond trauma and loss, the bombings prompted deep introspection in Japanese society. They grappled with questions surrounding accountability warfare practices and their nations' role in the international community. This introspection laid the groundwork for Japan to adopt a stance after World War II and commit to never engage in war again.

Furthermore, Japan experienced cultural and societal changes as well. Post-war Japanese literature, art, and cinema often incorporated themes of loss, rebirth, and haunting memories associated with the bombings. Books such as "Black Rain" by Masuji Ibuse explored the stories of those who survived Hiroshima. At the same time, filmmakers like Akira Kurosawa pondered the deeper philosophical questions that arose from the bombings.

Essentially, the atomic bombings of Hiroshima and Nagasaki impacted Asia, shaping political perspectives, cultural expressions, and societal narratives. These events triggered introspection and transformation, influencing the paths of nations and impacting lives.

Latin America and Africa: Calls for Peace and Disarmament:

The impact of the bombings in Hiroshima and Nagasaki was deeply felt in Latin America and Africa, two continents with rich histories of colonization, independence struggles, and the search for national identity. These regions interpreted the bombings through their unique experiences.

In Latin America, a continent that had been largely removed from the theaters of World War II, the bombings served as a stark reminder of the devastating capabilities of global superpowers. Countries like Brazil, Argentina, and Mexico had progressed significantly in modernization and international integration in the 1900s. However, they were now compelled to reassess their positions in a world overshadowed by the looming threat of destruction. The bombings underscored the importance of unity and cooperation, leading to initiatives aimed at promoting solidarity and collective security. An example is the Treaty of Tlatelolco, which emerged decades ago, establishing a nuclear-weapon-free zone in Latin America and the Caribbean as a testament to their commitment to peace and disarmament.

Meanwhile, Africa was experiencing colonial movements during the 1940s. Although geographically distant from Hiroshima and Nagasaki, these bombings carried symbolic significance for many African leaders and intellectuals. They saw them as examples highlighting the dangers of unchecked Western power and imperialism. The immense extent of the devastation served as a reminder of the importance of independence and self-determination. Leaders like Kwame Nkrumah from Ghana and Jomo Kenyatta from Kenya drew parallels between the bombings and the exploitation and subjugation experienced by nations under colonial rule. The pursuit of disarmament became intertwined with the broader fight for autonomy and self-governance.

These bombings sparked discussions across Africa about the role of science and technology in development. While the atomic bomb represented a pinnacle of achievement, it also symbolized the potential dangers of unchecked technological progress. This led to debates on a modernization approach that prioritized human values and ethical considerations.

Furthermore, both Latin America and Africa witnessed an impact on their artistic expressions due to these bombings. Poets, novelists, and musicians grappled with themes such as destruction, renewal, and resilience of the spirit. The atomic age, characterized by its nature of progress alongside devastation, inspired numerous works exploring existential dilemmas faced in the 20th century.

Although geographically distant from Hiroshima and Nagasaki epicenters, Latin America and Africa felt reverberations through their socio-political, cultural, and intellectual landscapes following these shocking bombings. The happenings in August 1945 brought these areas together, inspiring a renewed dedication to peace, unity, and a common goal of creating a world without the threat of warfare.

The Intellectual and Cultural Response: Art, Literature, and Philosophy:

The bombings of Hiroshima and Nagasaki impacted not only the geopolitical landscape but also the intellectual and cultural aspects of the world. With their scale and the contrast between human ingenuity and its destructive potential, these events sparked deep introspection and creative expression across various artistic and intellectual domains.

In literature, writers grappled with questions raised by the bombings. They produced novels, poems, and essays that explored themes such as mortality, humanity's inclination toward self-destruction, and the quest for meaning in an atomic world. In Japan, authors crafted poignant accounts of the immediate aftermath of the bombings and their long-lasting effects on survivors. These literary works shed light on the profound psychological wounds inflicted by these events through narratives and personal memoirs. They delved into themes like survivor's guilt, trauma, and the search for redemption.

Artists also felt compelled to respond to these events. Paintings, sculptures, and installations emerged as vehicles to capture the emotions of that time. Some artworks depicted scenes of horror associated with the bombings—desolate landscapes filled with suffering. Others took an abstract approach using symbolism and allegory to comment on the broader implications of this atomic age. With its mix of awe-inspiring implications, the mushroom cloud served as a recurring symbol representing humanity's complex relationship with its creations.

The world of cinema was not left untouched either. Filmmakers from different backgrounds crafted movies that approached the bombings and their aftermath from various perspectives. Some depicted the events, while others explored the political maneuvers that led to the bombings. Additionally, some films delved into the societal changes in a world constantly living under the specter of nuclear destruction.

Even philosophers found themselves grappling with the ethical dilemmas brought forth by these bombings. These events forced them to question beliefs about warfare, ethics, and what it truly means to be human. Philosophical works emerged, discussing the justifications for employing devastating weaponry and contemplating their broader impact on human civilization. The bombings became a point for discussions regarding power dynamics, the responsibilities tied to scientific progress, and establishing ethical boundaries for human actions.

Often considered a language, music became an expressive outlet for collective grief, anger, and introspection triggered by these bombings. Compositions spanning genres—from classical symphonies to folk songs—captured the spirit of that era. The lyrics mourned the loss of innocent lives, while the melodies expressed a deep and thoughtful reflection on a world that had been forever transformed.

In essence, the bombings of Hiroshima and Nagasaki became a cultural and intellectual milestone that profoundly affected people's lives and prompted a global surge of contemplation and creativity. Through forms of art, literature, philosophy, and other means of expression, humanity endeavored to process, comprehend, and ultimately reconcile with the profound impact of the events that occurred in August 1945.

The bombings of Hiroshima and Nagasaki were historically significant events and deeply impactful moments that reverberated throughout human civilization. As the world confronted the political and societal consequences of these bombings, a profound sense of introspection and contemplation permeated the global consciousness.

From the halls of power in Washington and Moscow to the streets of Hiroshima, these bombings evoked many reactions. Political leaders debated the ethical implications while nations adjusted their geopolitical positions. However, within the realms of art, literature, and philosophy, some of the profound reflections on these events took place. Writers, artists, filmmakers, and philosophers delved into questions raised by these bombings and produced works that captured the intricate complexities of collective consciousness.

Literature bore witness to both the trauma endured by survivors and their resilience. Artists grappled with portraying the nature of human potential juxtaposed with its capacity for destruction through their paintings and installations. Philosophers engaged in discussions about boundaries associated with power, while filmmakers brought multifaceted narratives depicting a post-atomic world to life. Music—communicating through its language—echoed sentiments encompassing grief, introspection, and hope.

The global reactions, whether discussions, pleas for disarmament, or artistic expressions, emphasized a shared desire to comprehend and make sense of the challenges of the atomic age. The bombings served as a representation of both the possibilities and the negative tendencies inherent in human progress.

Upon reflecting on the events that took place in August 1945 and their aftermath, it becomes clear that Hiroshima and

Nagasaki are not merely locations or historical incidents. They serve as enduring reminders of the obligations that accompany knowledge and power. They compel us to confront the aspects of our actions and motivate us to strive for a world where the atrocities of atomic warfare remain relegated to history books.

CHAPTER 11: GEOPOLITICAL IMPLICATIONS OF THE ATOMIC AGE

The advent of the era marked a significant turning point in human history. It brought about advancements in technology but also posed profound ethical dilemmas and drastically changed the geopolitical landscape on a global scale. The detonation of the bombs over Hiroshima and Nagasaki not only ended World War II but also initiated an era where power, politics, and strategy became inseparable from the looming threat of nuclear devastation.

The atomic age wasn't a period of scientific exploration and technological marvels; it witnessed a fundamental transformation in international relations. Diplomacy, alliances, and global priorities underwent a metamorphosis due to the newfound power and responsibility of possessing nuclear weapons. In this era, conventional military strength was no longer sufficient for nations to maintain their status. The possession or potential possession of weapons became crucial factors in determining a nation's position on the world stage, influencing its diplomatic engagements, strategic partnerships, and domestic politics.

Humanity had ventured into territory; the devastating power of atomic bombs introduced an entirely new dimension to warfare that had never been experienced before. It wasn't about the immediate destruction that a nuclear explosion could cause; it involved considering the long-term consequences, such as the lingering effects of radiation, the impacts on future generations, and the irreversible environmental damage. The bomb was more than a weapon; it represented power, served as a symbol, and served as a constant reminder of how close we are to both control and devastation.

Apart from the physical aftermath, the atomic age brought numerous ethical and philosophical dilemmas. How could we morally justify developing and potentially using a weapon to wipe out entire cities instantly? How did nations reconcile their pursuit of knowledge with the ethical implications that accompanied these discoveries? In positions of power, how did leaders balance the strategic advantages of nuclear deterrence against potential global consequences in case of a nuclear confrontation?

The United States and Soviet Union emerged as superpowers following World War II, finding themselves at the center stage for these discussions. Their conflicting ideologies and their possession of capabilities set the scene for a new kind of rivalry. This rivalry wasn't simply about ideologies; it was like an intricate dance or chess game with existential stakes.

As we continue our exploration in this chapter, we will dive into the web of events, ideologies, and individuals that influenced the geopolitical consequences of the atomic era. From the stages of atomic research to the intense diplomatic maneuvers during the Cold War, this narrative provides a thorough and captivating understanding of one of the most significant eras in 20th-century history.

THE COLD WAR'S INCEPTION AND THE INFLUENCE OF THE ATOMIC BOMB

Ideological Foundations and Early Tensions:

The divide between the West and the communist East did not emerge suddenly after World War II; it had been brewing for many years due to deep-rooted philosophical, economic, and political differences. The global stage during and after the Second World War highlighted these differences in a manner.

At the core of this division was a fundamental disagreement about the state's role in society and how economies should be organized. The United States, especially, strongly advocated for a system that valued freedoms in both economic and political realms. They believed in a market capitalist model where individual or corporate interests drove economies rather than state control. This economic model was not just seen as a system but also reflected broader societal values that prioritized individual liberties and democratic governance.

On the other hand, inspired by Marxist Leninist principles, the Soviet Union envisioned a world where state control over the means of production served as representation for the proletariat. However, their stance went beyond economics; it encompassed politics, society, and even culture. The Soviet model rejected individualism and emphasized collective welfare along with state-led development.

These different perspectives on the world were not limited to debates or policy discussions; they had real-life consequences. After World War II, Europe, in particular, was left devastated economically. The reconstruction efforts in Europe became a battleground for these competing ideologies. The U.S., through the Marshall Plan, aimed not only to provide economic assistance but also to strategically prevent communism from spreading in a vulnerable and ravaged Europe.

In response to intentions and with a desire to establish its own sphere of influence, the Soviet Union consolidated its control over Eastern Europe, forming the Eastern Bloc. As it became known, the Iron Curtain represented more than a physical boundary between East and West; it symbolized the profound ideological divide between the two superpowers.

This period also witnessed leaders emerging who would shape the course of the Cold War. Figures like Harry Truman and Joseph Stalin, each driven by their convictions and strategic goals, defined how the early Cold War era unfolded. Their decisions, often guided by a blend of ideology, realpolitik, and personal convictions, laid the groundwork for tensions and confrontations that would characterize the following decades.

As the 1940s transitioned into the 1950s, it became increasingly evident that the ongoing battle between capitalism and communism was not merely a passing phase but an enduring struggle that would shape geopolitics throughout much of the 20th century. The stakes were incredibly high; with the emergence of the atomic age, they had taken on an existential significance.

The Atomic Bomb: A New Dimension of Power:

The atomic bombings of Hiroshima and Nagasaki went beyond showcasing strength. They represented a shift in global geopolitics and the concept of warfare itself. These bombings marked the beginning of the age which introduced new technologies and redefined notions of power, strategy, and diplomacy.

Before the development of bombs, power was primarily measured by factors such as army size, territorial control, and economic strength. However, with nuclear weapons entering the picture, a nation's power could also be assessed based on its capabilities. The destructive potential of a bomb was unprecedented, rendering traditional power metrics almost irrelevant in comparison.

This reshaped power dynamic became immediately apparent in war interactions between nations. The United States was uniquely positioned on the world stage as the first nuclear-armed nation. Its decisions, policies, and even statements carried a weight. Allies sought its protection, while enemies feared its retaliation. Neutral countries closely observed their actions with anticipation. The atomic bomb had become a diplomatic tool in many respects. However, along with this newfound power, a series of challenges and responsibilities also emerged. Decision-makers felt the weight of the implications associated with utilizing such a weapon. The devastating human toll of warfare was starkly demonstrated by the bombings of Hiroshima and Nagasaki. The destruction of cities, loss of lives, and enduring effects of radiation served as a testament to the harsh reality brought about by this novel form of conflict. The world caught a glimpse into a strife-filled future, leaving an indelible impact.

The influence wielded by bombs extended far beyond military strategy alone. It permeated into domains including science, culture, and society at large. Pursuing atomic energy for peaceful purposes, like power generation, became a fervent endeavor. Notably, the age also deeply affected the cultural spirit of that era. Literature, films, and art began reflecting the anxieties, aspirations, and moral dilemmas arising from living under the shadow cast by these bombs.

Within halls of authority and leadership circles, strategists grappled with adapting their approaches in light of capabilities. Deterrence theories that were once focused on military strength had to factor in these new realities brought about by atomic weapons. Defense strategies underwent reevaluation while military budgets were reallocated accordingly; doctrines required rewriting to accommodate these transformations. The atomic bomb not only altered the way wars were fought but also profoundly impacted the thinking behind geopolitical strategies.

As the United States navigated through this territory, it became clear that its monopoly on nuclear weapons would not last long. Information from intelligence reports and geopolitical analyses indicated that other nations, the Soviet Union, would eventually develop their own atomic weapons. This realization brought a sense of urgency to strategic discussions. The world stood at the threshold of an era with the atomic bomb as its herald. The challenge was to wield this power responsibly and prevent an escalation into a nuclear arms race that could potentially bring about humanity's downfall.

The Nuclear Arms Race and Mutually Assured Destruction:

The Cold War era was marked by the nuclear arms race, which went beyond stockpiling weapons. It involved a mix of technological advancements, strategic calculations, and psychological warfare as the United States and the Soviet Union competed for supremacy; the world anxiously watched, fully aware of the high stakes.

Initially, the United States held a monopoly on weapons. However, when the Soviet Union successfully conducted its atomic test in 1949, it became clear that one side's dominance was no longer guaranteed. This development sparked a competition between the superpowers. Both nations invested resources into research, development, and espionage to gain an advantage. The race wasn't about quantity; it also focused on quality and technological superiority. The creation of hydrogen bombs with power demonstrated how this competition escalated.

As these arsenals grew, so did concerns about the consequences of a potential nuclear war. The doctrine known as Assured Destruction (MAD) emerged as a sad but stabilizing factor in this race. MAD suggested that if a scale nuclear conflict occurred, the attacker and defender would face complete annihilation. This understanding led to a situation; even though both superpowers were heavily arming themselves, possessing these weapons served as a deterrent against their use.

However, this delicate balance was not without its moments of danger. Developing ballistic missiles (ICBMs) capable of delivering nuclear warheads across continents within minutes reduced the time for making decisions during a crisis. As seen during the Cuban Missile Crisis, deploying these missiles could bring the world close to war within days or even hours.

The arms race was not limited to the United States and the Soviet Union. As the Cold War progressed, other countries, driven by rivalries and a desire for strategic independence, also aimed to develop their nuclear capabilities. This proliferation added complexity to an intricate equation and further complicated the global nuclear landscape.

The psychological aspect of this arms race was equally important. Propaganda campaigns, civil defense drills, and public demonstrations showcasing missile capabilities were just as crucial as the weapons in this competition. The objective was clear, demonstrating strength, determination, and readiness toward adversaries.

Yet amidst this rivalry, there were moments when clarity and cooperation emerged. In addition to their demonstrations of power, both superpowers during the Cold War also engaged in backchannel communications, summit meetings, and diplomatic gestures. They were well aware of the threat they posed to each other and would occasionally attempt to reduce tensions through arms control agreements and confidence-building measures.

Looking back, we can see that the nuclear arms race and the concept of Mutually Assured Destruction capture the contradictions of the Cold War. Despite being an era marked by competition and mistrust, there were moments of cooperation and acknowledgment of shared interests. The lasting impact of this period serves as a testament to the nature of geopolitics in the nuclear age.

Proxy Wars and the Global Chessboard:

The clash of ideologies between the United States and the Soviet Union, representing the West and communist East, respectively, extended beyond just diplomatic negotiations and arms races. It also played out in conflicts across the world. These conflicts, known as wars, were not confrontations between the superpowers but battlegrounds where they supported opposing sides by providing military support, financial aid, and strategic guidance.

One significant example of these conflicts occurred in Asia during the Korean War (1950 1953). The Korean Peninsula, divided between a North and a capitalist South, became a major point of contention. The United States supported South Korea, while the Soviet Union (alongside China) backed North Korea. This war reflected the dynamics of the Cold War on a smaller scale. Although it ended in a stalemate, with the peninsula remaining divided to this day, it serves as a reminder of Cold War tensions.

Africa was another region where Cold War competition played out due to its independent nations. Countries like Angola, Mozambique, and Ethiopia experienced civil wars, with both superpowers supporting opposing factions. The Soviets and Cubans assisted movements, while the United States often backed conservative or authoritarian regimes out of concern for communism's potential spread in this resource-rich continent.

Throughout history, Latin America has been considered an area of interest for the United States. However, it was not unaffected by the games of the Cold War era. 1959, the Cuban Revolution brought Fidel Castro, a leader, to power. This sparked a series of confrontations, such as the Bay of Pigs invasion and the Cuban Missile Crisis. Apart from Cuba, the U.S. intervened in countries like Nicaragua, Chile, and Guatemala to contain influences.

The Middle East was another significant region affected by Cold War dynamics due to its importance and oil reserves. The Soviet Union supported socialist regimes and movements, while the U.S. Formed alliances with countries like Israel, Iran (before the 1979 revolution), and Saudi Arabia. Conflicts such as the Yom Kippur War, the Lebanese Civil War, and the Soviet invasion of Afghanistan were influenced by varying degrees of Cold War tensions.

These proxy wars were complex. They were influenced by geopolitical rivalries and regional dynamics, long-standing animosities between nations, and struggles for national identity. However, it is important to note that throughout these conflicts, Cold War dynamics between the United States and the Soviet Union played a role in exacerbating tensions and prolonging resolutions.

Although direct confrontations between superpowers never occurred on battlefields, they resulted in immense human suffering during these wars. Millions of lives were lost, and numerous regions, such as the Middle East, are still grappling with the lasting impacts of these conflicts.

Additionally, the proxy wars inadvertently resulted in another consequence. As the United States and the Soviet Union competed for supremacy, they supplied weaponry and established military bases worldwide. This militarization in volatile areas has had long-term effects since many of those weapons provided during the Cold War continue to fuel ongoing conflicts even to this day.

Essentially, although the Cold War remained "cold" in that direct clashes between adversaries were avoided, its influence was felt extensively worldwide. It left behind scorched landscapes and visible scars on nations' geopolitical landscapes and socio-economic structures.

Diplomacy, Treaties, and the Quest for Stability:

In the aftermath of the mushroom cloud, the world recognized the need for diplomatic efforts to prevent a potential nuclear disaster. The Cold War period, characterized by moments of tension, also witnessed significant diplomatic initiatives to maintain stability and prevent an all-out nuclear confrontation.

During the years of the Cold War, both superpowers firmly held onto their ideological and strategic positions. However, as the reality of a nuclear arms race became increasingly clear, there was a growing understanding that unrestrained competition could result in destruction. This realization paved the way for dialogue and negotiations, even though they were marred by suspicion and mistrust.

One notable milestone in this endeavor was the initiation of Strategic Arms Limitation Talks (SALT) in 1969 between the United States and the Soviet Union. These talks aimed to restrict the expansion of their nuclear arsenals. Signing the SALT I agreement in 1972 introduced limitations on missile launchers for both sides. This historic achievement marked a step forward as it was the first time major powers agreed to restrain their nuclear capabilities.

Alongside SALT negotiations, discussions were also taking place concerning missile systems. Starting in 1972, the Anti-Ballistic Missile (ABM) Treaty was signed to limit the deployment of missile defense systems, ensuring that neither side could gain an advantage by neutralizing the other's deterrent. The main idea behind this agreement was to keep a balance of power intact, making sure that both superpowers were susceptible to each other's nuclear arsenals. This doctrine was known as Mutually Assured Destruction.

In addition to these treaties, various diplomatic efforts were made to address specific aspects of the nuclear problem. For example, the Intermediate-Range Nuclear Forces (INF) Treaty in 1987 eliminated a category of nuclear weapons, representing a substantial stride toward disarmament.

However, these diplomatic endeavors faced challenges along the way. One major point of contention revolved around verification mechanisms designed to ensure compliance with treaty provisions. Espionage and intelligence gathering confirmed that both sides adhered to their commitments. Furthermore, domestic political dynamics in the United States often influenced negotiation processes since treaties required Senate ratification.

The pursuit of stability during the age extended beyond just the United States and the Soviet Union relationship. Initiatives like the Nuclear Non-Proliferation Treaty (NPT), established in 1968, aimed to prevent weapons proliferation in other nations. Recognizing the risks associated with a world with nuclear powers, the Nuclear Non-Proliferation Treaty (NPT) aimed to find a middle ground. Its objective was to allow non-nuclear states access to nuclear technology while preventing them from acquiring nuclear weapons.

Looking back, the diplomatic efforts during the Cold War era highlight the significance of dialogue and negotiation in situations where trust and rivalry were deeply ingrained. The treaties and agreements, although not flawless, played a role in ensuring that the Cold War remained relatively peaceful. They prove that diplomacy can lay the foundation for stability and peace in extremely difficult circumstances.

The Atomic Age brought about technological advancements and raised ethical dilemmas, causing a major shift in the global geopolitical landscape. The bombings of Hiroshima and Nagasaki not only marked the end of World War II but also signaled the beginning of a new era where power, politics, and strategy became intertwined with the fear of nuclear destruction.

The ideological divide between the West (represented by the United States) and the communist East (represented by the Soviet Union) created a rivalry that shaped much of the 20th century. Despite their collaboration during the war, their differing ideologies and the development of weapons led to complex political, military, and ideological conflicts.

The subsequent nuclear arms race was not about building weapons; it reflected deep-rooted mistrust and strategic calculations on both sides. The principle of Assured Destruction emerged as a key concept ensuring that any all-out nuclear conflict would result in mutual devastation. Though tense, this delicate balance of terror brought about a kind of stability.

Nonetheless, it's important to note that the Cold War was far from stagnant or unchanging. The struggle between capitalism and communism impacted the world, from the forests of Vietnam to the deserts of the Middle East. These conflicts, though localized, carried symbolic meaning and had far-reaching consequences.

Amid this rivalry, diplomatic efforts were vital in preventing the Cold War from escalating into direct military confrontation. Important agreements like the Strategic Arms Limitation Talks and the Anti-Ballistic Missile Treaty aimed to establish stability in the face of tensions. These diplomatic endeavors have highlighted the significance of dialogue and negotiation in maintaining global peace.

The Cold War era was greatly shaped by weapons development, which profoundly influenced power dynamics, politics, and ideology. The lessons learned during this period remain relevant today as a reminder of how delicate power balances can be, how scientific progress can have significant consequences, and how essential diplomacy and dialogue are when navigating complex global geopolitical challenges.

CHAPTER 12: THE ATOMIC RENAISSANCE - SCIENCE AND SOCIETY IN THE NUCLEAR AGE

The detonation of the bombs in Hiroshima and Nagasaki marked a crucial turning point in human history, introducing an era that would forever be remembered as the nuclear age. This period, often associated with the haunting images of mushroom clouds and the immense devastation they caused, also brought about a rebirth in thinking, exploration, and discovery. The phrase "Atomic Renaissance" encapsulates this nature. The contrast between the destructive power of atomic bombs and the numerous positive advancements that have emerged from nuclear research for human civilization.

The 20th century was characterized by technological progress and significant geopolitical changes that set the stage for the atomic age. The world was transforming as nations competed for dominance, ideologies clashed, and scientific boundaries were pushed to new limits. In this backdrop, unraveling the secrets of atoms became a focal point for scientists and governments. Atoms, being the units of matter, held an extraordinary potential for energy and power within them. The race to harness this potential was a scientific endeavor with significant geopolitical implications since nations recognized that controlling atomic mastery could determine global power dynamics.

However, it is important to note that the story of the age goes beyond just pursuing atomic weaponry. The development of the bomb occurred alongside an exploration into how nuclear energy could be used for peaceful purposes. Many scientists who had feelings about their involvement in creating a weapon of mass destruction were equally enthusiastic about discovering ways to utilize atomic power for the betterment of humanity. This duality lies at the core of what we call the atomic renaissance. Alongside the haunting imagery of devastation, countless untold stories highlight how nuclear research has positively influenced various aspects of human life.

The Atomic Renaissance serves as a testament to creativity and resilience. Despite facing destruction, our drive to innovate, explore, and improve shone through. Instead of being characterized by widespread devastation, the atomic age transformed into a diverse breakthrough, challenges, ethical dilemmas, and advancements.

As we delve further into this chapter, we will explore the nuanced impact of the atomic age on science and society. We will embark on a journey through time as we trace the footsteps of those pioneers who dared to dream big, push boundaries, and challenge established norms. From the revered halls of academia to the laboratories of Los Alamos and from the intricate maneuverings of global superpowers to the ethical debates that ensued after the tragedies of Hiroshima and Nagasaki, our exploration promises to be enlightening and thought-provoking.

The resurgence of power is a poignant reminder of the dual nature inherent in scientific discoveries. It emphasizes the responsibility that accompanies knowledge and the ethical considerations that should guide its application. As we navigate through the nuclear era, we are reminded of Robert Oppenheimer'ss words, often referred to as "the father of the atomic bomb," who, upon witnessing the first successful test of an atomic bomb, quoted from Bhagavad Gita; "Now I am become Death, the destroyer of worlds." This solemn reflection underscores both progress and our immense responsibility.

In this chapter, we aim to provide an understanding of this atomic renaissance by capturing its essence, exploring its challenges, and delving into its profound implications for our future. Through research and deep introspection, we will unveil numerous ways the atomic age has influenced—and continues to influence—the course of human civilization.

POSITIVE ADVANCEMENTS IN NUCLEAR RESEARCH

Although tainted by the tragic events in Hiroshima and Nagasaki, the beginning of the era also shed light on opportunities for various scientific and societal advancements. Nuclear studies, often seen in weapons and international relations, have been a catalyst for progress, fueling innovations across disciplines.

Medicine: The Radiant Revolution:

The field of medicine, with its pursuit to heal and unravel the mysteries of the human body, has greatly benefited from advancements in nuclear research. The era of energy has ushered in a remarkable transformation, revolutionizing diagnostics, treatment methods, and scientific exploration beyond what was once considered mere imagination in science fiction.

Diagnostic Marvels:

Using radioisotopes in diagnostics has brought about a new era of precision and clarity. Techniques like Positron Emission Tomography (PET) and Single Photon Emission Computed Tomography (SPECT) scans utilize these isotopes to generate dynamic images of the body's internal processes. These imaging methods enable doctors to observe metabolic processes, blood flow, and even the activity of neurotransmitters in time. These valuable insights have played a role in early disease detection, understanding brain disorders, and customizing treatments to meet each patient's needs.

Therapeutic Breakthroughs:

Aside from diagnosis, the medical field has seen advancements in utilizing nuclear medicine for therapeutic purposes. A prime example is radiotherapy, which has become a tool in fighting against cancer. By employing radiation, it is now possible to effectively eliminate or reduce the size of tumors while minimizing harm to surrounding healthy tissues. Furthermore, innovative techniques like brachytherapy, where radioactive seeds or sources are implanted directly into or near the tumor, offer more targeted treatment options that result in fewer side effects and improved patient outcomes.

Radiopharmaceuticals:

The introduction of radiopharmaceuticals has greatly advanced the field of medicine. These medications, which contain elements, have proven valuable in diagnosis and treatment. For example, some radiopharmaceuticals can specifically target organs, bones, or tissues to enable imaging or therapy. They have shown potential in addressing conditions such as hyperthyroidism and alleviating bone pain associated with certain types of cancer.

Safety and Precision:

Safeguarding safety is an aspect of harnessing the potential of nuclear medicine. This field has witnessed an evolution toward ensuring utmost security. Utilizing state-of-the-art equipment and protocols guarantees that patients are exposed to radiation levels typically lower than the natural background radiation experienced in a year. The accuracy provided by techniques allows for more precise targeting of treatments, thereby minimizing the chances of complications.

Future Horizons:

The field of medicine holds immense potential for the future. Scientists are currently researching to investigate types of radiopharmaceuticals, improved imaging techniques, and even the use of radiation to target and treat diseases other than cancer. With advancements in technology and a better understanding of the body, nuclear medicine is set to continue leading the way in medical innovation.

The fusion of research and medicine has been a shining light of optimism and advancement. By providing an understanding of the human body and delivering precise therapies, the remarkable evolution in medical radiation exemplifies the positive possibilities of nuclear progress. As we persist in pushing the limits of what can be achieved, nuclear medicine holds promise in shaping the future of healthcare, bringing hope to countless individuals across the globe.

Energy: The Nuclear Promise:

The Genesis of Nuclear Energy:

The journey of nuclear energy commences with the unearthing of fission during the late 1930s. The remarkable breakthrough came about through the efforts of scientists Otto Hahn and Fritz Strassmann, along with Lise Meitner and Otto Frisch, who provided valuable interpretations. They revealed how an atom nucleus can be split into two nuclei, resulting in a significant release of energy. This groundbreaking revelation hinted that harnessing and controlling this process could pave the way for a formidable energy source.

The Rise of Nuclear Power Plants:

After the end of World War II, when the devastating effects of warfare still haunted people, there was a strong push to redirect nuclear research toward peaceful purposes. As a result, the first civilian nuclear power plants were established. The idea was captivating; a tiny uranium fuel pellet, bigger than a fingertip, could generate as much energy as 150 gallons of oil. It became clear that nuclear power could transform the energy industry. Consequently, in the mid-20th century, countries worldwide started utilizing fission for electricity production, significantly departing from traditional fossil fuels.

Challenges and Controversies:

However, the path of energy has not been without its difficulties. The very nature that makes nuclear energy so powerful also raises concerns. Events like the Chernobyl disaster in 1986 and the Fukushima Daiichi nuclear disaster in 2011 have raised questions about the safety measures associated with nuclear power plants. These incidents have shed light on the catastrophic consequences of operational failures.

Furthermore, managing waste remains a significant challenge. It poses a risk for thousands of years. Finding long-term storage solutions, such as deep geological repositories, has been the subject of extensive research and debate.

Innovation and the Future of Nuclear Energy:

Despite the challenges, the potential of nuclear energy remains vast. The advancements in technology have paved the way for safer designs of reactors. For instance, introducing thorium reactors provides an alternative to conventional uranium reactors. Thorium is more abundant than uranium. It produces less radioactive waste with a shorter half-life.

The global energy landscape is changing. In light of escalating climate change threats and the urgent need to reduce carbon emissions, nuclear energy is being reconsidered as a substitute for fossil fuels. The next generation of reactors, commonly called "Gen IV reactors," are being developed with enhanced safety measures, improved efficiency, and minimized waste production.

The story surrounding energy is full of hope, difficulties, and constant advancements. From its inception in physics to its present-day potential as a solution to global energy issues, nuclear power plays a crucial role in the resurgence of atomic science. As we progress, it becomes essential for scientists, policymakers, and society to harness the potential of energy responsibly, ensuring that we fulfill the promise it holds while safeguarding our planet and all living beings.

Agriculture in the Atomic Age: Harnessing Nuclear Science for Food Security:

The Global Challenge:

During the period after the war, when countries were dealing with the consequences of the atomic age, another significant issue was quietly becoming prominent: ensuring global food security. With growing populations and shifting climate patterns, the agricultural industry faced the responsibility of guaranteeing steady and plentiful food production. Although proven over time, conventional farming techniques were insufficient to address these emerging challenges. In this context, nuclear science unexpectedly became a valuable resource for farmers and agricultural scientists.

Mutation Breeding: A New Dawn for Crop Varieties:

Mutation breeding has emerged as a use of nuclear research in agriculture. Scientists achieve this by subjecting seeds to controlled doses of radiation, which prompts genetic mutations and ultimately creates novel and enhanced crop varieties. These "mutant" crops frequently possess characteristics like higher yields, improved resistance against pests and diseases, and the ability to thrive in various climatic conditions. Notably, cultivating drought strains of wheat and rice has played a crucial role in ensuring food security in regions with unpredictable rainfall patterns.

Soil and Water Conservation:

In addition to crop breeding, nuclear techniques have also been crucial in soil and water conservation. Isotopic tracers, which are isotopes, are utilized to investigate soil erosion, water retention, and nutrient absorption. These valuable insights enable farmers to improve their irrigation methods, minimize water usage, and boost soil fertility. These nuclear techniques have been vital in advancing sustainable agricultural practices in areas like Africa and Asia, where water scarcity is a significant issue.

Pest Control: The Sterile Insect Technique (SIT):

Pests have always been a problem in agriculture, causing farmers substantial crop damage and financial difficulties. Although chemical pesticides are effective, they also raise environmental and human health concerns. The Sterile Insect Technique (SIT) offers an eco-friendly solution. Releasing sterilized insects into the environment disrupts the pests' breeding cycle, resulting in a gradual decrease in their populations. This approach avoids using chemicals, ensuring that crops remain uncontaminated and promoting well-being and human health.

Food Preservation and Safety:

Advancements in science have also greatly improved food preservation techniques. One such method is food irradiation, where food products are exposed to ionizing radiation. This process effectively eliminates pathogens and extends the shelf life of the food. Not only does this help minimize food waste, but it also ensures that the food remains safe for consumption, particularly in areas with limited access to refrigeration facilities.

The merging of science and agriculture showcases how humanity can adapt and develop innovative solutions when faced with challenges. Although the atomic era raised ethical and geopolitical questions, it also presented opportunities for growth and success. In agriculture, nuclear science has become a source of optimism, guaranteeing food security, encouraging methods, and leading us toward a future where hunger and malnutrition are things of the past.

Water Resources in the Nuclear Age:

Water is important and is often called the 'elixir of life.' Its significance cannot be emphasized enough. In light of the issues we face today, such as climate change, urbanization, and growing demands, managing our water resources sustainably has become crucial. The nuclear era has brought forth scientific breakthroughs that offer creative solutions to tackle these challenges effectively. These advancements ensure that water accessibility and sustainability are prioritized for everyone.

Isotope Hydrology: A Revolutionary Tool:

Isotope hydrology has become a tool in the field of managing water resources. By analyzing water composition, scientists can gain valuable insights into groundwater's age origin and movement. This information plays a role in understanding aquifer systems, which serve as the primary source of freshwater for many regions.

Unlike surface water, groundwater is shielded from external factors, making it a more stable and dependable source. However, excessive extraction and contamination pose threats to these reserves. Isotope hydrology helps identify areas, assess the rate at which groundwater is replenished, and evaluate the sustainability of extraction practices. For instance, by determining how old groundwater is, scientists can estimate how long it takes for an aquifer to recharge. This knowledge guides policies aimed at ensuring extraction practices.

Combatting Saline Intrusion:

Coastal areas experiencing rapid population growth encounter the problem of saltwater infiltration. When freshwater is extracted from coastal sources, there is a potential for seawater to seep, making the water unsuitable for drinking or agricultural purposes. Isotope techniques can be utilized to track where the salinity originates, aiding in developing strategies to prevent or reverse this intrusion. By comprehending how fresh and salty waters move and mix effective barriers or extraction methods can be devised.

Nuclear Techniques in Ecosystem Conservation:

Wetlands, mangroves, and estuaries have a role in preserving ecological equilibrium. They serve as barriers against flooding, offer habitats for various species, and are essential for capturing carbon. Nevertheless, these ecosystems face threats from actions and climate change. Nuclear methods and radiotracers aid in comprehending the movement of water and sediment within these regions. Conservationists can develop strategies to safeguard and revitalize these ecosystems by monitoring the flow of nutrients and pollutants.

Water Quality and Pollution Tracking:

Ensuring the quality of our water is extremely important for the public's well-being—contaminants, whether from waste runoff, farms, or even natural sources, can cause serious problems. Radiotracers provide an accurate way to trace where pollutants come from and how they spread. By understanding their origin and how they move, we can take targeted actions to prevent contamination and keep our water sources clean.

The convergence of science and water resource management showcases the beneficial progress made during the atomic age. As we face increasing challenges concerning water scarcity, quality, and sustainability, the innovative tools and techniques developed in the era will guarantee that water, essential for all life on Earth, remains accessible and sustainable. By combining water conservation methods with nuclear approaches, we can adopt a comprehensive approach that addresses immediate needs and long-term sustainability goals.

Space Exploration: A Nuclear-Powered Odyssey:

The Quest for Deep Space Exploration:

The sheer expanse of the cosmos, with its enigmas and obstacles, has forever fascinated the human mind. As we venture into realms beyond our celestial abode, we recognize the shortcomings of traditional means of propelling ourselves. All the vast gaps between heavenly bodies demand a propulsion system that is highly effective and incredibly potent. Thus came about nuclear propulsion—a visionary concept poised to redefine the very essence of space exploration.

Nuclear Thermal Propulsion (NTP):

Nuclear Thermal Propulsion (NTP) has emerged as a solution for overcoming the challenges of deep space exploration. In contrast to chemical rockets that rely on burning fuel, NTP utilizes a nuclear reactor to heat hydrogen, which serves as the fuel to extremely high temperatures. Once heated, the fuel is expelled through a nozzle-producing thrust. The efficiency of NTP measured in terms of impulse greatly surpasses that of chemical propulsion. This means that spacecraft can achieve speeds and carry larger payloads, opening the possibility of embarking on missions to far-off planets and venturing into interstellar travel.

Safety and Sustainability:

While it's clear that there are benefits to using nuclear propulsion, it also presents a range of safety challenges. When deploying reactors in space, strict safety measures must be implemented to avoid potential accidents during launch and while in space. Additionally, the long-term viability of propulsion depends on the advancement of lightweight and reliable reactors that can operate efficiently with minimal risk. Researchers are focused on developing these reactors to ensure the safety of the spacecraft and its crew.

The Role of Miniaturized Reactors:

As space missions strive for durations and greater distances, ensuring a steady and dependable power supply becomes incredibly important. Compact nuclear reactors specifically designed for space applications offer a solution. These small-scale reactors can generate electrical power to support spacecraft systems and habitats. In addition to propulsion, they play a role in maintaining the functionality of life support systems, scientific instruments, and communication devices throughout the entire mission.

The Future: Project Prometheus and Beyond:

NASA's Project Prometheus began in the 2000s and represented an ambitious vision for exploring space using nuclear power. Although the project was eventually put on hold, it established a foundation for future endeavors. The project's main objective was to create nuclear-powered systems to support extended space missions targeting the outer planets. The impact of Project Prometheus still resonates with scientists and engineers today, igniting aspirations for missions propelled by nuclear propulsion.

The field of space exploration is on the verge of a revolution powered by nuclear technology. As we envision galaxies and interstellar voyages, harnessing the power of atoms could be crucial in transforming these dreams into reality. The obstacles are diverse. So are the potential opportunities. In the words of renowned astrophysicist Carl Sagan, "We carry within us the wonders of the universe. Our very composition consists of materials. We serve as a means for the cosmos to understand itself." With propulsion, we may uncover new ways to comprehend and explore our vast cosmos.

Space Exploration: A Nuclear-Powered Odyssey:

The Quest for Deep Space Exploration:

The enormity of space, with its enigmas and hurdles, has forever fascinated the human mind. As we look beyond our planet, we've realized the shortcomings of traditional means of propulsion. The immense gaps between bodies require an effective and robust propulsion system. This is where nuclear propulsion comes into play—an idea that holds the potential to transform space exploration as we know it.

Nuclear Thermal Propulsion (NTP):

Nuclear Thermal Propulsion (NTP) has emerged as a solution to overcome the challenges of deep space exploration. Unlike chemical rockets that rely on burning fuel, NTP utilizes a nuclear reactor to heat a propellant, usually hydrogen, to extremely high temperatures. Once heated, the propellant is ejected through a nozzle, creating thrust. NTP's efficiency, measured by impulse, greatly surpasses that of chemical propulsion systems. This means spacecraft can travel at speeds and carry more payloads, opening up exciting possibilities for missions to faraway planets and interstellar travel.

Safety and Sustainability:

Although the benefits of using propulsion in space are clear, significant safety concerns also need to be addressed. To ensure the use of nuclear reactors during launch and in space, strict safety protocols must be implemented. Additionally, the long-term viability of propulsion relies on developing advanced reactors that can operate efficiently while minimizing risks. Current research focuses on creating durable reactors that prioritize the safety of the spacecraft and its crew.

The Role of Miniaturized Reactors:

As space missions strive for durations and greater distances, consistent and dependable power sources are essential. Miniaturized nuclear reactors present a solution to this challenge. These compact reactors, specifically designed for space applications, can effectively generate power for spacecraft systems and habitats. Apart from propulsion, they also play a role in maintaining the functionality of life support systems, scientific instruments, and communication devices throughout the entire mission.

The Future: Project Prometheus and Beyond:

The ambitious vision for nuclear-powered space exploration was exemplified by NASA's Project Prometheus, which was started in the 2000s. Although the project was eventually put on hold, its impact can still be seen today as it paved the way for ventures. The primary goal of this project was to create nuclear-powered systems that could support long-duration space missions specifically targeting the planets. The influence of Project Prometheus continues to motivate scientists and engineers, instilling a sense of optimism for missions driven by nuclear propulsion.

The future of space exploration is on the verge of a revolution powered by nuclear energy. As we imagine venturing into galaxies and embarking on interstellar voyages, harnessing the potential of atomic power could be the key to transforming these dreams into reality. The challenges we face are numerous. So are the possibilities that lie ahead. In the words of Carl Sagan, "We are connected to the cosmos. Our very existence is intertwined with stardust. We serve as a means for the universe to comprehend itself." With propulsion, we may discover new ways to understand the vast cosmos better.

The atomic era, with all its complexities and contradictions, has undoubtedly made a lasting impact on society. Although it began with the force of atomic bombs, the following years witnessed a surge in scientific advancements and exploration. This transformative period, known as the "Atomic Renaissance," showcases humanity's pursuit of knowledge even amidst challenging ethical dilemmas.

Space exploration has been one of the captivating and promising fields during this renaissance. The vastness of the universe filled with mysteries has always fascinated us. However, venturing into space requires innovative propulsion systems beyond traditional methods. Nuclear propulsion emerged as a solution in this endeavor by offering faster and more efficient journeys to distant celestial bodies. Nuclear Thermal Propulsion (NTP), known for its efficiency, holds tremendous potential to revolutionize our approach to space travel and make interplanetary or even interstellar voyages possible.

Nevertheless, we must remember that great power comes with responsibility. Employing reactors in space necessitates strict safety measures and protocols. Developing reactors designed for space challenges emphasizes our commitment to safety and sustainability. These reactors offer efficient propulsion and ensure the smooth operation of life support systems, scientific instruments, and communication devices that are crucial for the success of long-duration missions.

Projects like NASA's Prometheus have paved the way for future endeavors in nuclear-powered space exploration, even though they haven't been fully realized yet. Such initiatives showcase the potential of research to propel humanity into new frontiers, enabling us to explore deeper into the vast cosmos.

When we contemplate the Renaissance and its profound impact on space exploration, we are reminded of the limitless possibilities that lie ahead. The challenges we face—both scientific and ethical—are substantial but not insurmountable. As we find ourselves at this juncture looking toward a future illuminated by atomic power, hope and anticipation fill our hearts. The universe beckons us forward, armed with advancements born in the age of energy that equips us better than ever before for this magnificent journey. The path ahead promises to be enlightening and transformative as we continue pushing boundaries driven by curiosity and fueled by the promise of a renaissance.

CHAPTER 13: THE FUTURE OF NUCLEAR TECHNOLOGY

Few discoveries have profoundly impacted human progress and sparked as much debate as nuclear technology. Since scientists first unlocked the power hidden within the atom, humanity has stood on the threshold of a new era—a time when we can harness and manipulate the very building blocks of our universe. This atomic age promised advancements in energy, medicine, and science. However, it also brought forth ethical, environmental, and geopolitical concerns.

The narrative surrounding technology is fundamentally one of duality. On one side, it represents the epitome of ingenuity—a testament to our tireless pursuit of knowledge and ability to harness natural forces. The potential applications for the technology are extensive and diverse. Just imagine a world where clean and abundant electricity replaces fossil fuels, liberating us from the looming threat of climate change. Envision breakthroughs in science that enable precise diagnosis and treatment of diseases using atomic tools—unlocking the mysteries of our bodies. These possibilities are not dreams; they are concrete opportunities well within our reach, thanks to the power held within atoms.

However, there is another side to the story. The atomic age has presented us with some of the challenging ethical dilemmas of our time. While nuclear power can bring light to cities and drive advancements, it also possesses the capability to cause immense destruction. The bombings of Hiroshima and Nagasaki serve as reminders of the devastating potential of nuclear technology. Apart from the impact, incidents like Chernobyl and Fukushima highlight the long-lasting environmental and health consequences of atomic power.

Nuclear technology carries geopolitical implications. In a world where nations compete for dominance, possessing capabilities can tip the power scales in their favor. The delicate balance of deterrence has shaped international relations for many years, resulting in a complex network of treaties, alliances, and rivalries. The pursuit of supremacy has even brought nations dangerously close to conflict on occasions, emphasizing the high stakes involved in this nuclear game.

As we delve into this chapter, our goal is to navigate the landscape of the atomic age while examining its potential benefits and inherent dangers. We will journey through the pages of history, tracing how atomic science has evolved from theoretical origins to practical applications in modern times.

Throughout our journey, we will. Grapple with the moral, ecological, and political hurdles of nuclear technology. We aim to comprehend the consequences of the atomic era on humanity and our planet.

The destiny of technology remains an unfinished story, influenced by scientific advancements, political determinations, and societal principles. As we find ourselves at this crossroads, it becomes essential to approach this subject matter with an open mind, a discerning perspective, and a strong sense of accountability. All our decisions today will shape the lasting impact of atomic energy for future generations.

Section 1: Revolutionizing Energy Production - A Deeper Dive:

The appeal of energy as a sustainable power source goes beyond its minimal carbon footprint; it also lies in its remarkable efficiency. One uranium fuel pellet, about the size of a fingertip, can generate as much energy as 3.5 barrels of oil.

This exceptional energy density enables nuclear power plants to produce electricity using relatively small quantities of fuel despite their intricate infrastructure.

A promising advancement in energy is the development of fast breeder reactors. These reactors are designed to generate fissile material and consume effectively "breeding" fuel. This not only maximizes uranium utilization but also potentially reduces the amount of radioactive waste produced. By converting fissile isotopes into fissile ones, fast breeders can extend the lifespan of our uranium resources and potentially create a more sustainable nuclear fuel cycle.

Another avenue being explored is fusion energy. Unlike fission, where atoms are split to release energy, fusion combines atomic nuclei—typically hydrogen—to create heavier nuclei. This process, which fuels our sun, has the potential to provide an almost limitless source of energy by utilizing abundant fuels, like deuterium, from seawater. While fusion energy is still in the stage, projects such as the International Thermonuclear Experimental Reactor (ITER) lead the way, showcasing its potential as a clean and abundant energy source.

However, there are challenges to overcome on the path toward a nuclear-powered future. One of the concerns is the issue of nuclear proliferation. As more countries aim to harness energy, there is an increasing risk of nuclear materials falling into unauthorized hands. To ensure that nuclear technology is solely used for purposes, it is crucial to establish strong international oversight and foster cooperation between nations.

Decommissioning nuclear reactors poses both technical and financial difficulties. Reactors must be safely dismantled and their sites decontaminated when they reach the end of their lives. This process entails expenses and necessitates specialized expertise to guarantee safe execution.

Public perception also presents an obstacle. Despite advancements in nuclear safety measures, incidents like the Fukushima disaster have impacted opinion. Building trust and fostering transparency in all operations is vital for gaining wider acceptance of nuclear energy. Ultimately, nuclear energy offers the potential for a greener and sustainable future. However, achieving this vision demands a strategy beyond solving technical hurdles. It necessitates addressing the political and environmental considerations linked to atomic power.

Section 2: Pioneering Medical Innovations:

The impact of technology on the field of medicine has been truly revolutionary. Its applications go beyond what's commonly known in diagnostics and therapy, and it has the potential to reshape our understanding of human health and disease.

One area that holds promise is molecular imaging. This technique allows us to see molecular processes in real-time, giving us insights into disease mechanisms that were previously inaccessible. By using labeled molecules that target specific cellular receptors or processes, doctors can observe how molecules interact within living tissues. This helps with early detection and enables personalized treatment approaches for each patient, marking a new era in medicine.

There is a growing interest in using alpha-emitting isotopes for radionuclide therapy. Unlike the commonly used beta-emitting isotopes, alpha-emitters deliver radiation precisely to targeted cells while sparing surrounding tissues. This precision makes them highly effective against resistant cancers, offering hope to patients with previously untreatable conditions.

Another exciting application lies in the treatment of malignant diseases. For example, researchers are exploring radiopharmaceutical's potential in managing conditions like rheumatoid arthritis. Targeting inflamed joints makes it possible to administer therapeutic doses of radiation that can alleviate pain and inflammation without causing the systemic side effects often associated with conventional treatments.

Neurological disorders are also benefiting from the advancements in medicine. Radiolabeled compounds capable of crossing the blood-brain barrier offer insights into conditions such as Parkinson's, Alzheimer's, and multiple sclerosis. Through visualizing the brain's biochemistry, researchers are gaining an understanding of these disorders, paving the way for innovative therapeutic interventions.

However, these advancements bring their share of challenges. The production of radiopharmaceuticals requires facilities and expertise. Given their short half-lives, ensuring a supply of medical isotopes necessitates a coordinated global effort. Regulatory obstacles can also impede the translation of research findings into practice. Furthermore, ethical considerations surrounding treatments for terminal conditions require thoughtful deliberation.

In essence, while nuclear medicine holds the potential to revolutionize healthcare, it is a journey riddled with challenges. Nonetheless, through endeavors, ongoing research efforts, and an unwavering focus on safety and ethics, we can bring the promise of nuclear technology in reshaping medicine within our grasp.

Section 3: Societal Implications and Ethical Dilemmas:

Technology's impact on society goes beyond just energy production and geopolitics. It has fundamentally changed how societies function, influencing narratives, shaping public perceptions, and challenging traditional ethical frameworks.

The cultural narrative surrounding technology is diverse and captivating. From portraying power as a possible savior or an impending apocalypse during the Cold War era to today's discussions on sustainable energy, it has been a recurring theme in literature, film, and art. This cultural engagement reflects society's fascination with and concerns about atomic energy. Movies like "Dr. Strangelove" or books like "On the Beach" capture the fear of nuclear warfare, while more recent stories explore the complexities of nuclear energy in a world grappling with climate change.

Public opinion about technology is equally intricate. While scientists generally recognize its benefits for energy generation, public perception often varies. Memories of incidents like Three Mile Island, Chernobyl, and Fukushima have left impressions on people's minds, leading to heightened fears and skepticism. Grassroots movements advocating for disarmament or opposing the construction of nuclear power plants often gain support as they reflect broader societal concerns. Finding a balance between addressing these concerns and meeting the need for sustainable energy solutions is a complex challenge that policymakers and industry leaders grapple with.

The ethical dimensions of technology are vast and multifaceted. One of the pressing ethical dilemmas revolves around our responsibility toward future generations. How can we justify storing waste for thousands of years knowing it remains radioactive, and what right do we have to burden future generations with potential risks? This unique intergenerational ethical issue arises in relation to nuclear technology, demanding careful thought and innovative solutions.

The equitable distribution of technology and its benefits poses another ethical challenge. While developed nations have the resources and expertise to safely harness nuclear power, developing nations often face obstacles related to infrastructure and regulations. The question of whether or not to share technology, along with determining the conditions under which it should be shared, sparks international debate. The ethical considerations surrounding proliferation treaties—aimed at preventing the spread of nuclear weapons while facilitating peaceful use—are intricate and often fraught with political tension.

Lastly, there is an ethical concern regarding the potential militarization of nuclear technology. The concept of deterrence, whereby nations maintain arsenals to discourage adversaries from launching nuclear attacks, has long played a central role in international relations. However, the ethical concerns associated with this doctrine, which essentially relies on the threat of destruction, run deep. The moral dilemmas posed by using or possessing weapons with immense destructive capabilities challenge traditional ethical frameworks and call for a reassessment of global priorities.

When navigating nuclear technology's implications and ethical problems, it becomes clear that the atomic age is not simply about scientific progress. It reflects humanity's profound aspirations, fears, and moral dilemmas. As we continue to harness the power of atoms, these societal and ethical considerations will remain at the heart of discussions shaping the course of the atomic age.

Section 4: Environmental Considerations:

The environmental considerations surrounding technology go beyond the immediate area around nuclear power plants. While nuclear energy is often touted as an option with reduced greenhouse gas emissions, we need to delve deeper into the broader ecological impact.

One aspect that doesn't get attention is the water usage associated with nuclear reactors. Cooling systems in these plants require water, usually taken from nearby rivers or lakes. Although most of this water is returned to its source, the higher temperatures can disrupt ecosystems, affecting aquatic life and potentially reducing biodiversity. Changes in water temperature can interfere with the reproduction patterns of species, disrupt migration routes, and make aquatic populations more vulnerable to diseases.

The process of extracting uranium, which serves as the fuel for most nuclear reactors, presents environmental challenges. Uranium mining through open pit methods can cause significant damage to land. This process contributes to soil erosion and habitat destruction while releasing dust into the air. Additionally, the byproducts of uranium extraction, known as tailings, contain materials and heavy metals. If not properly managed, these tailings can contaminate groundwater. Pose risks both to the environment and human health.

Another important factor to take into consideration is the long-term storage of waste. Although scientists are exploring geological repositories as potential solutions, numerous challenges are involved in selecting suitable sites. The ideal location must remain geologically stable for thousands of years to ensure the waste is effectively contained. This requires understanding geological processes, the possibility of seismic activity, and the long-term effects of storing radioactive materials underground.

In addition to these aspects, we must also acknowledge the psychological impact on communities living near nuclear facilities. The fear of accidents and concerns about long-term waste storage can create higher anxiety and stress levels among local residents. Consequently, this can affect community dynamics and property values. It may even lead some individuals to consider moving away to distance themselves from perceived risks.

Overall, while nuclear technology offers environmental advantages in terms of reducing carbon emissions, it is crucial to recognize that there are complex ecological and societal implications associated with its use. Understanding these challenges through thorough research and adopting responsible practices will be vital as we navigate the future nuclear energy path.

The journey into the realm of technology has shed light on the immense possibilities and complex hurdles linked with harnessing the power of atomic energy. As we have delved deeper, nuclear energy emerged as an eco-friendly alternative to traditional fossil fuels, offering hope in our battle against climate change. The advancement in reactor designs and the exploration of fuels like thorium further highlight the ever-evolving landscape of nuclear innovation.

Nuclear technology has had an impact on medical science. From precise diagnostic tools to groundbreaking cancer treatments, atomic advancements have transformed the boundaries of medical research, presenting new avenues for healing and optimism.

Nevertheless, societal and ethical dimensions surrounding nuclear technology exist that give rise to debates and dilemmas. The geopolitical power dynamics and moral questions related to disarmament efforts and the potential misuse of atomic power contribute to a complexity that extends beyond scientific realms.

One significant consideration revolves around the consequences associated with nuclear energy. While it is undeniable that it offers reduced greenhouse emissions, ecological aspects need careful examination, such as water usage in cooling systems and challenges related to uranium mining. These factors paint a nuanced picture when evaluating its overall impact. The storage of waste for long periods, the search for stable locations to store it underground, and the impact on communities living near nuclear facilities all emphasize our complex challenges.

When considering both the advantages and disadvantages of technology, it becomes clear that our exploration of the atomic age requires finding a delicate equilibrium. It involves harnessing the power of atoms while carefully navigating through ethical, environmental, and societal dilemmas. As we peer into the future, this delicate balance will determine how history remembers the age, shaping our choices and influencing the world we leave behind for future generations.

CONCLUSION AND REFLECTIONS

The era of energy, with its countless complexities, demonstrates humanity's insatiable curiosity and unwavering pursuit of knowledge. As we've ventured into the realm of nuclear technology from its inception to its current implications, we've grappled with the profound duality it presents. On the one hand, the atom promises a more sustainable future by offering solutions to our pressing challenges. On the other hand, it casts an uncertain shadow that raises ethical questions, prompts us to consider our responsibility, and even challenges our human nature.

Throughout this exploration, we have witnessed how nuclear technology possesses the power to bring about transformation. Its potential to revolutionize energy production, drive advancements in healthcare, and reshape politics is undeniable. The prospect of a world fueled by abundant nuclear energy – free from fossil fuel limitations and the looming threat of climate change – inspires hope for a better future. Similarly, the medical breakthroughs made possible by science – ranging from precise diagnostic tools to targeted treatments for cancer – highlight the positive impact that the atomic age has brought about in terms of human well-being.

However, this journey has also forced us to confront some of society's challenging moral dilemmas in present times. The immense power that can illuminate cities and propel advancements also carries the potential to devastate them. The haunting memories of Hiroshima and Nagasaki stand as reminders of nuclear technology's immense destructive force. Beyond these tragedies, the long-term consequences on the environment, society, and human psyche resulting from nuclear incidents such as Chernobyl and Fukushima emphasize the complex challenges associated with atomic energy.

The environmental considerations surrounding technology further highlight the importance of a balanced approach. While nuclear power offers environmental advantages by reducing carbon emissions, it is crucial to conduct extensive research and adopt responsible practices due to its wider ecological impact encompassing aspects like water usage and uranium mining.

As we contemplate the era of energy, it becomes clear that our interaction with this technology requires equilibrium and responsibility. It is a relationship shaped by our choices, values, and vision for the future. The atomic age urges us to think, question assumptions, and engage in meaningful discussions. It compels us to consider the scientific and technological dimensions, broader ethical concerns, societal consequences, and environmental implications.

Ultimately, the story of nuclear technology mirrors our human narrative. It chronicles our ambitions, trials, and collective journey toward a brighter tomorrow. At this juncture, we hope our exploration has provided valuable insights, sparked curiosity, and inspired deep reflection. Our decisions today will shape the legacy of energy influencing the world we live in and future generations.

As we conclude our journey through the era of advancements, let us take a moment to ponder the path we have walked together;

We began by immersing ourselves in a world before the emergence of atomic bombs, understanding the geopolitical and scientific landscape on the verge of transformation. This backdrop allowed us to truly appreciate the contributions made by brilliant minds like Einstein and Bohr, who laid the groundwork for this atomic age through their pioneering work on atomic theory.

Our expedition led us to delve into the heart of the Manhattan Project, where we unraveled the efforts and encountered challenges in harnessing atomic energy. This exploration revealed intricate processes in creating a bomb—a convergence of science, strategy, and secrecy.

Equipped with an understanding of technical complexities, we witnessed world-altering events like the Hiroshima and Nagasaki bombings. We felt not only the immediate aftermath but also recognized their profound impact on global consciousness that endures till today. This thoughtful reflection brought us into the period known as the Cold War, where the competition for nuclear weapons and global power dynamics took center stage.

As we navigated the complexities of the age, we grappled with important moral questions, such as whether it was right to use nuclear bombs and the ethics surrounding nuclear proliferation. We also delved into the impact of nuclear technology, weighing its benefits against its challenges.

Our contemplation deepened as we explored how Americans viewed the bomb in contrast to hearing heart-wrenching personal stories from survivors of Hiroshima. This chapter served as a reminder of both the human toll and worldwide ethical dilemmas presented by the atomic age.

Looking ahead, we contemplated what lies on the horizon for technology. Considering potential advancements in applications and identifying challenges and opportunities that await us.

This book has taken us on a journey through aspects of the atomic age, from breakthroughs to ethical dilemmas, from environmental considerations to future possibilities. Our narrative has been filled with valuable insights, challenges to overcome, and hope for what lies ahead.

As we look back on this journey, I truly hope the information and insights we've shared can encourage conversations, foster deeper comprehension, and ignite a collective vision for a better and more accountable future.

Reflections:

The study of the era goes beyond just being an intellectual pursuit; it delves into a deep contemplation of the human essence, our potential, and the moral limits that shape us. Numerous thought-provoking themes arise as we ponder the interplay between science, ethics, and society, beckoning us to delve deeper into self-reflection.

The Dual Nature of Discovery:

Every major scientific advancement brings both possibilities and dangers. The finding of fission, which can both provide light to cities and destroy them, exemplifies this dual nature. It makes us ponder: How can we responsibly utilize the potential of our discoveries? On a deeper level, how do we ensure that our quest for knowledge doesn't inadvertently steer us toward our demise?

Ethical Stewardship:

The era of power has placed a great burden of ethics upon us. The choices related to technology go beyond just technical or political aspects; they have a profound moral dimension. From the scientists involved in the Manhattan Project to present-day policymakers, the gravity of these choices echoes throughout time. It compels us to reflect on the consequences of our actions and to prioritize the common good over immediate advantages.

The Interconnectedness of Life:

The environmental impact of technology highlights the fragile equilibrium of our ecosystem. From the water bodies impacted by nuclear power plants to the communities residing near facilities, we are reminded of the intricate interconnectedness of life. Each choice and every action carries consequences, emphasizing our shared duty to protect our planet and its inhabitants.

The Power of Dialogue:

Throughout the age, we have learned a valuable lesson about the significance of open communication and collaboration. It is essential to recognize that the complexities brought forth by technology cannot be tackled in isolation. Instead, they demand an endeavor that connects various fields of study, cultures, and countries. Embracing an environment of dialogue enables us to explore inventive resolutions and fosters mutual understanding and a collective vision for the future.

Resilience and Hope:

Despite the difficulties and ethical issues associated with the era, there is also a narrative of resilience and optimism. We see communities coming together to rebuild after incidents and global movements advocating for disarmament and sustainable energy. These stories highlight the unyielding spirit of humanity, showing our ability to adapt, learn, and strive for a future.

301

Reflecting on our age is like looking into a mirror that reflects our hopes, fears, and collective journey. It's a journey filled with challenges but tremendous potential. As we navigate the complexities of today's world, may we find inspiration in the lessons of the past. Let us be armed with knowledge, empathy, and foresight to construct a world characterized by peace, sustainability, and shared prosperity.

As we end this journey through the atomic age, it's a moment for reflection, gratitude, and hope. The pages you've explored, the stories you've encountered, and the insights you've gained are a testament to your dedication to understanding one of the transformative periods in human history.

Congratulations on reaching the end of this journey. By accompanying us on this journey, you have expanded your knowledge and engaged with the profound ethical, scientific, and societal implications of the atomic age. From the thinkers who established atomic theory to the poignant narratives of Hiroshima survivors, from grappling with environmental challenges posed by nuclear technology to envisioning its bright future possibilities, you have navigated a narrative that is both intricate and captivating.

What you have learned surpasses facts and figures. You have delved into depths that reveal humanity's resilience, our pursuit of knowledge, and the moral boundaries that shape our decisions. You have wrestled with the nature of discovery—witnessing its promises and perils that go hand in hand with significant advancements.

As you close this chapter, remember that knowledge acts as a guiding light illuminating our path forward. The era of power, with all its intricate intricacies, reminds us of our shared duty to utilize knowledge for the betterment of society, to inquire, to contemplate, and to take action with forethought and compassion.

We appreciate your participation in this endeavor. May the wisdom you have acquired ignite discussions and curiosity. Help you comprehend the world we live in. Cheers to a future brimming with enlightenment, empathy, and optimism.

The End

If you're interested in exploring more about Oppenheimer's, I invite you to check out my other book titled **"Oppenheimer's Beyond the Blast,"** which offers a deep exploration into J. Robert Oppenheimer'ss life and enduring legacy at:

https://www.amazon.com/dp/B0CF47FMBK

LIST OF SOURCES

Books:

The Making of the Atomic Bomb by Richard Rhodes
A comprehensive account of the history of the atomic bomb, from its scientific origins to its geopolitical implications.

Dark Sun: The Making of the Hydrogen Bomb by Richard Rhodes
A sequel to Rhodes' earlier work, focusing on the development of the hydrogen bomb and the Cold War era.

Manhattan Project: The Birth of the Atomic Bomb in the Words of Its Creators, Eyewitnesses, and Historians by Cynthia C. Kelly
A compilation of firsthand accounts, documents, and narratives surrounding the Manhattan Project.

On Nuclear Terrorism by Michael Levi
An exploration of the threats of nuclear terrorism and the measures to prevent it.

The Second World War: A Complete History by Martin Gilbert
A detailed account of World War II, providing context for the development and use of the atomic bomb.

The Physics of the Manhattan Project by Bruce Cameron Reed
A deep dive into the scientific and technical challenges of the Manhattan Project.

Research Papers and Articles:

The Manhattan Project: Making the Atomic Bomb by the U.S. Department of Energy, Office of History and Heritage Resources.

The Environmental and Health Legacy of the Manhattan Project and Cold War by the National Institutes of Health.

The Decision to Use the Atomic Bomb by Gar Alperovitz, published in Foreign Affairs.

The Legacy of Hiroshima and Nagasaki: Reflections 60 Years Later by the Bulletin of the Atomic Scientists.

Nuclear Energy: Current Status and Future Prospects by the International Atomic Energy Agency (IAEA).

The Ethics of Nuclear Weapons Dissemination: Moral Dilemmas of Aspiration, Avoidance, and Prevention by James F. Doyle, published in the Journal of Ethics.

The Geopolitical Implications of the Atomic Age: A Historical Analysis by the Journal of Contemporary History.

The Atomic Renaissance: Nuclear Science and Society Post-WWII by the American Institute of Physics.

This list provides a foundation of credible sources that have informed the content of the book, ensuring accuracy and depth in the exploration of the atomic age.

Oppenheimer's movie 2023, written and directed by Christopher Nolan

A MESSAGE FROM THE PUBLISHER:

Are you enjoying the book? We would love to hear your thoughts!

Many readers do not know how hard reviews are to come by and how much they help a publisher. We would be incredibly grateful if you could take just a few seconds to write a brief review on Amazon, even if it's just a few sentences!

Please go here and find the book to leave a quick review:
https://www.amazon.com/review/create-review

We would greatly appreciate it if you could take the time to post your review of the book and share your thoughts with the community. If you have enjoyed the book, please let us know what you loved the most about it and if you would recommend it to others. Your feedback is valuable to us, and it helps us to improve our services and continue to offer high-quality literature to our readers.

Made in the USA
Las Vegas, NV
07 September 2023

77210445R00174